HARD SELL

Now a Major Motion Picture Love & Other Drugs

Jamie Reidy

Andrews McMeel
Publishing, LLC

Kansas City · Sydney · London

Andrews McMeel Publishing, LLC
an Andrews McMeel Universal company
1130 Walnut Street, Kansas City, Missouri 64106

www.andrewsmcmeel.com

10 11 12 13 14 FFG 10 9 8 7 6 5 4 3 2 1
ISBN: 978-0-7407-9913-6

The Library of Congress has cataloged the hardcover edition with the title *Hard Sell* as follows:

Reidy, Jamie.
    Hard sell : the evolution of a Viagra salesman / Jamie Reidy.
        p. cm.
    ISBN: 0–7407–50`39–9
    1. Selling—Drugs—Popular works. 2. Sildenafil—Popular works. I. Title.

HF5439.D75R45 2005
381'.456151—dc22
[B]

2004046212

ATTENTION: SCHOOLS AND BUSINESSES

For my parents, Rich and Loretta

They gave me my sense of humor

and the confidence to believe that

people want to hear my stories.

You can blame them.

We couldn't all be cowboys,

So some of us are clowns

—*"Goodnight Elisabeth"*
by Counting Crows

Contents

Acknowledgments

I'D BE NOWHERE without the thick skins of my brother, Patrick, and sister, Anne-Marie. Thanks for not smothering me in my sleep.

In the summer of 1990, Joe Mileti wrote me a letter at basic training saying, "You'll be a fine writer when your day comes, Jamie." He probably doesn't even remember that, but I never forgot it. Thanks for being the first, Papa Joe.

Egomaniacs sometimes need tough love to see the truth. To that point, I thank Shelley (Guilbault) Curry for giving me a well-deserved kick in the ass.

Thanks to screenwriter Ted Griffin for talking me out of another title and into *Hard Sell*.

After shamelessly taking advantage of their willingness to read this book multiple times, I am impossibly indebted to Maureen Lynch, Carol Quigley, and Steve Egan for their encouragement, keen eyes, and quick turnaround time. Hopefully all of you will still work for beer the next time around.

Thanks to Adam Duritz, for allowing me to use the Counting Crows quote that opens the book, and Nicole Duritz for talking her big brother into it.

Still dizzy from reading my publishing contract, I must thank Patrick Sweeney, a great attorney and an even better friend.

I got published without an agent. Really. I owe that to Ed Trifone, whose insistence on using his connections to get this book to Andrews McMeel made this "acknowledgments" section necessary. Eddie, we are ND.

I'm eternally grateful to my editor, Chris Schillig, who saw something in an unsolicited manuscript someone dropped on her desk. Thanks for believing in me, Chris, and for making me look better than I really am.

Without my number one fan's unflagging optimism and ceaseless editing efforts, I never could have reached this point. Mary Harder, M.D., part of this is yours.

Lastly, to the men and women I worked with at Pfizer (especially the Vipers, El Ninos, and Bricklayers), I thank you for the laughs, the lessons, and the stories. Good selling.

Prologue

"TAKE THE FIRST PILL ONE HOUR BEFORE SEX!" The urologist's voice boomed from down the hall, loudly enough that I—along with the twenty-five men jamming the waiting room—could hear. I froze, mortified by the realization: That's how Viagra is dosed!

At that point in my three-year pharmaceutical sales career, I had witnessed numerous violations of patient confidentiality. In spite of their best efforts to avoid doing so, doctors often dispensed advice in front of other patients. When discussing bronchitis or allergies, it wasn't that big a deal, but never before had I heard a physician inform everyone within earshot that, basically, "This guy can't get it up!" Viagra was really making people crazy.

And I should have seen the insanity coming. A phone call from my father two months earlier had provided all the evidence necessary.

Growing up in my parents' home, conversations about sex were as common as visits from the Pope and about as comfortable. My dad had so looked forward to our "birds and bees" talk that my mom finally had to step in and explain things to me. Consequently, I was caught off guard when, during a phone conversation in mid-March 1998, just days before Viagra received FDA approval, he jokingly referred to having s-e-x.

In January of that year, I had been promoted, along with 119 other sales reps, into Pfizer's new Urology Division, one created specifically to sell Viagra to the specialists who most often treated erectile dysfunction (ED). We had used the first two months of the year to begin establishing rapport with our new customers—it might be awkward to meet a physician for the first time and immediately begin discussing blood flow to the penis—and to sell the other three products in our division's portfolio. The urologists didn't want to hear about our drugs to treat infected prostates or help men pee less often at night, though. All they wanted to know was when the wonder pill would be on the market. Referring to this, I told my father I was looking forward to the Viagra launch meeting.

"I just know Pfizer stock is going to explode," he said optimistically. *Sure, Dad.* I nodded at the phone the way all sons do at some point when talking with their fathers. If I'd have hung up right then, we might never have had "the conversation." After a pause, Dad continued with the strange, forced chuckle I would become quite familiar with over the next few months. "Well, ha-ha, Jamie, when you get some samples, how about you send the old man some? Ha-ha, ha-ha."

My father and I had had only one successful sex talk ever. On the night of my tenth Christmas, he and I sat downstairs after the last guest had departed. Over the humming of the dishwasher, we could hear my mother moving between rooms, clearing innumerable plates and glasses. My dad gazed around the room, nodding contentedly, his eyes glassy with Christmas cheer and a half-dozen whiskey sours. Just us guys enjoying a postholiday moment; I'd never get a better chance to bring up an issue that had been bothering me for a few days. With an exaggerated cough, I interrupted the silence. Swirling the ice in his drink, he looked at me with raised eyebrows. Emboldened, I asked him what would happen if a man's penis got stuck in a woman's vagina while they were having sex. (To a ten-year-old boy, one could not imagine finding oneself in a worse predicament.) He replied, without hesitation, "You should be so lucky." Alas, the rest of our sex talks were neither memorable nor comfortable experiences for either one of us. Consequently, we silently agreed not to have them anymore.

Yet there he was on the phone talking about doing it with my mom! *Ewwww.* The thought of my parents having sex—*still* having sex in their mid-fifties—made me shiver. I was not so naïve to think that my parents had never done it. I knew that they had. Three times. And they had kids named Jamie, Patrick, and Anne-Marie to prove it. I'd rather kneel on jacks for half an hour than joke with my father about his having intercourse. Something needed to be done to prevent this discussion from ever happening again.

"You know, Dad," I began, as he continued chuckling over the preposterous idea of his needing Viagra. "This is so weird."

"What is?"

"Well, *Mom* called me two months ago and asked me to send you Viagra samples."

The startling silence was followed by a quick change of topic. Mission accomplished.

Nonetheless, when Viagra had prompted our first mentions of copulation in fifteen years, I should have realized that Pfizer's little blue pill was going to change the world. Standing in that urology office two months later, I got a peek at life A.V.—After Viagra.

"Take the first pill one hour before sex!"

Moments earlier, as I had squeezed my way toward the reception counter, I had mentally double-checked that it was, in fact, Friday. Like pharmaceutical salespeople, patients tried to avoid visiting physician's offices late on the last afternoon of the workweek. After all, who wanted to start the weekend at the doctor's? In spring 1998, a *lot* of men scheduled appointments with their urologists on Friday or any other day they could manage. Following the FDA's approval of Viagra, urologists, like American steel mills during World War II, could have stayed open 24/7 and still not met demand.

In this particular office, I had been chatting with a few staff members through the reception window when we heard the urologist's voice steadily rise to the point of yelling. I expected one of the nurses to run back there to find out what was going on. Instead, they shared a knowing look and just started laughing. When the doctor screamed out the dosing instructions for Viagra, I blanched at the thought that everyone in the waiting room would now know this man needed Viagra. Little did I realize that the guy had nothing to be embarrassed about.

"If that doesn't work tonight, tomorrow night take two pills!" A minute later, the door opened, and the physician strode toward us. He removed his glasses, rubbed the bridge of his nose, and shook his head with a broad grin. Shortly after, the door opened again and would have closed had something not propped it open. I almost fell over when I saw what that something was.

The bottom of the aluminum legs appeared first. The rest of the walker eventually caught up, but its owner took a bit longer to come into full view. I had to give the guy a break, though; it could not have been easy to use a walker *and* pull an oxygen tank at the same time. He was at least seventy, but the tubes hanging from his nostrils made him seem older. *This guy is getting Viagra?*

Reading my mind, the urologist assured me that this patient was a solid candidate for it. "I know he looks like he's ten minutes from the funeral parlor," he said, in a possible overestimation of his patient's appearance. "But he's really in decent shape. No heart problems at all, and he doesn't need the oxygen, it's more mental than anything else."

We watched the man "walk" into the waiting room, prompting a gasp from the other patients. Their thoughts were unanimously transparent: There's hope for all of us.

I turned to the office staff for an explanation of how such an old man could still be having sex, could still desire sex. "Everybody wants it," a nurse said with a shrug. And a little blue pill could help them get it.

Standing in a crowded urology office with my mouth agape seemed like an unusual circumstance for engaging in prayer, but pray I did: "Lord, please let me still be having sex after seventy." As I walked through the parking lot, I laughed at this crazy place at which I had arrived in life. I had to ask myself: How the hell did I get here?

GETTING IN

"WHAT ARE YOU, AN IDIOT?"

That was my father's reaction to my decision to get out of the army early. Thanks to the military drawdown in 1994, I was one of one hundred army lieutenants allowed to leave the service prior to completing our four-year active duty commitments. I expected Dad to be surprised by my decision and perhaps even a little upset, but I did not anticipate his questioning my intelligence. That was a bit much, I thought. An idiot?

After attending Notre Dame on an ROTC scholarship, I spent the majority of my three years on active duty at Camp Zama, Japan, hating every second in fatigues. From the moment my mom pinned those lieutenant's bars on my shoulders, I dreamed of nothing but tearing them off. The instant that became possible, I jumped all over the opportunity, and my dad jumped all over me.

"Uh, no, Dad, I'm not an idiot, it's just that—"

"Jesus Christ, Jamie, I know you're not an idiot. But this is a big decision, and it's not something you should run into half cocked. Have you even thought about this?"

Maybe he really did think I was an idiot. "C'mon, Dad, obviously I've been thinking about this a lot. I know what I'm giving up, and—" I would finish very few sentences in this conversation.

"You know! What do you know? You're only twenty-five years old; you *don't* know, okay? You have no idea what you're giving up. Jamie, you are an army *officer*. You have absolutely no appreciation for that. You're going to be promoted to captain in six months. Before you know it, you'll be collecting a pension at age forty-two and playing thirty-six holes every day." Bam! The sound of the liquor cabinet closing was unmistakable, as was the subsequent tinkling of ice in a cocktail glass.

"But, Dad, that's in seventeen *years*. I don't want to be in the army for seventeen more days, let alone seventeen years," I said, bouncing a Nerf basketball off my wall and displaying the very lack of maturity my father had referred to earlier.

"Why the hell not? It's a solid career. Look at all it's given you so far: the experience, the discipline, and the travel. You're in Japan, aren't you? What would you be doing now if it wasn't for the army?"

He did have a point there. A point, I might add, that he had managed to work into every conversation we'd had since I began active duty. Yeah, as an English major—and a not-so-motivated one, at that—my postgrad job prospects had not been so hot. I probably would've ended up at some northeastern prep school teaching English and coaching wrestling for about $1.37 per hour. Before taxes. So, in hindsight, the army had definitely been a "great place to start," but its usefulness had come to an end.

"Fine," my father spat. "It's your life, and you can do with it what you like. Speaking of which, what are you going to do?"

"What do you mean?" I asked, crushing the Nerf in my fist.

"When you get out." At this point, he raised his voice and slowed his rate of speech, enunciating each syllable as if speaking to a foreigner. "What are you going to do for a job when you get out of the army?" Bam! I could picture him pouring the second drink, more vodka than tonic.

A smart guy would've been ready for this question. A smart guy would've rehearsed his answer over and over until he had it just right.

"I don't know."

"You don't know?" I still get a bit weak-kneed when I imagine the look on his face as he turned to Mom in disbelief. "He doesn't know." Dad paused at this point, possibly searching for the nitroglycerin tablets to prevent his second heart attack.

"You don't *know?* You just made the biggest decision of your goddamned life, and yet you *don't know* what you're going to do next?"

That would have been a good time to say something reassuring, something to indicate that this decision had been made by a mature adult after a great deal of objective analysis.

"Jeez, Dad, what are you getting so worked up about? It's really not that big a deal."

Strangely, he did not seem reassured. "I . . . I . . . I can't talk to you. Normally, I'd say, 'I hope you know what you're doing,' but, ha-ha, you've already made it pretty damned clear that you don't. Here, talk to your mother."

I almost cried tears of thanks. *Mom* was getting on the phone! She'd understand what I was going through. She'd appreciate my throwing caution to the wind. Mom would make it all better.

"Do you *really* not know what you're going to do?"

"Oh, I'll be fine, Mom. Don't worry about me. I'm just going to wing it, and we'll see what happens."

Without going into all the boring, profanity-laced details, suffice it to say that "winging it" was not a concept with which mothers—mine, in particular—were comfortable. Moms prefer a specific flight plan and a destination.

Thankfully, the latter was one thing I *did* have. I may not have had any idea what I'd be doing once I got there, but I knew where I was going: Chicago, home of my girlfriend, Katey.

In fact, that was the only certainty in my life. I was head over heels in love, and I had promised her, *guaranteed* her, that I'd move to Chicago after spending a leisurely June at my parents' house forty-five minutes north of New York City.

Alas, my father had a different plan for his eldest son's first thirty days back in the States. The grass was at least a foot high, the dining room needed to be painted, and the leaves from the *previous* autumn had yet to be raked.

"Why doesn't Patrick mow the lawn like I used to have to do?" I whined, referring to my teenage brother.

My dad shook his head. "He's allergic to grass."

"Allergic to grass? Dad, he plays on the football team."

I didn't win many arguments that summer, but I did mow, paint, and rake my unemployed ass off. All in addition to the daily dose of grief I got from my father concerning my lack of direction or paycheck.

Dad was not a big fan of his twenty-five-year-old son's sleeping past eleven o'clock each morning in a bedroom still decorated with the athletic and beer posters I had hung in high school; such behavior did not provide my two younger siblings with the sterling example of go-getter-ness he desired. Before getting into the shower every morning, he'd come into my room and shake the bed just enough to disrupt the coma. Twenty minutes later, as he left for work, he'd throw the door open, turn on the lights, and begin his daily "pep talk."

"Hey, GI Joe, how about you look for a job today?" he'd ask, not waiting for a response. "It's been three weeks, and you haven't had one interview. I hear McDonald's is hiring: fun, food, and friends. At least mow the damn lawn, would ya?" Twenty-five years after leaving the Bronx, his accent was still strong.

For his coup de grace, my loving father would yank the covers off me on his way out the door to a job that most certainly involved kicking puppies. He left the bedroom lights on, of course. That month, I learned a lot about my ability to sleep while shivering and squeezing my eyes shut tight.

The torture didn't end there, though. From his office, he'd call the house over and over again, knowing that the phone was located close enough to be annoying yet too far for me to answer without getting out of bed. In any other American home, an answering machine would have limited my suffering. Not in the Reidy house. Maintaining their perfect record of ignoring technological advances—we had been the last family on the block to get cable, a VCR, or a video-game system—my parents owned no such newfangled gadgetry. As a result, the rotary-dial phone would ring for as long as Lord Vader liked.

On one of those fun mornings, my career in pharmaceutical sales got started.

Having already suffered through several "ringings," I finally got up and staggered to the bathroom. As I turned off the faucet, the phone began ringing again. I sprinted toward it, pleased to show my dad that I had gotten up before noon. After about eight rings, I picked up.

"Hello?" My voice sounded as if I had just awakened after drinking until three A.M. What a coincidence.

A man who was not my dad said, "Oh, good, I didn't think anyone was home. The answering machine didn't pick up."

"Really? That's weird." I pegged the guy for a telemarketer, and saw no reason to ration the sarcasm. "Can I ask who's calling?"

The guy cleared his throat, embarrassed. "Oh, sure. Sorry, I should have introduced myself up front. I'm John Dryer with Orion Recruiters. I'm trying to get in touch with a Jamie Reidy."

I stood up a little straighter. "That's me." Before leaving Japan, I had floated my résumé to Orion Recruiters, a firm "specializing" in placing junior military officers.

"Oh, great! Well, we received your résumé, and I've gotta say that you are very impressive on paper. Let me ask you: What do you think about pharmaceutical sales?"

Although I did not have a clue as to what I wanted to do with my life, I knew that sales was not it. Not that I had anything against salesmen, I just thought of them as short, sneaky guys who tried to sell you shit you didn't need.

"Uh, I don't," I said in a monotone. Mr. Dryer was undeterred.

"Okay, well, what do you think about a base salary of forty thousand plus bonus, an expense account, a company car, and a laptop computer?"

Forty thousand dollars? In my last year as a lieutenant, I had made $31,000. Maybe. Forty thousand seemed like a lot of money to a twenty-five-year-old guy standing in his boxers three feet from his boyhood bedroom. I ditched the attitude.

"Oh, did you say pharma*ceutical* sales? I'm sorry, I thought you said *farm tools*." I paused, shaking my head. *Farm tools?* "I am very interested in pharmaceutical sales, John."

Having hooked his fish, Mr. Dryer continued. "All right! The company's name is Pfizer. I'm sure you've heard of them."

I had not. For a guy conducting a "job search," I knew amazingly little about the business world. Outside of IBM, Microsoft, and Abbott Labs, I had not heard of many companies. The only reason I knew anything about Abbott was because they had, amazingly enough, hired a college buddy who spent more time on academic probation than off and didn't get his driver's license until two weeks before the job interview.

"Uh, yeah, uh, no, no, I don't think I have. To tell you the truth, I'm not very familiar with the pharmaceutical industry. How do you spell that, F-y-z . . . ?"

If John had ended the conversation right then and there, Pfizer would have been a lot better off.

"No, no. It's P-f-i-z-e-r. Believe me, Pfizer is one of the best corporations in the nation, and you should be honored that they've selected you for an interview."

"Oh, I'm honored, John. I am honored." I was so honored that I missed the next few things he said, as I kept mouthing, "Forty thousand dollars!" I had some questions as to why such an outstanding company would want to hire a guy who nearly flunked high school chemistry and had no sales experience, but I kept such thoughts to myself.

"Okay, Jamie, then I'll put an information packet on Pfizer in the mail to you today. Can you be in Chicago next Friday for an eight o'clock interview?"

"Uh, hang on a second while I check my calendar." Putting the phone down, I checked my "calendar," which bore a striking resemblance to the *New York Post*'s sports section, crinkling some pages to make it sound as if I was checking a daily planner.

"Next Friday? Uh, yeah, I think I can make it then."

"Super. I've got a good feeling about this, Jamie. I'll be in touch."

As he said his good-bye, Katey's face exploded into my mind.

"Wait! John, there's one more thing. I know when I filled out your information sheet that I listed Chicago as my preferred city; this job *is* in Chicago, right? Because that's the only place I want to live."

He didn't hesitate. "Sure, Jamie, they have plenty of openings in Chicago. You just knock 'em dead at the interviews, and everything will fall into place."

Relieved, I hung up the phone and immediately called my dad.

"Reidy."

He always answered the phone as if he was an FBI agent bunkered down in a command post, not a financial planner.

"Hey, Dad. Listen, what do you know about Pfizer?" I asked, uncertain whether I was even pronouncing the name correctly.

He paused for a long second before answering.

"Take the job! Take the job!" He pounded his desk as he spoke, and I imagined his suffering chest pains as the result of his exuberance.

"Dad, relax, they just called to set up an inter—"

"Take it! They are a *great* company. The *best!* We rated their stock number one in the industry this year. Jamie, listen to me, you are an *idiot* if you do not take this job."

Again with the idiot thing! I had graduated from the University of Notre Dame and earned a commission as an officer in the United States Army, yet my old man acted as if I had gotten an AA from

West Texas State–Southern and had spent the past three years working at a car wash. The first time he called me an idiot, I pretty much
blew it off. This time, however, I really believed him. Truth be told, I
was starting to sweat not having a job. Hence, I wussed out.

Fortunately, I was a lucky wussy. At a wedding the weekend
before my interview, a friend told me about his fraternity brother
who worked for Pfizer. "You need to give him a call," Michael said.
Dismissing it as typical drunken nonsense, I nodded and ordered
another round. Michael was serious, though, and he called me the
next day with his buddy's number. "You know, you can make a lot
of money as a drug rep," Michael said. "Like, a hundred grand."
Suddenly, he had my full attention. "He's expecting your call.
There's a bunch of stuff in pharma sales that you have to know to ace
the interview, and he can help you out. Have you done any research
on your own?" *Good one.* "Yeah, you really should call him."

I called him. Man, did he help me.

"The whole thing is about getting scripts," he said matter-of-
factly. He correctly interpreted my silence as confusion.

"Scripts. *Prescriptions.* That is what this job is all about: getting
docs to write prescriptions for our drugs instead of another drug." I
nodded as I scribbled on the pad: Scripts!

He continued, discussing HMOs, samples, company cars, nurses,
daily routines, and so on. He gave me a nice tip on a possible interview question—What is something you worked and worked and
worked for, but ultimately failed at?—that I was asked on Friday.
Most important, however, he taught me how to act like a "closer."

"What's a closer?" I asked, as my mind raced with images of
baseball relief pitchers like Dennis Eckersley. His sigh was audible.

"A closer is a guy who asks for the business, a guy who breaks
docs down and gains a commitment to use our product." I was very
confused.

"How am I going to show the interviewer I'm a closer if I have
never sold anything?"

His answer was the money shot, a piece of advice that has made me—and a number of people with whom I have shared this story—a lot of money. "You just have to make him believe in you, make him see that you have it in you to be a closer." He paused dramatically before continuing.

"At the end of the interview, he'll ask you, 'Jamie, do you have any questions for me?' You'll ask him the typical ones: 'How long is training? When can I get promoted? Do I get stock options?' And after he has answered them, you drop it on him." I stopped scribbling the three questions he assumed I would know to ask but that I had, in fact, never thought of. *It?*

"You get on the edge of your seat and look him right in the eye and say, 'Mr. Interview Guy, I *know* I'm the right guy for the job. I *know* I'm going to blow it out sales-wise and do great at this job, but I'm wondering if there is anything—*anything*—that would stop you from hiring me right now?'"

All that sounded a bit cocky, even for an egomaniac like me. I said as much.

"That's the point!" he said. "Sales guys *need* to think they are the best, and you have to get that across in the interview or you're finished. Even if the rest of the interview went shitty, you *have* to close him at the end. See, a big part of our job is simply asking doctors for the business, 'Doc, will you use our drug first to treat bronchitis?' If the guy says yes, great! If he says no, that's okay, too, because then that's when the *real* selling starts."

I hung up the phone with my head spinning.

The interview took place at eight A.M. on a Friday in late June. I reported to the hotel at 7:45 in a blue suit, white shirt, red tie, and wing tips, and immediately spotted ten other guys with short haircuts dressed exactly like me—my first introduction to the fact that Pfizer *loved* military guys. Pfizer had just added a new sales force specializing in pediatrics and, as a result, had to hire 150 new reps by August 1.

After filling out the typical paperwork, I was ushered into a hotel suite to meet with the local HR director, Brandon Somethingorother. Bearing more than a slight resemblance to Nick Tortelli, Carla's ex-husband on *Cheers*, Brandon exuded an annoying "I'm-*the*-HR-guy!" vibe. He waved me in with a hurried motion, suggesting that every minute of his time was precious. Somehow, his day was already going poorly at eight A.M., and he greeted me tersely. "So, you're willing to relocate anywhere in the Midwest, right?"

"Uh, excuse me?"

His condescending stare suggested that I was less than intelligent. *What was with these middle-aged guys thinking I'm stupid?*

A sigh. "The Midwest. You're willing to relocate anywhere in the Midwest, right?"

There must be some mistake, I told myself. He must have me mixed up with some poor guy who didn't have a *recruiter* set up his interview, a recruiter who knew that his candidate would only work in Chicago and had guaranteed his candidate that the job was, in fact, in Chicago.

"Uh, no, no, I'm not." The look got worse. "I was told the job was in Chicago."

Brandon-the-HR-guy closed his eyes and rubbed the bridge of his nose where his glasses had left a mark.

"Then don't interview."

"Excuse me?"

He had already begun gathering my résumé and other papers to put them back into their manila folder. "Don't interview." He stood, hands on hips. I sat, mouth agape. "I don't have a spot in Chicago. I don't want to waste your time, and I don't want to waste my time. So, don't interview."

I should have walked out. Better yet, I should have said, "Blow me," before leaving. And then I should have called ace recruiter John Dryer and told him to go screw himself. (Imagine, a recruiter misleading a job candidate?) I did none of those things.

Instead, I asked Brandon-the-HR-guy what territories *near* Chicago he had open. He stared at me silently, as though I was now officially wasting his time. I quickly explained that, due to the stipulations of my early out from the army, I had to live within a seventy-five-mile radius from an Army Reserve unit outside Chicago. Still silent, he began nodding up and down. Grabbing a sheet of paper, he read off the names of various cities with openings. When he said, "South Bend, Indiana," I jumped out of my chair. "I'll take South Bend!" Brandon squinted at me suspiciously and asked why. I pointed out that I had graduated from Notre Dame and was familiar with the area.

At this, his face underwent a complete transformation from total jerk-off to long-lost buddy. Extending his hand for a hearty handshake, he smiled. "Brandon Riley, Class of '68." I was in.

Which wasn't good, at least not according to my girlfriend. The way I later unsuccessfully explained it to Katey was, "I dunno what happened. It was like when my freshman football coach told me I might never set foot on the field or my drill sergeant said I wouldn't be able to climb his wall; it was some kind of challenge, and I just couldn't let him get away with it."

Girlfriends do not want to hear about former coaches or army guys and the pointless challenges they may have made to your machismo years ago. Nor do girlfriends want to hear about how "South Bend is just a two-hour drive from Chicago, which is quite an improvement on the twelve-hour flight from Tokyo." The only thing girlfriends want to hear about is when you are moving into their neighborhood.

Even though Brandon Riley, Class of '68, had welcomed me to the club, I still had to interview with a regional manager, for whom approximately seventy-five reps worked. Brandon came out from behind his desk to give me the skinny on this guy.

"He is going to want to hear examples of your overcoming challenges, and he loves to hear about competitiveness. He may give you a hard time about your lack of sales experience." He paused, as if he had forgotten something. "Don't forget to close him. Tell him that you and I discussed it, and South Bend is the place for you. Now, you go in there and show him what an ND man is all about!" *Go Irish!*

The regional manager barely got out of his chair to shake my hand. He showed even less energy during the rest of the interview. Livelier fish could be found at Tokyo's famous seafood markets. I regurgitated Michael's friend's hip terminology such as "scripts" and "asking for the business," but got no reaction. It was as if this guy was an energy vampire, sucking the life out of me in order to (barely) keep himself alive. My voice lacked its usual enthusiasm, and I slouched in my chair. As I mumbled on about overcoming great odds to get a B in German 201, he interrupted me.

"So, how'd you like Zama?" he asked, relevant to nothing. *How'd I like what? Did he say something?*

Somewhere in the back of my nearly numb brain, his question struck a chord. Zama, Zama, yeah, sounds familiar . . . oh, yeah! I had been stationed at Camp Zama in Japan. A tiny army post that served little purpose, most *soldiers* had never heard of it, let alone civilians. My friends and family routinely butchered its spelling and pronunciation—Zuma, Zema, Zoma; only people who had been there called it Zama, for short.

Waking from my coma, I looked at him with my head cocked to the side, my brow furrowed with confusion. He smiled briefly.

"I did some R and R there while flying in Korea," he said, suddenly sitting straighter in his chair, his voice displaying a timbre absent during the previous thirty-five minutes. We quickly struck up a lively and entertaining conversation about serving in the military in Asia. He had been a Marine pilot, as my father had hoped to become before blowing out his knee at Marine basic training at Parris Island. "Semper Fi!" I said, before sharing my dad's story, which garnered an approving nod.

We spoke no more about pharmaceuticals. Twenty minutes later, we both seemed surprised when Brandon Riley, Class of '68, knocked on the door, indicating that our interviewing time was up.

"Where do you want to work?" the regional manager asked. This caught me off guard; I had been readying myself for the all-important "Do you have any questions for me?" question.

"Uh . . . South Bend," I replied, thinking the words sounded strange. He smacked the desk.

"Sounds good," he said, standing to shake my hand. "Good luck out there." I hadn't even gotten the chance to close him.

That was it. I got a job in pharmaceutical sales, not because of my qualifications, but because the HR guy went to Notre Dame, and the man who did the hiring had spent three days at an obscure army post in Japan forty years before.

I ended up losing a girlfriend because I took a job I hadn't sought—in a town I hadn't considered—all because my daddy told me to do so.

Two

BOOT CAMP

HAVING BEEN HIRED WITHOUT SALES EXPERIENCE or a science background, I was in serious need of training. Fortunately, Pfizer took its training very seriously.

Although the circumstances could not have appeared more different, I felt the same queasiness in my stomach walking into the hotel for Pfizer Initial Training as I had experienced five years earlier while climbing onto a bus headed for boot camp at Fort Knox.

The two situations were not without similarities. For starters, just as I hadn't planned on working for Pfizer, I'd never intended to join the army. Having put my family on the hook for $45,000 in unexpected tuition costs by quitting *navy* ROTC three weeks into my freshman year—because it "was a hassle"—I felt a nagging sense of guilt, one that my more business-minded classmates did a superb job of heightening. "Dude, your dad is a broker? He must've gotten *wrecked* by the stock market crash in '87!" *Uh, yeah, I guess I remember his being a bit moodier than normal that autumn.* Apparently, at the time, there were more important issues on Planet Jamie—trying not to set a school record for dropped passes and wondering why none of the cheerleaders would date me, to name two.

After becoming the fifth of five Reidys to recognize the drain I'd become on our family, I applied for a two-year army ROTC scholarship in 1990. I didn't receive one, but I was given the opportunity to spend six fun-filled weeks in Kentucky, competing against six hundred other juniors-to-be for a scholarship. That June, the only thing heavier than the humidity in the Blue Grass State was the weight on my shoulders. I rallied, though, and won the $20,000, which my mom promptly spent on a new car. Which I was not allowed to drive for a year.

I didn't feel any pressure as I entered Pfizer training—I already had the job this time—but I did have the same "What the hell am I doing?" chorus running through my head. Curiously, boot camp and Pfizer training each lasted six weeks, an ominous parallel. In both places, I was told when to eat, and my dining options were severely limited.

The strangest similarity, though, concerned my parents' behavior prior to my departures. Drinks in hand while reclining on chaise lounges, my mother and father somehow concluded that what I needed most in my final hours of unemployment was to hear *every* sales tip they had ever learned. They could have filled an entire Ken Burns documentary called *Sales*. Listening to them drone on, I flashed back to driving with my dad to the airport for my flight to Fort Knox. He talked continuously for the forty-five-minute trip, relating tales from his Marine Corps boot camp, tips on how to handle drill instructors, and so forth. He meant well then, just as they both had good intentions in the backyard lecture series, but these occasions called for less, not more. Having learned through years of product testing that my parents hadn't come equipped with a "less" switch, I decided to get to Pfizer training early.

It didn't take long to get there. In a nice twist of fate, training was held at the Marriott Hotel in Park Ridge, New Jersey—ten minutes from my folks' house. This proved extremely convenient when my fellow trainees and I wanted to do laundry for free or enjoy gratis Oreo Blizzards courtesy of my sister, Anne-Marie, who worked at the local Dairy Queen.

A cacophony of voices greeted me at the lobby of the hotel; 150 salespeople make quite a racket. Sizing up the crowd, two thoughts came to mind: "Wow, more guys who look like me!" and "Check out all the babes!" As I skirted the group's edge looking for a place to break in, I sensed a commonality among my classmates, a uniformity that seemed familiar but which I could not place. Men and women of differing nationalities and ages filled the room, but they had something identifying them as a group, as part of the same team. Then it hit me: Everyone was *in uniform*, yet another similarity between the army and Pfizer.

Not that a camouflage-clad regiment had invaded the Marriott. Rather, the males were dressed alike, as were the females: "business casual." Resembling the cast of extras in a Dockers commercial, the guys—myself included—all sported golf shirts or button-downs with their pressed khakis. The ladies appeared to have been invited to a different party. They wore business suits with scarves (Pfizer girls love their scarves), unless they were from California, in which case the fashion daredevils traded pants that matched their suit jackets for skirts that matched their suit jackets. Later that night, a woman explained the disparity in dress in this way: "It's total bullshit, to be completely honest. There's just no way for us to dress casual without looking slutty, so we have to wear what we'd normally wear to work, which means that even though they say 'business casual,' it might as well be 'business standard' 'cause that's how it ends up. Yet, you guys get to look like you just walked off the eighteenth green." This would not be the only time in my career that I would hear, in no uncertain terms, about the injustices suffered by women in our male-dominated world.

Having exhausted all delaying tactics, I took a deep breath and approached the first cluster I saw. Extending my right hand toward an attractive, dark-haired woman, I leaned in, read the name tag hanging from a cord around her neck—yet *another* military parallel; everyone had to wear name tags—and introduced myself to my first Pfizer pfriend. This began a series of introductions that lasted approximately three days. With few exceptions, every one of my 149 classmates was impossibly friendly. I had never spent time with so many people who were as chatty as me, and it was fairly annoying. When would I get to talk?

My chance arrived soon enough, allowing me quickly to shove one of my size-twelve loafers squarely into my mouth. Standing in a group of five, someone tossed out the conversation starter, "How about those interviews?" Three people rolled their eyes and nodded knowingly. Not sure why they had nodded knowingly but certain that I did not want to be the only one not doing so, I nodded knowingly, too. "One after another and they just kept getting harder," a woman offered, sparking a flurry of comments around the circle, all of which focused on the number of interviews each of these people had endured. Finally, a guy trumped everyone by revealing he'd had *seven* interviews. Jaws dropped in empathetic horror. I could no longer contain myself.

"Yeah," I began, wanting to join the crowd. "Mine was a *killer*." Four confused looks came my way.

"What do you mean, 'Yours *was* a killer'?" the topic originator asked. "Didn't you have more than one?" The eyes of the group bored holes in my forehead. *Bridge out. Turn back! Turn back!*

"Uh, no," I laughed. Alone. "I had only the one." Word of the "one-interview guy" spread faster than pinkeye through a kindergarten. Had I not snagged a beer cooler from my dad's garage the next afternoon—fifteen of us played volleyball after class every day—I may not have made any friends.

Ah, if only that had been my sole blunder in the early days. When I met Gina, the director of initial training, who, with her blond bob, glasses, and striped button-down shirt, looked as though she had just fallen out of a Brooks Brothers ad, I did not thank her for the opportunity or ask for a pearl of advice on successfully completing what would surely be a challenging month and a half. Ignoring all the signs screaming "Caution: ultraconservative ahead!," I told her, "The beers in the hotel bar are four dollars apiece! I was thinking maybe you could talk to the manager and explain that, with over a hundred and fifty of us drinking here for the next six weeks, we deserve a Pfizer discount." Gina peered through her glasses at me for a long moment before suggesting that perhaps the price of alcohol should not have been the most important thing on my mind on the eve of training. Apparently, she did not see the humor in this. There was another person who did not guffaw at my request: my district sales manager, Bruce. My *Mormon* district sales manager.

Of course, I didn't realize he was Mormon right away. If I had, maybe I would've tried to cut down on my cursing a bit. Not that it would have been easy; after three years in the army, I couldn't complete a sentence without tossing out, at a bare minimum, three "F Bombs." See, soldiers didn't listen to anything that was not preceded by and finished by a profanity, preferably a strong one. "Shit" barely rated as a curse in the army. Conversations with troops went something like this:

Me: Sergeant Santiago, did you get me the colonel's personnel file like I asked?

Sergeant Santiago: (No reaction at all. Since I hadn't followed standard operating procedure by saying "fuck" within the first five words of the sentence, he did not process the question.)

Me: Sergeant Santiago, where the fuck is the colonel's personnel file?

Santiago (Head turned toward me, eyes registering the briefest recognition): Did you say something, sir?

Me: Holy fuck! I need the fucking colonel's fucking personnel
   file. Fucking Santiago, why is it not on my fucking desk like
   I fucking told you fucking yesterday?
Santiago: Look under the *Sports Illustrated,* sir.

So, having succeeded in that colorful world, I transferred that
style to the real world, where it wasn't necessarily embraced.

I hadn't met many Mormons in the army, and there hadn't been
a large number of Latter-Day Saints majors at Notre Dame, but I
was familiar with the basics: They were all great quarterbacks from
Utah who lived according to some *Footloose*-esque rules prohibit-
ing dancing, drinking, and fun, in general. Although Bruce had
never enjoyed a cocktail with me or cursed in my presence, he
didn't fit "the profile." A taller, bug-eyed version of Michael J. Fox,
he displayed a materialistic vein, wearing Polo clothes as though
his dad was Ralph Lauren. He could quote any line from *Raising
Arizona* and Andrew "Dice" Clay's first HBO special. Finally, his
extensive music collection contained lots of angry young men (the
Cult and Nirvana) and few happy young men (the Tabernacle
Choir). This guy was a Mormon? Regardless, complaining about
"four fucking dollars for a Bud Light bottle" was not the best way
to begin a career with a new manager. Fortunately, I was able to
blame my fellow trainees for my gaffe. I mean, one of the, like,
eight hundred other Mormons in my class could have warned me.

Pfizer *loved* its Mormons. Allegedly, more than one-third of
Pfizer's entire sales force could sing the BYU fight song. I heard
different theories explaining this high percentage, with the best one
stating, "If you can sell religion door to door in a foreign language,
you can sell *anything.*"

Almost equaling the number of Mormons, though, was the
number of former military officers in the group, hence the bevy
of short haircuts I noticed upon entering the hotel. I commented
on the coincidence that Pfizer had hired all these ex-military guys,

and one of our trainers, a former naval officer, revealed that it was no accident. "We need self-starters, people who can be counted on to get up every morning and go to work and be trusted with an expense account and a car. People who are used to managing people, but will now manage only themselves." This would later prove to be a *teeny* crack in the system.

Pfizer prided itself on being a company for the twenty-first century, and the demographic makeup of the remainder of my class reflected that attitude. In addition to the Mormons, military guys, and attractive women, there were sizable percentages of black, Asian, and Indian people. Our trainers joked that the sales force was comprised of the "Three M's"—Military, Minorities, and Mormons—and it was easy to believe. An extremely diversified group entered "boot camp" that day in August 1995, emerging six weeks later not as trained killers, but as trained closers. *Highly* trained closers.

Our indoctrination into the Pfizer Way began one second into our first class. The schedule stated that training would commence at eight A.M. Accordingly, a large number of people arrived at 7:58 and took a few minutes to fill coffee cups. Wrong.

As 150 of us wandered around looking for our assigned seats, Gina stood at the front of the room looking less than pleased. When the herd had finally settled, she spoke.

"It is now eight-oh-four. Class begins at eight. This does not mean you arrive at eight, but that you will be seated and ready to participate *before* eight. We operate on Pfizer Time, meaning if you are not ten minutes early, you're late." I glanced about the room to gauge the reaction. While the military people nodded along as if to say, "Business as usual," there were more than a few trainees with their heads on a swivel, looking around for someone to let them in on the joke. In complete possession of everyone's full attention, Gina began our training.

Any drug rep from any company will tell you that he left initial training thinking that his drugs were the best in the industry, such was the power of pharmaceutical brainwashing. Pfizer reps departed training with a "Pass me the Kool-Aid" conviction that not only were our drugs the best in the industry, but also that our company was the best in the world. Doctors and competing reps alike routinely commented on a "Pfizer attitude," a tangible vibe suggesting we were intrinsically better than any other salespeople. Interestingly, army trainees emerge from boot camp with a similar sense of indestructibility, an unshakable belief that there could not be a more prepared soldier on earth. The key to creating this self-confidence in both arenas was the same: an endless repetition of message and task.

In basic training, the drill sergeants sent a message that was simple, but not subtle. The U.S. Army was the pinnacle of military preparedness, and you should thank your lucky stars you were given this opportunity. You were shit, and you would always be shit, unless you got with the program. Who wouldn't want to go from the shithouse to the penthouse? One glance at a drill sergeant showed a recruit what a real soldier looked like: perfectly pressed uniform, boots shining like the freshly waxed hood of a black Lexus, body ready to snap off one hundred push-ups at any time. They were the living embodiment of what we were supposed to become and what we wanted to become.

Few Pfizer trainers could have dropped and given us one hundred, but there were no out-of-shape instructors, either. Former fighter pilots and army Rangers and college athletes and cheerleaders trained us. We repeatedly heard about how then-CEO Bill Steere took his family heli-skiing every winter and how a rep in California was a world-champion arm wrestler. The message was clear: There were few fat people at Pfizer. Though not all supermodels, every one of the trainers was well dressed and somewhat attractive. Universally quick on their feet, with smooth, confident deliveries, none of them appeared older than thirty-five. Each had an encyclopedic recall of the most minute product details and perfect pronunciation of complex scientific terms. Young, smart, and talented, they represented what we were supposed to become and, in many cases, what we wanted to become. "In the training department," I responded when Bruce asked me where I wanted to be in two years.

Over beers, I grew to like the trainers even more. Away from their stage, they proved to be funny people who didn't take themselves too seriously, willing to share stories and buy rounds. We learned a lot about them—sometimes too much.

Two of the most popular trainers were guys in their mid-twenties, Matt and Edward. A typical Italian guy from the Northeast, Matt was a bit on the cheesy side, a weight lifter who changed his voice to a softer pitch when he talked to women, but he was a good guy nonetheless. A tall, former college pitcher, Edward drove the women *crazy* with his killer wardrobe and smooth style. With his shaven head, he resembled Michael Jordan. Drinking beers one night, we heard a story about Matt and Edward as hotel roommates at a Pfizer meeting.

Edward awakened one morning to the sound of his electric razor. He thought this was weird, seeing as how Matt shaved with a disposable razor and shaving cream. Edward got out of bed and walked toward the bathroom area, which had two sinks located just outside the shower and toilet room. Turning the corner, he stopped in his tracks. Matt did not see Edward, which was understandable: A guy really *should* be staring intently at his testicles while shaving them. Edward found Matt standing naked with one foot on the countertop and Edward's electric razor buzzing in his hand.

"What the fuck are you doing?" Edward asked.

Matt looked up, surprised. "Shaving my balls," he said matter-of-factly.

"I can see that! But that . . . that's my razor!"

Matt nodded. "I'll be done in a minute."

Edward told Matt to *keep* the razor.

Fortunately for Matt and us, Pfizer didn't select its trainers based on their personal grooming habits or adherence to etiquette; sales success, personality, and career ambition stood out as prerequisites. We as trainees were fortunate also because Matt was a great trainer. He brought a real world perspective to training, rolling his eyes at some of the things the company required him to teach us, and people listened to him because of it. In front of a crowd, he, like all the trainers, was impressive.

Apparently, we were an impressive group ourselves. From Day One, people told us how great we were. "Pat yourselves on the back," our first speaker said, "because you are the cream of the crop." I had already noticed that our class did not lack confidence, and the knowing grins on people's faces confirmed my perception. The speaker went on anyway. "We interviewed ten people for each one of your jobs." This sparked some surprised looks. "You are a mature group. The vast majority of you have previous sales experience, or at least have been in the workplace for a few years."

I didn't grasp the significance of that comment, but it was later explained to me that most pharmaceutical companies hire recent college graduates. Pfizer being Pfizer, however, it didn't have to resort to trolling college campuses; Pfizer could pick and choose its sales force from candidates who got their start at other companies. (This changed in the late 1990s as several expansions inside and outside Pfizer thinned the talent pool, forcing the company to hire twenty-two- and twenty-three-year-olds. The difference in maturity and talent was quite evident to veteran reps.) "So, you *are* the best, and now you *work* for the best. Congratulations." Wild applause and cheering followed. *I could really get used to someone telling me I'm as great as I already think I am,* I remember thinking.

The brainwashing was not limited to our view of ourselves, however. Rather, the Pfizer training staff instilled within us indelibly negative impressions of our competitors, creating a hatred for people we had yet to compete against, let alone meet. The swiftness and lasting effect of their mental manipulation reminded me of an experience at Notre Dame.

During the first week of my freshman year, in 1988, a guy in a neighboring dorm hung a bedsheet out his window, reading, BEAT THE RUSH; HATE MIAMI NOW. Two seasons prior, the Miami Hurricanes had humiliated the Fighting Irish on national television by running a reverse for a last-second touchdown, despite their 40-plus point lead. During the 1987 contest, Miami dominated 24–0, again on national TV. The losses hurt ND fans, but it was the cockiness of the Hurricane players and coaches that sparked a blood feud. Those games had had little impact on me while I was a high school student, but within days of reading that bedsheet, I had worked up a powerful hatred of Miami. Likewise, after two days of training, I absolutely despised the Biaxin (an antibiotic from Abbott Labs) and Prozac (Eli Lilly & Co.) reps.

They lied. They cheated. Their women dressed slutty. They bought physicians' love with extravagant dinners and golf at Pebble Beach, instead of earning it through ethical practices. (I later learned that *every* company told its reps that they did things the "right way," while the other companies cheated.) What would you expect, though, from reps who sold substandard drugs for substandard companies? Their headquarters were in the *Midwest,* for crying out loud, as opposed to midtown Manhattan, two blocks from the United Nations. With our white hats firmly in place, we would ride off to victory, both moral and financial.

Accordingly, at least once a week another big shot—a sharply dressed, in shape, well-spoken big shot—would come in and tell us how great Pfizer was. Having heard over and over about our strong stock performance, unparalleled drug pipeline, and ethical superiority, I began to understand why my dad had "encouraged" me to take this job.

Having pumped us up, the trainers pumped us full of everything we needed to know in order to keep Pfizer at the top. The first week of initial training covered the basics of anatomy and pharmacology (how drugs affect the body), and we were given exams daily. I wasn't crazy about taking a test every day, but my mood brightened considerably after learning that 80 percent was a passing grade. Other than naming an honor grad—the trainee with the highest GPA got a gift certificate (I think) and an attaboy—there was no significance placed on excelling academically. Or maybe I just didn't pay attention when any significance was applied. Faced with the option of studying to become number one or doing the bare minimum to get by, I headed to the bar. I wasn't alone.

There was something refreshing about entering a hotel bar to find friends with their feet up, textbooks strewn among beer bottles. Refreshing, or *concerning,* as Bruce described the scene. "Okay, all right," he told Steve, a district teammate, and myself, nodding excitedly. "I see how it's going to be with you guys." We exchanged "Oh shit, here comes the big speech" looks. Bruce's eyes narrowed as he continued. "If you guys want to do it this way, fine. Can't wait to see how you do on the exam." He definitely scared us a bit, and we buckled down to do some studying. Then the game came back on and somebody bought us another round, and we kinda lost momentum. When Steve and I both scored 90s the next day, Bruce had mixed emotions. We, on the other hand, did not. *Uh, two Bud Lights, please.*

The next fortnight consisted of intense instruction on the drugs we would be selling to pediatricians, ENTs (ear, nose, and throat docs), and ob-gyns. The level of difficulty of the exams increased dramatically, as the trainers drove home the point that we had to be the experts on our products. In essence, we had to know everything. God forbid a tough-to-see doctor asked us a question we couldn't answer; we may never again have the opportunity to see that particular doctor. We also had to have a firm grasp on our competing products. Frequently referencing Sun Tzu's *The Art of War,* our instructors urged us to know our enemies better than we knew ourselves. Consequently, we memorized dosing schedules, side-effect profiles, and efficacy rates, searching for weaknesses. At first, I struggled to adjust to the elevated intensity and sweated out a few scores in the low 80s. This embarrassed the hell out of me because, for all the stroking the trainers did in telling us how smart and successful we were, it wasn't as though Pfizer had raided NASA's recruiting pool. Sufficiently motivated to step it up a notch, I started studying more and sat in on a few study groups. I had never seen so many flashcards. "What's the dose of Zithromax for chlamydia?" Flip. "One gram, one time!" By the end of the first three-week session, I felt very confident about my product knowledge.

Phase II bore no resemblance to Phase I. Sayonara, Dockers and golf shirts; hello, suits and ties. Training took place not at the Marriott, but at IBM's corporate training site in Palisades, New York, where Pfizer had leased space prior to building its own training center. The new site, an impressive facility that screamed of professionalism, alerted us to the fact that our collegiate atmosphere was over. Business had begun.

Whereas Phase I provided us with the knowledge the job required, the second three-week session was designed to turn us into walking, talking Pfizer sales reps, armed and dangerous. In the first two weeks, the trainers taught us our sales pitches—known as "details"—for each of the three drugs we would be selling: Zithromax (ear infections), Zoloft (depression), and Diflucan (oral thrush in babies, yeast infections in women). We then rehearsed the details intensely, repeating them over and over in front of trainers and among peers. For the finale, Week Three introduced us to the dreaded video recorder, and we were videotaped "detailing" trainers pretending to be doctors, and not always friendly ones. We heard so many horror stories about Week Three that the Hell Week of SEAL training infamy practically paled in comparison.

From the start of Week One, it was obvious that the train-ers' attitudes mirrored that of our new training site: serious and focused. Immediately, two of them—playing the roles of sales rep and doctor—demonstrated what a successful call was like. The rep was impressive, confidently delivering his sales pitch while smoothly flipping through the twenty-plus pages of his visual aid, aka "vis aid." When he finished, we applauded enthusiastically. The trainer who played the doctor provided commentary. "Did you see the way he started out with an attention grabbing IBS [Initial Benefit Statement], then gave me a trial close halfway through, then handled my objection, and, finally, closed me for a specific number of patients?" People all around me nodded, signifying that they had, in fact, noticed all those things. I, on the other hand, had not. My main takeaway from the scene was: "I wonder where he bought that shirt."

We were taught all we needed to know about Initial Benefit Statements, trial closes, and so on. In fact, we were instructed to detail doctors *exactly* the way the trainer had, leaving me feeling as though I had seen this movie before.

In the army, when a drill sergeant conducted a class on tossing a hand grenade, he expected each soldier to follow his instructions precisely. Nobody could say, "But throwing it sidearm feels more comfortable." The army knew best, period. Researchers had spent hundreds, perhaps thousands of hours perfecting every technique used by soldiers in battle, and accommodating individual preferences was simply not an option. Everybody did it the same way, regardless of whether they had been through basic training in Georgia or Colorado. Uniformity saved lives.

Likewise, at the University of Pfizer, the individualizing of sales presentations was not encouraged. Pfizer had spent countless hours and tens of thousands of dollars accruing market research to help determine the most effective way to present the advantages of our drugs over the competition. Following the formulation of the sales strategy for a particular drug, Pfizer's brain trust created the accompanying detail, which was then presented to managers and trainers, who memorized it and subsequently taught it to their sales reps. The script in Atlanta was the same as the one in Denver. This uniformity may not have saved lives, but it did ensure that the Pfizer message—the thoroughly studied, tremendously expensive message—was consistently delivered.

Several years into my career, a colleague pointed out another benefit to hiring military officers, one that I had never considered. "They want guys who are used to taking orders," he theorized. "Pfizer needs to push its message exactly the way it was intended. Who better to do that than people who are used to following instructions perfectly?" It was not lost on me—the fact that a free thinker such as myself had not considered this theory was the exact reason Pfizer had hired me.

For starters, we learned that an Initial Benefit Statement, or opener, such as, "Dr. Brown, how would you like to get thirty percent fewer phone calls in the middle of the night from angry mothers?" was key to grabbing a physician's attention and engaging her in a discussion. Obviously, everybody would like fewer interruptions at three A.M., so she would be likely to respond affirmatively and then ask how that could be achieved. The trainers constantly emphasized "features to benefits" in our selling, meaning taking the positive aspects or advantages of our drugs and highlighting the impact they could have on the patients and the doctor in everyday life.

For example, Zithromax caused 33 percent less diarrhea than Augmentin, then the leading antibiotic for ear infections in children. This was an advantage we *had* to get across to physicians. However, just because we clearly saw that benefit did not mean every doctor would automatically transfer that feature to her own practice. We were instructed to constantly ask ourselves, "So what?" meaning, "So what does that mean to a nurse or physician?" A physician might hear "thirty-three percent less diarrhea" and think, "Okay, that sounds good," but not necessarily make the connection between less diarrhea and fewer phone calls in the middle of the night. However, when told she would get 33 percent more sleep during nights when she was on call, that doc would think, "That sounds great! Zithromax can help my practice." Most benefits revolved around saving a physician or her staff time and hassle or saving mothers time and hassle, which normally then resulted in the former as well.

Having garnered a doctor's attention with a snappy IBS, we shifted our focus to efficacy, or how well a drug worked. When all was said and done, if a doctor didn't consider a drug as effective or better than its competitors, he wouldn't use it. Fortunately, we had solid data demonstrating that Zithromax, Zoloft, and Diflucan were equal to or superior to the other drugs in their respective classes. The trainers taught us to emphasize the trade journal in which a study had been published, the medical school or research group that conducted the trial, and the number of patients involved (larger numbers meant stronger data and were more convincing).

Once we had gained a doctor's agreement that the drug worked, we highlighted safety advantages as well as concerns, if there were any. We were reminded time and again that it was absolutely critical to inform medical professionals of any patients who should *not* be given one of our drugs, as well as any potential problems due to drug-to-drug interactions. Our credibility was everything, Bruce told us, and trying to hide something from a physician because we were afraid it might keep him from prescribing our product was not only irresponsible, it would also ruin us in the eyes of the customer.

Finally, we would explain the dosing schedule to the physician, since an incorrect dose could be ineffective or, worse yet, harmful. Then, being true "closers," we'd ask for the business. Every once in a great while, the trainers informed us, we'd get it without objection.

Unless a drug had been universally hailed as a panacea for a particular ailment or disease, doctors rarely agreed to start prescribing it in their "next ten patients." Cautious creatures of habit, physicians stuck to the products they had been trained to use during their residencies and with which they had subsequently grown comfortable. Having studied biology, chemistry, and so forth for years, doctors developed a scientist's natural skepticism and learned to question the validity of findings and doubt the results of pharmaceutical trials, especially those sponsored by the maker of the drug in question.

Physicians, then, often had issues and questions, aka objections, that the sales reps had to be able to answer satisfactorily before the physicians would be willing to prescribe the drug. Most of these were legit, but some were merely smoke screens designed to conceal the real reason the doctor refused to use the drug, i.e., he was sleeping with the Bristol-Myers Squibb woman. Of course, some physicians just enjoyed busting the balls of a new rep, so they asked ridiculous questions ("How will Zithromax affect my patients with Lou Gehrig's disease?" As panic sets in, "Uh, Doctor, aren't you a pediatrician?") or raised nonsensical issues ("I don't like the color blue, so I can't prescribe any Pfizer products"). Regardless of the motivation behind the objection, successfully handling it was the biggest part of a drug rep's job.

Not surprisingly, Pfizer had a formula for doing just that. When faced with an objection ("Once a day dosing for just five days? That's the silliest thing I've ever heard of. I'm not going to use Zithromax because of it"), we were to do these six things in order: Listen, clarify, empathize, provide proof, verify, and trial close. Faced with an objection to a drug that had been on the market for a while (if the product was new, obviously few people would have had the chance to try it out), a rep initially asked, "Is this something you've seen or heard, Doctor?" This determined whether the doctor had actually used the drug or if a competitor had planted the concern. It was far easier to handle the latter as opposed to an objection prompted by a physician's personal experience.

The first step—listen—seemed fairly obvious, but it was an important reminder to chatty salespeople to shut up and pay attention to the customer. Chock full of data and hell-bent on dispersing *all* of it, many reps, especially new ones, continued talking even after being interrupted by a medical professional. As a result, they missed hearing a crucial objection that would preclude the guy from prescribing the drug whose data spewed from the rep's mouth Dick Vitale–style.

Having listened effectively to an objection, the salesperson then had to clarify what he had heard: "So, Doctor, what is it about Zithromax's unique dosing schedule that worries you? Are you worried that your patients won't receive enough medicine to cure their ear infections?" Pfizer cleverly trained us to answer just about every possible objection, enabling us to extract specific concerns from nonspecific comments.

If the doctor agreed that, yes, he was concerned that the two-year-old he tried Zithromax on would remain sick and that he'd have to deal with her mother *again*, the rep had to empathize with the problem. "Well, Doctor, I can understand why you would be concerned about that. Obviously, getting your patients better is your primary goal, as it is for Pfizer. Admittedly, Zithromax's revolutionary dosing schedule of *just* once a day for *only* five days [subtle plug for the drug's biggest advantage over its competitors] has raised some eyebrows here in the States, where everyone is used to twenty or even *thirty* doses with *older* agents. But if I can show you efficacy data that proved to the FDA that Zithromax works as well in otitis media patients as your current gold standard Augmentin with *one-third* of the doses, would you like to see that?" This normally prompted something sounding like "Humph."

Pulling out the detail piece and flipping it open to the "efficacy" page in one smooth motion, the salesperson then explained the trial design and the results. Having provided proof, Johnny Drug Rep moved to step five—verifying. "Doctor, have I addressed your concern that Zithromax's unique dosing schedule of just once a day for only five days will not provide the efficacy you are looking for in your otitis media patients?" If he said no, then the rep asked more questions to drag out the true objection. Perhaps the rep did a poor job of presenting the data, or maybe this was just a smoke screen. Either way, more probing was needed. If the doctor agreed, though, it was time for the close: "Doctor, given Zithromax's demonstrated efficacy, strong side-effect profile, and ease of dosing, will you prescribe it first line in your next ten ear infection patients?"

Which was exactly how the trainer posing as a rep finished his detail demonstration with the other trainer posing as a doctor. Closing a physician is vitally important because of a factor unique to pharmaceutical sales compared to sales in other industries. When a Xerox salesman leaves a customer's office she either holds in her hand an order form for two new copiers or nothing. She always knows whether she made a sale or not. The same goes for surgical equipment or steel or software. Drug reps, however, walk out the door without knowing if they've sold any of their products. Doctors agree to write prescriptions for Drug X, but there's no contract signed, no check written. Only weeks later will a drug rep find out if the physician kept his word to prescribe a drug. (Pharmaceutical companies pay hundreds of thousands of dollars to third-party firms that gather sales data from the nation's pharmacy chains; reps get detailed reports informing them how many prescriptions—of their own drugs, as well as those of their competitors—each doctor has written in a particular week. Many physicians are unaware that their reps have access to this information.) Without the standard business agreement, then, a rep *has to* close a doctor in order to establish some sort of commitment that can be followed up on later. *Now, Doctor, last month you agreed to try Zithromax in your next ten otitis media patients. What stopped you from doing so?*

Shortly after seeing how a pro did it, we received our own vis aid. Idly flipping through the laminated pages, I had no inkling as to how familiar I would become with the data they contained. Just as army trainees learn to disassemble and reassemble their M-16 rifles while blindfolded, we could turn without hesitation to any page of the vis aid and regurgitate the verbiage we'd been taught. I began dreaming at night about detailing trainers playing the role of doctor, and I wasn't the only one. Again and again, we detailed each other; people rehearsed over lunch, in the hallways, even in the bathrooms. No one wanted to blow it on camera.

The use of videotaping as a training tool was still relatively new to the pharma industry in the mid-1990s. With the red light on, reps detailed trainers playing doctors, and later they rewound the tape and critiqued the performance. When asked what the taping sessions were like, a fellow trainee with previous pharmaceuticals experience said with resignation, "It's gonna suck." Reports of fitful nights of sleep increased dramatically.

We had to pass another unnerving obstacle first, however: detailing our manager in front of the team. We were scheduled to divide into our respective districts on a Sunday night. Up until then, I had yet to sweat detailing in front of a group. So I was quite surprised to feel knots in my shoulders as I walked into our district's meeting room. This discovery made me even more nervous; dating back to the second grade, I had never gotten rattled by speaking in public.

In 1978, I was selected to appear at a Board of Education meeting and read my one-page "essay" on the purchase of Manhattan Island. On the drive there, my parents kept reminding me, already a loud child, to "speak very, very loudly, so even the people in back can hear." The message stuck. The room was packed with parents, but there were twenty open seats in the front, reserved for the readers. Each chair had a sign with a student's name on it. We walked over to take a look and JAMIE REIDY—EL DORADO ELEMENTARY was taped to the chair on the far left, front row. I was going first.

Standing onstage, holding my essay written in large block letters, I stared at the crowd while a nice woman adjusted the microphone for me. *Microphone?* My parents had not anticipated the use of a mike, but it was too late to deprogram their eight-year-old speech giver, who had been told to speak very loudly, and, by golly, he was going to do as he was told. "THE INDIANS SOLD MANHATTAN FOR SEVENTEEN DOLLARS IN TRINKETS. . . . " My parents never urged me to "speak loudly" again.

Over the years, I sang solos in school concerts, did readings at Masses, and briefed commanding generals in the army without pause, yet I was still nervous before my first official detail in front of my manager and nine teammates. Bruce gave a little pep talk about it being a "no-pressure environment" and then asked for a volunteer to kick things off. This request was met with lots of paper shuffling, neck scratching, and shoe gazing, but very little hand raising. The humming of the fluorescent ceiling lights seemed deafening. Finally, in what would turn out to be a brilliant move and become a staple in the Reidy arsenal, I said I'd do it. Everyone, Bruce especially, looked stunned. *The drunken guy with the potty mouth wants to go first?*

My logic was simple: If I went first and stank, people would still give me credit for having volunteered. Had I gone fifth or sixth and stank, well, that would have really stunk. Or, had I gone fifth or sixth and done well, it could still have been argued that I had benefited from hearing four or five other details. If I went first *and* did fairly well, though, I'd look like a superstar.

Bruce fell in love with me that night. In one ten-minute period, I went from problem to asset, clown to go-to guy. Consequently, I started volunteering to go first all the time. Soon, Bruce stopped accepting my offers, privately explaining that other people needed to learn to detail under pressure. Thwarted, I amended my strategy: Try to go first, but when unable to do so, offer to go *immediately* after the worst person on the team. After all, how could I not look good on the heels of a terrible performance? Thankfully, we had some less-than-stellar detailers on our team who provided me with numerous opportunities to shine.

Too bad I didn't sparkle so much when the cameras first rolled. The format was simple: A rep would detail a "doctor" using her vis aid—the pages covered with cheat-sheet notes on yellow stickies ("Fewer phone calls to nurses during the day!" or "Gold standard!")—which took anywhere from seven to twelve minutes. Four or five more reps followed, and then they would gather to watch their tapes together and get feedback from the trainer.

It was truly amazing to watch what happened to people after that red light flicked on, myself included. Former fighter pilots froze, veteran sales guys stammered and stuttered. Seemingly superconfident people collapsed in front of the camera. "One of the benefits of Mithrozax, Doctor . . . " While my detail itself went fine, I was humiliated to see on tape that I had developed, out of nowhere, a nervous tic. Cruising along, I suddenly, briefly, touched the area between my upper lip and nose—think Hitler's mustache—and then returned to normal behavior. It reminded me of a frog snatching a fly out of the air, not exactly the image of professionalism I was hoping to convey. This happened at least ten times during the five-minute detail, and it caused me to nearly retch while viewing it with my teammates. "What the hell am I *doing* with my finger?" I asked. Between giggles, they tried to tell me it was barely noticeable.

My second taping featured no amphibian traits, which was good. Also absent were my normal enthusiasm and smoothness of delivery, which was bad. Apparently, the tic and a quality performance were inseparable. I started to worry when I developed a zit at the point of contact. Fortunately, as I grew more comfortable with my detail and the process, the constant touching stopped. Had it not ceased, a friend pointed out, I could have simply taken Zoloft to treat my obsessive-compulsiveness.

As we progressed and improved, the trainers cranked it up a notch to make it seem more real. Coincidentally, the amount of crying increased. In fact, some "doctors" seemed to enjoy making people squirm, and purposely tried to rattle reps by being unresponsive or contentious. Bruce, sensing that I was getting a little big for my britches, tried to rattle me one afternoon.

As I detailed him with the tape rolling, he suddenly stood up and asked, "Is Zithromax going to kill my patients?" I just looked at him, incredulous. He continued, "I had a patient last week whose head just *exploded* after taking one of those new drugs! Is that going to happen with yours?" My heart pounded as my mind raced.

"Uh, well, uh, Doctor," I began inauspiciously. "Is this something you've seen or . . . " My voice trailed off as I realized he had, apparently, seen this. There seemed little need to clarify ("So, Doctor, what I'm hearing is that you are concerned that your patients will die as the result of cranial explosion after taking Zithromax?") or empathize ("I can see, Doctor, why you'd be concerned about that"), so I decided to audible. "Well, Dr. Bruce, it sounds like that patient may have taken Pop Rocks with Coca-Cola, which, as you probably know, can be fatal. After all, it killed Mikey." Bruce paused for a moment, and I chastised myself for omitting the six-step objection-handling algorithm. He stared straight into my eyes with his face turning beet red. When he finally started to speak, he burst into laughter and pounded the desk between us. After he hit the Stop button and rewound the tape in the camcorder, deleting the evidence of non-Pfizer-esque role-play, he nodded approvingly.

"You keep your cool like that out in the field, and you're gonna be great, Jamie." At that moment, neither of us knew that out in the field I would never actually sit down and detail a real doctor for ten-plus minutes, but it was nice to know Bruce had confidence in me.

And, just like that, training was over. When I graduated from army boot camp, my drill sergeants had convinced me I was a lethal weapon, ready to march to Baghdad and take out Saddam Hussein by myself. Upon completion of Pfizer training, I felt a similar confidence, albeit with a vis aid rather than an M-16. Our trainers assured us that we were now *closers,* ready to snatch as much market share from Abbott Labs and Eli Lilly as we wanted.

It was up to each of us to decide how much that would be—some of us would choose less than others.

Three

BABY STEPS

FRAMED GRADUATION CERTIFICATES IN HAND, we landed in our respective territories believing we were trained and ready for action. We were wrong.

Having invested nearly $100,000 to hire and instruct each of us, Pfizer wasn't about to let us take the training wheels off and head out onto the open road without some "real-world" coaching. Our district managers (DMs) required a few days of one-on-one time to explain policies and provide additional instructions, the most important of which involved packing our car trunks. Before I could do that, though, I needed to get a car.

Just about every pharmaceutical company leased cars exclusively from American automakers. Four-door sedans were the norm, and the Ford Taurus was the most common rep ride. Management assured us, though, that because we were not typical reps, we would not get typical cars. In fact, Pfizer told the members of its new, crackerjack Pediatric Division that we could get whatever car we wanted. As long as it was a white Chevy Lumina. My girlfriend's grandma had a Lumina, too.

I had vastly underestimated the significance the company car would take on in my life. Basically, it was an office on wheels. Rather than report to a central Pfizer office every day, drug reps worked from home. Consequently, each salesperson had to have enough room in her home to provide a workable office area with desk, filing cabinets, fax machine, and printer. Aside from those items, the company car contained everything a rep would ever need in the field: studies, dosing charts, pens, pads, giveaway items, and, most important, samples.

Upon arrival in Indiana, I found waiting for me thirty-two cardboard boxes, each big enough to hide a preschooler. Full of samples and sales materials, they provided a fitting introduction to the industry-wide paranoia concerning "branding." Drug companies took to another level the advertising concept of distributing items imprinted with product names. Like the arms race between the United States and Soviet Union during the Cold War, pharma firms engaged in a never-ending race to see who could make the most notable (or simply the most) giveaway items. Each product had its own color scheme and font, which were printed on everything from the practical (pens, pads) to the preposterous (long-distance phone cards). The logic held that in a harried moment of prescribing indecision, a doctor might look down, see a drug's name on the pen in his hand, and exclaim, "Yes, of course! Drug X works for genital warts!" and write a prescription for Drug X. Reps cheesily referred to this alleged phenomenon when distributing pens: "Now, Dr. Jones, keep in mind that this pen *only* writes prescriptions for Zithromax."

Over postwork beers, I once asked an ob-gyn if he and his colleagues really paid attention to which company or product had the coolest pens. His happy-hour smile vanished into an icy stare. "Don't you think I have better things to do than worry about crap like that?" Apparently, the marketing teams employed by the various pharmaceutical companies didn't think so, because we kept getting more and more stuff. In the pediatric marketplace especially, branding took greater precedence as companies sought to establish "mascots" with which children could identify.

For example, Pfizer created a marketing campaign for our antibiotic based upon its generic (azithromycin) and brand names

(Zithromax), using an "A thru Z" theme—Azithromycin is for Apple and Zithromax is for Zebra. Thus was hatched a zebra mascot with purple stripes (all Zithromax packaging was purple) named "Max," short for Zithromax. Consequently, we got hundreds of items with zebras and "Zithromax" printed on them; we received slightly fewer items for our other drugs.

Hence, the thirty-two boxes that greeted me upon my arrival in Indiana. This taught me a basic tenet of working for Pfizer: Expect FedEx boxes every day. They never stopped coming, so much so that a woman in my sales district ended up marrying a neighbor in her building who had talked the FedEx guy into letting him sign for her packages every day. This gave the stalker, that is, the neighbor an excuse to knock on her door every night. (She heard the story later, yet was not at all alarmed by it. She got promoted before I did.) Rumor had it that Pfizer was Federal Express's second-biggest customer behind L.L. Bean. It was easy to believe.

I had a harder time accepting the fact that Bruce thought I had packed my trunk improperly. *Who can't pack a trunk?* I wondered.

Just as a mechanic sets up his toolbox according to how often he uses each tool—most often closest, least often farthest away—a drug rep was supposed to pack her trunk with the most commonly given out items in front and the rarely used things stuffed way in the back. The first time I packed my trunk, everything was packed in the exact opposite position of where it should have gone, according to the Pfizer Way. I had placed the items according to monetary value: bulky, plastic models of the respiratory system up front, cheap pens and sticky notes in the back.

Standing in a pediatric parking lot with Bruce, I watched with my mouth agape as he unloaded the entire contents of the trunk, spreading everything out in the vacant spot next to my car. Boxes of pens, pads, magnets, stickers, Kleenex boxes (a single buddy of mine would later develop a crush on the Diflucan model who graced a tissue box in my house, only to lose interest when he learned Diflucan was a one-tablet cure for yeast infections), zebra-shaped stethoscope ID tags, zebra puppets, coffee mugs (my mom loved hers), antibacterial soap dispensers, and cherry-flavored tongue depressors lay strewn across the blacktop like remnants from a car crash. (In the late 1990s several of these giveaway items reprised their real-life roles on the small screen, giving Pfizer exclusive, *free* product placement on television's top-rated program: *ER*. The Hollywood-area physician serving as *ER*'s on-set consultant was the good friend of a Pfizer rep, who gave the doc various Pfizer items that were then strategically placed in scenes; only Pfizer had this access. Dr. Mark Green even mentioned Zithromax by its generic name, azithromycin, in one episode.) Bruce would not allow me to begin making sales calls until my trunk was packed in the proper order. As mothers and their sick children walked past us en route to the pediatrician's office, I wished I could pack *myself* into the trunk.

My first mistake was failing to insert the Pfizer sign into the bottom of the trunk. This was a major problem, he explained. It wasn't that I hadn't noticed the thin blue piece of rubber, approximately thirty-six inches wide and sixty inches long. I simply thought it a bit much to cover the samples and materials with a huge sign that screamed PFIZER to the world every time I opened the trunk. Egomania, it turned out, was not its inspiration.

The sign did scream PFIZER on one side. On the other side, however, it screamed HELP, and was to be left hanging from the trunk in case of emergency. Not only that, but the sign was intended to be placed like a liner on the floor (samples and so on placed on top), with two feet left slack so it could be dropped down over the side to protect a rep's clothes from getting wet or muddy when touching the bumper. The latter resulted in tremendous dry-cleaning savings.

Bruce explained that the pens and sticky notes I had stashed in back were a form of currency that could buy entry at myriad levels of a doctor's office. Like cash, pens came in differently valued "denominations": cheap, flimsy writing instruments were the one-dollar bills, given out indiscriminately to any office employee in sight; sturdy, brightly colored pens were the twenties of the rep world, distributed to overvigilant gatekeepers and reticent nurses much the way handshake tips were given to maître d's at crowded restaurants. Similarly, since the amount of paper used in medical offices would've made trees shake with fear, sticky notes and scratch pads were accepted like manna from heaven. "You're going to give these away on *every single* call, so they go up front, where you can grab them easily." Pens were stored vertically to save space, divvied up according to the name of the drug printed on them. Likewise, all other giveaways were kept together to reduce the odds of a mix-up. "Zoloft here, Diflucan over here."

In a specific order retreating toward the back, the most commonly requested samples followed. We had three different forms of Zithromax: an oral solution for children with ear infections, capsules for adults with bronchitis, and a 1 gram powder to be taken only one time to treat chlamydia. Without thinking, I had packed the latter up front and the former in back. Bruce pointed out that this made no sense, since the majority of my customers were pediatricians and would be more likely to be treating kids who could not swallow pills, rather than promiscuous, non-condom-wearing adults. The studies touting our drugs' effectiveness or highlighting our competitors' weaknesses were kept in folders hanging in a plastic milk crate placed in the center of the trunk. The other items were often left in their shipping boxes with the box tops cut off for easy access.

Forty-five minutes later, I again stood with my tonsils exposed, only this time with disbelief as I realized how much stuff—how much *more* stuff—Bruce had been able to fit in there (I had thrown a number of boxes in the backseat). The bulky, plastic models of the respiratory system could barely be seen.

Thankfully, I hadn't been the only "packing challenged" new hire; several fellow rookies described similar scenes via voice mail. The packing system made sense, I'd grudgingly admit weeks later. As Bruce pointed out, by setting up the trunk improperly, a salesperson doomed himself to wasting time searching for things—time that might allow a competitor to get into an office first.

My makeover was not yet complete. Bruce next turned his attention to the cumbersome, square, shiny black valise I had been trying to avoid since it arrived on my doorstep. "Dude, you gotta load up your bag." I quickly learned that a rep's detail bag was a smaller version of his company car, filled with studies and pens and pads and samples and, most important, the detail book with the vis aids for each of a salesperson's drugs. Sometimes, detail books grew to more than a hundred pages. I saw doctors flee from their favorite reps after spotting the dreaded "book" on a medical counter. After Bruce finished packing my detail bag in a similar anal fashion to that which he had employed with the trunk, I cautiously hefted it, testing its weight. Taking a practice stroll in the parking lot, I came to an immediate realization: It was impossible to look cool carrying The Bag.

Having squared me away, Bruce took off to do the same with the other seven new reps in our district. I still was not ready to unleash my talents on the unsuspecting pediatric and ob-gyn communities of northern Indiana, though. Before letting me pedal on my own, Pfizer needed one last assurance that I was ready for my first solo ride.

Since Bruce was busy unpacking and packing trunks throughout Indiana, Michigan, and Ohio, he had a senior rep on our team give some of us a two-day indoctrination. In Jack, a sarcastic twenty-eight-year-old who had been with Pfizer for four years, I could not have gotten a better mentor; we shared both a similar sense of humor and the desire to drink beer after work. Carrying less hair and a few more pounds than he had displayed on the ice, the former collegiate hockey player also assumed an "I can still go into the corner and knock you on your ass" air. Jack knew what worked and didn't work in the field (Detroit Red Wing tickets did, tongue depressors—regardless of flavoring—did not) and he had little tolerance for corporate efforts to alter his style.

He laughed when I relayed the details of Trunk 101. "Don't worry," he assured me. "Nobody knows how to do it at first. But since you're going to be spending a *lot* of time leaning into this fucking thing in the rain and snow, you want to make it as efficient as possible." Jack had my complete attention.

He spent the next two days monitoring my behavior in the field, including how I (A) schmoozed with receptionists, (B) introduced my products and myself to nurses, and (C) handled brief, unscheduled meetings with physicians. A and B went pretty well, but C demonstrated plenty of room for improvement. Having gained access to the Promised Land—the back office—I quickly established rapport with a nurse who subsequently asked the doctor to speak with me for a moment. *Bingo! This job is going to be even easier than I thought!* Jack and I exchanged knowing winks, neither one of us aware that the dam in my brain was about to burst, unleashing six weeks' worth of acquired knowledge.

Not wanting to scare off the first physician kind enough to take the time to meet me, I was simply supposed to introduce myself, give him a *brief* synopsis of Zithromax, and ask if he had any questions. If he did, then I could launch into my "detail," as I had been trained to do. To say that I dropped a torrent of information on the poor, unsuspecting pediatrician would be quite an understatement. To this day, he may never have spoken to another rep. Pfizer people called it "brain dumping"; even today, I can still hear the truck backing up. *Beep . . . beep . . . beep.*

"Hello, Doctor, my name is Jamie Reidy, and, having recently gotten out of the army, where I was an HR officer, I am a new member of Pfizer's new Pediatric Division, and I will be bringing you Zithromax, the world's first once-a-day for only five days oral antibiotic for your ear infection patients. Zithromax works great, as evidenced by its equal efficacy when compared to Augmentin in this six-hundred-thirty-plus patient study, and has thirty-three percent less diarrhea, which will give you one-third more sleep at night as you'll get thirty-three percent fewer phone calls from angry moms at three in the morning, and, with its cherry flavor, Zithromax tastes even better, and I know how important that is for your moms not to have to fight with the kids to get their medicine down because, after all, if they don't take it, it's probably not going to work. Am I right or am I right?"

I had plenty of time to ponder my own question as the previously nice nurse escorted us out of the office. Jack held a little coaching session with me in the parking lot. "Dude! You need to chill the fuck out!" Thus my first sales call proved both ironic, because rarely in my career would I ever again convey so much product information to a physician, and prophetic, because my postcall behavior revealed an innate desire to cheat the system.

I slunk into the Lumina and pulled out my laptop computer so I could enter my "postcall notes," a brief description of any information I learned or shared during the sales call. Before my next visit with that physician, I was expected to read through those notes and then use the information to my advantage. For example, "Doctor, the last time we spoke, you expressed interest in using Zithromax in your bronchitis patients. . . . " Of course, after that stellar debut, I could only say, "Doctor, the last time we spoke I verbally vomited on your loafers." As my laptop booted up, I turned to Jack and asked, "Does that count for four calls or just the one?"

He turned in the passenger seat to face me, his head tilted and eyebrows scrunched. "How many docs did you talk to?" he asked.

"One," I said.

"Well, then I guess you made only one call. You weren't a math major, were you?"

I shook my head. "No, it's just that he has three partners, so I thought maybe, 'cause I got to the back office, it counted for four calls."

Jack stared at me for a long time before the smirk crept into view. Nodding his head slowly, he started to laugh.

"You made only one call *today,* but in a few months, after you stop getting lost and doing twenty U-turns a day and people start to know your name, that'll count as four calls." I looked up from my typing to see him staring at me with a sparkle in his eye. "You're gonna do just fine at this job, Reidy. Oh yeah, *just fine.*" We drank a lot of beer that night, after Jack taught me how to chill warm beer in just two minutes by filling a hotel sink with ice and then spinning a beer can on top of the cubes over and over.

Before he departed the next day, he encouraged me not to say anything to our boss about how one call could someday be entered as four calls. I was sad to see Jack go; talk about a mentor.

When Bruce returned to South Bend for his first official field day with me, I felt an apprehensive curiosity regarding his management style. Bruce was a brand-new manager, a role I knew well. Having been a brand-new manager in the army only three years earlier, I was quite familiar with the myriad mistakes that such an individual could make. Army lieutenants were fortunate to have seasoned sergeants working for them, people who warned us to duck when approaching low-hanging branches. My right-hand man, Sergeant First Class Jose Santiago, had eighteen years under his belt prior to breaking me in. Although newly promoted sales managers underwent weeks of extensive training at the University of Pfizer, they had no one to lean on day in and day out.

In addition to my concern over the lack of a steadying hand, my fears multiplied after hearing several horror stories about other new managers, and I grew concerned that I might be forced to update my résumé shortly. One new DM in Cincinnati required his reps to fill out a time sheet broken down into fifteen-minute intervals specifying how they spent every minute of the day, "8:00—Drove to Dr. Johnson's office. 8:15—Arrived. 8:45—Departed to Dr. Smith's office." A manager in Kansas City forbade his salespeople from gassing up their Luminas between seven-thirty A.M. and five P.M., saying it was a waste of time that could be spent selling. When Bruce pulled into the parking lot at our designated meeting place, I was more than a bit nervous.

He quickly put my worries to rest. We were stuck in traffic on a two-lane road in rural Elkhart, Indiana, when Bruce began fidgeting in his seat. Soon after, he rolled down his window to lean out to see what was causing the delay. Banging out a drumbeat on the dashboard, he instructed me to pull onto the shoulder and go around the stopped cars. I looked in that direction and spotted a series of sizable potholes. "No can do," I explained. "Those things will wreck the car." The tapping stopped, and he stared intently at me.

"Jamie," Bruce began, clearly annoyed, "what's the difference between a company car and a four-wheel drive?"

I shrugged.

"A company car can go *anywhere*." He motioned to his right. "Now, hit it." Like Elwood Blues, I did as I was told, and my freshly washed Lumina lurched and bucked unhappily but successfully through the mud and past the traffic jam. Bruce nodded approvingly.

A district manager's main job was to monitor and modify behaviors. For a person managing new reps, however, his most important task was to *create* those behaviors, to instill in his people the need to make ten sales calls every day, during which they would detail at least two products and close the physician for a specific number of future patients. Having created such a behavior pattern over the course of several months, the DM could then encourage certain habits, tweak others, and overhaul the remainder. The creating, monitoring, and modifying of the behaviors took place during field rides.

As former salespeople, managers loved field rides. As *current* salespeople, reps felt differently. All salesmen thrive on their autonomy, their freedom to decide which customers to see when, and they hate the idea of reporting to the same office every day cooped up behind a desk. Once promoted out of the field and into management, though, DMs relinquish total control of their schedules, and they are suddenly forced to spend innumerable hours in management meetings or completing paperwork in their offices. Field rides gave managers an excuse to get out of their rut and do what they loved most: selling. Sales reps preferred their bosses indoors approving expense reports.

Bruce and I started off at the biggest pediatric office in northern Indiana, and he hung back in the waiting room as I approached the receptionist in my blue suit, white shirt, and red tie. An attractive woman with an approachable air, she smiled brightly at me while introducing herself as Brenda. I felt easy like Sunday morning. "Do you have an appointment?" she asked. I did not. "Our doctors only see reps who have appointments." No longer humming Lionel Ritchie, I began stammering about being a brand-new rep who only wanted to introduce myself to the office manager to find out what the practice's policies were. She tilted her head sympathetically. "*Amy* is our office manager, but she's busy all morning and asked us not to interrupt her."

Heart sinking, I glanced over my shoulder at Bruce, whose abnormally large eyes had been observing intently. Turning back to Brenda, I tried to look as pathetic as possible, hopefully appealing to her maternal instincts. Subtly motioning behind me with my thumb, I whispered forcefully, *"That is my boss! This is my first call ever! Is there any way I can see the office manager?"* She leaned toward me conspiratorially and said she'd see what she could do.

As Bruce nodded approvingly, I could hear Brenda telling no one in particular, "He looks like he's ten years old! You *have* to see this rep." At this, several administrative workers stood up to check me out, which resulted in a chorus of giggling hellos. Soon, a well-dressed, dark-haired woman emerged from behind a door in the back of the office. Brenda gave me a thumbs-up sign. It was Amy.

Amy opened the door leading from the waiting room to the back office, and I smiled and walked toward it. She then closed the door and met me in front of the receptionist's window; there'd be no back office invitation for me. After I introduced myself and she very pleasantly explained that she had little time to talk, I sensed some-one behind me; Bruce had stealthily crept up. Sweat beaded on my forehead. I explained to Amy that I was a member of Pfizer's new pediatric sales force and that we had a new antibiotic; could I leave information for the doctors? She asked for nine packets of informa-tion (six pediatricians and three nurse practitioners), saying she was certain they would be very interested. "Why don't you schedule a lunch for the office?" She winked at this last part, letting me know she knew how much she was helping me out.

Having handed over the product information, I asked her if the doctors needed any samples. Since both Zithromax and Diflucan oral suspensions were new, the physicians wouldn't use drugs about which they knew nothing. In training we had been told that "just about every office" would have employees taking Zoloft, Pfizer's antidepressant, and that when in need of a "Hail Mary" to keep a sales call alive, it was worthwhile to resort to the Zoloft play. I started to do so, saying, "You know, I also have Zoloft. Perhaps some of your coworkers—"

"Zoloft! My doctors use that for some of their teenaged patients. We've never had samples before, though." At this, Bruce winked at me. Pfizer based our division's antidepressant sales quotas on past ob-gyn prescribing history (Zoloft, Prozac, and Paxil were used according to FDA indications for depression and "off label" to treat extreme PMS symptoms), not on past pediatric history, since few physicians felt comfortable using medications that were not FDA approved in children under eighteen. Amy's comment pulled back the curtain on a potential gold mine of Zoloft sales. Excited, I asked how many samples they'd like. "As many as you can give us!" Amy had just become a Jamie fan. I turned to Bruce for guidance and he said nonchalantly, "Ah, give them a case."

I skipped across the parking lot to the Lumina, grabbed a large box containing 144 bottles of seven pills (most physicians gave patients a bottle or two—one or two weeks' supply—with a prescription), and raced back inside to find Amy laughing along with Bruce. Her smile grew upon seeing the case, but his vanished.

Walking to the car moments later, Bruce lagged behind with his shoulders slumped. I waited for him to catch up, and he shook his head and muttered, "Those sample cases are *way* bigger than they used to be." It took more than a year for Amy's doctors to work through all that Zoloft; we had given away the gold mine. Changing the subject, I asked what he and Amy had been laughing about.

Bruce perked up at this. "I just asked her to keep an eye on you, to make sure no pretty nurses take advantage of the new *single* guy." He gave me a playful jab on the arm.

"But you know I have a serious girlfriend." He nodded, smiling devilishly.

"Yeah, but Amy doesn't need to know that."

I stopped outside my car door. "What are you talking about?"

"Jamie, you need to take advantage of what you've got," he explained impatiently. "You're a young, clean-cut, good-looking, funny guy; schmoozing receptionists and nurses will be your *in*. You've got to play that card for all it's worth. That's how you're going to make your money."

"But what happens when they find out I'm not single, that I have a girlfriend? Won't my credibility be shot?"

He shrugged. "There's only one way for that to happen, man, and they're not going to hear it from me." He paused for a moment, eyebrows raised. "All right, are we going to sell some Zithromax today, or what?" The message was clear: Give them whatever they want and tell them whatever they want to hear; just move product.

We didn't see many medical professionals that day, as we seemed to spend more time with our faces in a northern Indiana road map than we did inside offices. When actually in front of customers, I felt as if I was having an out-of-body experience. It was surreal to have someone follow me around all day, listening to every word I said and noticing every change in body language and speech. "You told him that Zithromax would mean one-third less phone calls for his nurses, but you didn't translate that into a benefit for him. Features to benefits, Jamie. Features to benefits."

Such close monitoring made me incredibly self-aware, and I found myself paying more attention to my physical reactions to a doctor's comments than the actual comments themselves. "Uh, Jamie? Dr. Smith just said he'd like to know how to dose Zithromax in a twenty-two-pound patient." *Yeah, fine, but did you notice that I'm not standing with my arms crossed anymore?* This was not healthy, or productive. Predictably, Bruce gave me feedback immediately after each call, making sure to begin with a few positives—"Nice tie" or "I *really* liked the way you handed the pen to that nurse"—before pointing out instances where I could have referenced a certain study or asked for the business based on "buying signals" I had not noticed. Unpredictably, however, he never stepped in to rescue a sales call gone awry.

Pfizer instructed its managers to refrain from interfering, even if the lack of action meant a loss of business. "It's like learning to ride without training wheels, man," Bruce said. "If your dad never let go of the back of the bicycle seat, you never would have learned on your own. This way, you'll fall a few times, but eventually you'll get the hang of it. If I jumped in every time a new rep struggled, he'd never learn how to overcome that on his own." His explanation made perfect sense, but he did little to convince me that he actually believed it. As evidenced by his impatience in traffic, Bruce craved action, and I knew that sitting on the sideline watching the game slip away must have driven a guy like that crazy. It did.

Few places were more chaotic than the middle of a pediatric practice on a late-autumn afternoon, with kids coming home sick from school as ear infection season found its groove. Appointment schedules, already a term used loosely, became even more of a working document as at least one family would invariably arrive late, throwing everything off. Further derailing the operation, Joey's nanny scheduled a visit for him, but brought his two siblings along, because, "They all have it." Impatient mothers quizzed harried nurses, who nagged doctors to stay on schedule—all of it occurring in an area rarely larger than a living room.

Squarely in the eye of the storm, the same doctors attempted to collect their thoughts long enough to remember what child they had just examined, what ailed said child, and what drug to prescribe for said said child. The last thing such a scene needed was a salesman trying to impress his boss. Yet there we were, two guys in suits standing in the midst of this tumult, as out of place as pork chops at a bar mitzvah.

My every instinct screamed, "Run away!" but Bruce sensed my discomfort and motioned with his hands to stay put. With an assuring nod, he nudged me in the direction of Dr. Jones, a pediatrician in his late thirties. Hair thinner than his runner's build, he leaned against the countertop, poring over a patient's chart. Of the three docs in the office, this was the guy I would have picked to approach first; weeks earlier my mentor, Jack, had tipped me off to the tendency of younger physicians to be more willing than seasoned doctors to talk with reps; the young ones were closer in age and would feel like jerks if they blew us off.

"Listen, guys, I'd love to talk, but"—he held his arms outstretched at the madness—"this isn't a good time." Apparently, Dr. Jones hadn't gotten the memo re: talking to reps. "I'm sure you can understand." I could and did understand, and I began to thank him for his, albeit brief, time, when I saw a strange gleam in my boss's eye. We weren't going anywhere.

Bruce was about to cross the manager–rep line. He had tried to stay out of the fray—I had to give him that. Like a medic, he did his best to remain a noncombatant, but in the end, he could not resist the urge to pick up a rifle and fight. I did not know it, but I was about to witness a master at work. Class was in session.

"I can see how busy you are, Dr. Jones," he began, "and that's why I'll be brief." As if. "I guess it's not surprising that your office is this packed, considering that it's prime otitis season," he said, referring to the clinical term for an ear infection. "Let me ask you, after amoxicillin fails in those patients, do you have an algorithm for deciding which antibiotic you'll use second or third line?"

Most reps considered directly asking a doctor what drugs he used to be a risky move under *good* conditions, let alone in the middle of a busy office when the doc had already told you he didn't have time. The noisy swirl of sick kids and moms and nurses seemed to increase in response to this bold overture. My throat went dry, and I braced for the explosion.

None came. The pediatrician cocked his head, squinted at Bruce with a "let's-mess-with-this-guy" kind of smirk, and said, "Yeah, as a matter of fact, I do. I like Cefzil, and if that fails, Biaxin." Amazing! He had just given up extremely valuable information that I'd be able to use to my advantage on my next call, as we would certainly be leaving now that we had overstayed our welcome. Or not. Bruce's eyes brightened as his mouth formed a similar smirk. He had stumbled upon a worthy opponent and had no intention of passing up an opportunity to spar.

"Interesting," Bruce continued. He turned to me. "Jamie, do you have a copy of the Block reprint?" *Of course I have a copy, Bruce. I have a thousand copies.* It occurred to me that he wanted Dr. Jones to feel unthreatened, as if they were simply engaging in a conversation, like, "Hey, Jamie, do you have the business card for that hardwood-floor guy?" I glanced apprehensively at Dr. Jones's nurse, who was staring unhappily at Bruce and me. Perspiring, I rummaged around in my bag for a while, as though it was hard to find the reprint he'd requested.

Bruce moved to the pediatrician's side, breaking down the spatial comfort zone most people preferred and throwing me into a near-panic state. We hadn't been invited into the office. We hadn't been asked to provide any information, just the opposite. Yet here we were, slowing down the entire operation. I began fidgeting like a nine-year-old during Adult Swim.

Pointing to the study he had placed on top of the patient chart the doctor had been reviewing prior to our interruption, Bruce explained, "As you can see from Dr. Block's data, Zithromax provides the efficacy you and your mothers are looking for. . . . " The pediatrician actually stopped and looked at the information. After a moment or two, he objected. "Yeah, but what about the gastrointestinal side effects associated with this class of drugs?" Bruce turned to me again and asked if I happened to have a "Slim Jim," or a pocket-size version of all the marketing pieces contained in our detail book. Like the Block studies, I had a ton of them. I quickly handed him the Slim Jim, which he used to point out Zithromax's tolerable side-effect profile. With that, Dr. Jones offered another negative comment about Zithromax. This time, like a veteran operating-room nurse, I handed my surgeon the sales scalpel he needed before he even asked for it.

The ticking of my internal clock pounded in my brain. We had been there way too long. Yet back and forth they went, like Borg and McEnroe at Wimbledon, until the pediatrician finally blinked.

As his face reddened, Dr. Jones turned to look Bruce squarely in the eye. "When I was doing my residency at the naval hospital [although the oral suspension for children was new, Zithromax capsules had been available for adult usage for two years], Zithromax cost more than any other antibiotic, and I swore I'd never use it again!" he sputtered, pounding the countertop once for emphasis. *Game over.* Bruce looked contrite.

"You know what, Dr. Jones?" Dr. Jones did not know what. "You're right," Bruce said, and I don't know who was more shocked, the doctor or me. "Pfizer overpriced Zithromax when it first came out, and we suffered for it. But we listened to the marketplace and have since cut the cost in half, so that now"—he extended his hand toward me without looking, and I smoothly gave him back the Slim Jim, which conveniently listed a pricing breakdown displaying Zithromax's cost advantage over our competitors, including the aforementioned Cefzil and Biaxin—"Zithromax offers the lowest cost for your patients." Dr. Jones had played his best card, and Bruce trumped it. "So, can we count on you to use Zithromax in your next ten otitis media patients?"

"All right, all right," the frustrated pediatrician said. "I'll use it! Now get out of here and let me see some patients." Dr. Jones would become the fourth biggest Zithromax writer in my territory.

In just under six minutes, Bruce showed me exactly what it meant to be a closer. He created positive tension with a physician, stood his ground in the face of disagreement, and moved in for the kill at the perfect time. It was like watching a great white shark from a steel cage, seeing it in its element: fearless, relentless, and indestructible. I should have been thrilled.

Instead, I left the office with a sweaty shirt, dry throat, and knotted stomach—physical evidence of my discomfort at interrupting a busy doctor and then practically arguing with him in front of thirty people. At that moment, I knew I'd never be able to swim with the sharks.

TRAINING WHEELS OFF

THAT PERSONAL DISCOVERY, however, did not prompt me to seek another career, one in which I'd feel more comfortable or fulfilled. I was self-aware enough to know that I harbored no deep-rooted desire for a "career" in the traditional sense, nor did I feel a need for job fulfillment. Simply put, I just wanted to have as much fun as possible. In my short time at Pfizer, I'd been able to figure out that the company car and the expense account and the ability to sleep till ten every morning (more on the latter later) provided a solid foundation from which to pursue my stated goal of having fun.

Having decided to forgo the confrontational selling style preferred by Pfizer, I became the "anti-closer," a sales rep who sought to increase sales through rapport and friendships rather than aggressive promotional tactics. Accordingly, I searched for a way to connect with physicians on a personal level, hoping that such relationships would improve access and opportunities to discuss my drugs in a casual manner. My lifeboat arrived in the form of the *preceptorship,* an opportunity to learn more about a doctor's specialty by tagging along for half a day while he made hospital rounds and saw patients in the office.

While such an experience was certainly educational, the key benefit lay in getting to know a doctor and, more important, his getting to know me. This personal relationship—and the $500 he'd receive from Pfizer—would hopefully nudge him toward writing more prescriptions for my products. Using this approach, I asked Dr. Fort Wayne, the second-highest prescription writer in my territory, if I could shadow him for an afternoon, and he agreed. Walking into his office, I was fairly nervous, primarily due to the fact that Bruce had reminded me a half-dozen times that as my number-two writer, this pediatrician could single-handedly determine whether or not I would make my Zithromax quota for the next year.

Thankfully, Dr. Fort Wayne turned out to be a laid-back guy who immediately put me at ease. He seemed to get a genuine kick out of explaining patient histories to the "medical student" assigned to him for the day. (In order to put parents at ease, I wore a white lab coat and played the role of a medical student trying to determine if I wanted to go into pediatrics.) For four hours I observed the standard bronchitis and ear infection cases, and he let me listen to coughs with the stethoscope (amazingly phlegmy) and look into eardrums (amazingly red). More important, we found out we both were from New York—hello, rapport building. Having accomplished my goals, I was ready to call it a day at four-thirty and thank him for the unique experience. However, my hopes for an early exit were cut short when Dr. Fort Wayne asked, "You mean you're not staying for the circumcision?"

At no point during my initial sixty-minute interview or subsequent six-week training session did anyone from Pfizer mention that there existed the slightest possibility that I would watch a physician sever a newborn's foreskin. For me, this would have been a deal breaker. Unable to sit through half an episode of *ER* without covering my eyes, I knew O.J. had a better chance of hosting a show on Lifetime than I did of remaining conscious through an entire circumcision.

Scrambling for an excuse that would allow me to avoid revealing my phobia of needles, specifically, and all medical procedures,
in general, I stood in embarrassing silence. This break provided
his four female medical assistants the opportunity to hurl stinging
barbs at me, calling me, among other equally clever names, "a girl."
Within three minutes I was scrubbed in.

Medically speaking, the procedure was a simple one, requiring
only the doctor and a medical assistant. Parents—fathers, in particular—were not allowed to observe due to the increased likelihood that
the physician would emerge from the room with a black eye. From
the moment patient Quentin was strapped down, we spent only
twenty-five minutes on the procedure, fifteen of which amounted
to waiting for the local anesthetic to take effect and the strategically
placed clamps to slow the blood flow to an acceptable level.

Finally, Dr. Fort Wayne pulled out a stainless steel device that
on first glance resembled a corkscrew. A plastic, disposable device
was more commonly used, but this veteran physician preferred the
old-school tool. Having seen the startled look on my face, he held
up the instrument and said, "It's called a Gomco clamp," which I
mistakenly heard as "Gumpco clamp," sparking giggles over the
idea of Forrest revealing the means by which he would touch the
most lives: "Momma says it's my magic clamp."

Designed specifically for circumcisions, the Gomco clamp actually worked in a manner similar to the aforementioned corkscrew.
After pulling back the surprisingly large amount of foreskin, the
physician slid the clamp down over the penis and let the loose skin
snap back over the device. Things then got a bit surreal as he began
tightening the clamp by turning it, making a *scrr, scrr* sound like
that of a ratchet. With the device secured, he grasped a scalpel and
simply moved it along a ridge ingeniously placed in the Gomco
clamp to guarantee a stable and accurate cutting path. When
using sharp objects in the vicinity of the penis, accuracy was a nice
feature.

Despite the apparent ease with which Dr. Fort Wayne performed the procedure, it was no breeze for the spectator. The evacuation of blood from my head coincided with the injecting of the local anesthetic, and if not for the industrial-strength doorknob that supported all of my 180 lightheaded pounds they surely would have been forced to call in medical assistance "stat!" Conversely, Quentin took it like the man I could only hope to be and *nodded off* for five minutes in the middle of the procedure.

Concerned that we had "lost" the patient, I asked why the baby, who just moments earlier been expressing his displeasure at high decibels, now looked as though he was not breathing. "Sometimes they fall asleep," the fifteen-year veteran said, shrugging. I mentioned that if a boy could snooze during a circumcision, he probably wouldn't make it to work on time very often as an adult. "I mean, if you don't wake up when a scalpel tickles you *down there,* I doubt the buzzer on the clock radio is going to do much good." Dr. Fort Wayne pulled his scalpel hand back from the patient. "Jamie, now's not a good time to make me laugh."

Poor comedic timing aside, the preceptorship had been extremely beneficial. All goals were met: Rapport had been established (the pediatrician asked if I wanted to start playing tennis with him), and he showed an interest in using my drug. "Hey, Jamie," he yelled after me as I left the office, "make sure you leave me a bunch of those Zithromax samples; I want to try that stuff."

Ah, samples. In the minds of most medical professionals, free drug samples were the raison d'être for the existence of pharmaceutical salespeople. Just as shoppers don't buy a car without taking it for a test drive, doctors rarely prescribed a drug without trying it out a few times. Since patients might get angry about paying for a drug being test-driven by their physicians, pharmaceutical companies provide free samples. While it is possible for a rep to go a day or two without speaking to a doctor, making it through a day without dropping off samples is next to impossible. The ceaseless delivering of said items to offices without being allowed to speak to physicians—in *our* minds the raison d'être for our existence—prompted many self-effacing references to ourselves as "well-dressed UPS guys." With samples being our lifeblood, we got a lot of them.

I learned quickly that having thousands of dollars' worth of drugs lying around really warps your concept of health maintenance. Prior to working for Pfizer, I avoided taking antibiotics whenever possible, choosing instead to combat illnesses with heavy doses of vitamin C. *Really* heavy doses. I got this regimen from my father, whose morning ingestion of vitamin C met the recommended daily allowance for a grammar school. Coughing in front of my dad ("I don't like the sound of that cough") earned you an immediate overdose of the orange pills. Since we rarely got sick, my old man stood by his theory. In Pfizer training, however, I learned that *most adults* rarely got sick simply because they did not have the day-to-day, close personal contact kids experience in school. Every so often, though, when a cough or sore throat would not subside, I was forced to go to the doctor's office.

Regardless of the city, state, or country in which I was examined, the physician invariably wrote me a prescription for amoxicillin. Three tablets a day for ten days? Please. There was no way I was finishing all that medication. As soon as I'd start feeling better—normally around day four or five—I'd forget I had ever been sick in the first place and stop taking the amoxicillin. Ask yourself, what do *you* do with your leftover medication?

As a drug rep, I learned that I was a "saver," meaning I'd save the remaining medication for the next time I got sick. Pretty smart, I thought. Turned out that a lot of other people thought the same way. I met nurses who gave the leftover drugs to their dogs and doctors who kept the remainder for sick family members. Turned out that we were all members of a very stupid club.

There is a reason antibiotics are prescribed for a specific number of days, and, surprisingly, it has nothing to do with corporations trying to wring every last cent from the pharmaceutical stone. Simply put, doctors prescribe an antibiotic for the amount of time specified in the drug's package insert. The FDA bases this time period on the dosing regimen used in the clinical trials that got the product approved in the first place. Finishing a course of therapy, then, is crucial to combating an illness successfully. Alas, many people—like me—stop taking their medicine after the symptoms subside.

Feeling better didn't guarantee that the bacteria inside my body were all dead. By day five, most were gone, but not all. Bacteria, like athletes suffering through grueling workouts, live by the credo "That which doesn't kill me makes me stronger." By surviving exposure to an antibiotic, pathogens can become, over time, resistant to that drug. Therefore, if a woman takes an antibiotic for only a few days, she can actually strengthen the very bugs she has been trying to destroy. Patient noncompliance is one of two major causes of the alarming spread of worldwide drug resistance.

If patients make up half the problem, doctors and mothers complete the equation. That's right; in trying to heal the sick, physicians sometimes do more harm than good. Antibiotics cure only *bacterial* infections. Unfortunately, bacteria do not cause every illness.

Viruses are responsible for a large number of respiratory infections, but doctors don't have any drugs in their arsenal to kill these organisms. Instead, someone suffering from a virus needs lots of rest and fluids as she simply lets the infection run its course. However, patients don't want to hear that. More specifically, *mothers* of patients don't want to hear that. "You've really got two patients when you treat a kid," a pediatrician once told me. "The kid and the mom."

Moms were the worst. I know. I have one. "Let me tell you something," my mother began defensively after I asked her if she ever badgered our pediatrician for prescriptions. "Do you think I was going to bundle up three kids in their winter clothes, drive twenty minutes through the snow to the pediatrician's office, where I would wait for another goddamned half hour, at least, to see the doctor for ten minutes, *maybe,* and have him charge me sixty bucks for that visit only to tell me your brother had a virus that couldn't be treated with antibiotics? I don't think so. I wasn't leaving there without a prescription!"

This perspective was not rare. Seeing my mom get that riled up twelve years after last bundling anyone up in winter clothes was nothing compared to watching a real live mom scream at a pediatrician in the middle of the office. Amazingly, there was no difference in the content of the rants. Likewise, in both cases the doctors caved in and wrote out a prescription. For amoxicillin.

Are doctors in the wrong when they buckle under such pressure? The Centers for Disease Control (CDC) would say so. On the flip side, I wonder what Harvard Business School thinks. All other considerations aside, a physician runs a business. So, if the customer is always right, that puts the doctor somewhere between the proverbial rock and a hard place.

Suppose Dr. Smith puts his foot down and, citing the CDC's guidelines, refuses to prescribe an antibiotic. On the one hand, he has done his part to curb one of the biggest crises facing the medical community today. On the other hand, he has angered a customer who may very well go to the next neighborhood playgroup session and tell all the other mothers that Dr. Smith is a quack. Consequently, he may lose not one but five or ten other patients. In my experience, the short-term bottom line trumps the big picture view almost every time, and will continue to do so until American mothers start listening to their doctors. Their kids' doctors, that is.

That being said, let me climb down from my sample box and admit that drug reps—especially those of us who sold Zithromax— were the worst offenders of all. *Wait a minute, Jamie; I thought you used antibiotics only as a last resort?* A little knowledge plus instant access added up to one big value change.

I have already explained that the one thing a rep learned in pharmaceutical training was that her drug(s) were the best. Period. I mean, would a company spend thousands of dollars on teaching its employees that their product is third best? Not surprisingly, I emerged from six weeks of training and brainwashing with the blind-faith belief that Zithromax was the best damn antibiotic under the sun, and I had $20,000 of the stuff sitting in my garage.

Suddenly, "staying drug free" had been replaced by "better living through pharmacology." Within weeks, I had begun self-medicating. If I happened to wake up in the morning with a scratchy throat, I'd start a Z-Pak. Even if the scratchiness had nothing to do with a bacterial infection and everything to do with having attended a rock concert the night before, I'd start a Z-Pak. Pretty soon, I began handing out samples to friends and family members who coughed in a way I didn't like. Without the aid of throat cultures or even a stethoscope, I became a de facto doctor, replacing *expertise in* medicine with *access to* medicine. Emboldened by my early success (funny how concert-caused scratchy throats went away in two days), I branched out into antihistamine prescribing.

Unlike the other drugs in my sales portfolio, Pfizer did not discover and develop Zyrtec. Rather, we paid the Belgian company UCB Pharma for the right to help them sell this soon-to-be billion-dollar product. Co-marketing has become more commonplace throughout the industry as small companies with promising molecules but in need of bigger sales forces sought partners with larger sales forces needing promising molecules. Pfizer did this twice more during my tenure, with Parke-Davis (Lipitor) and G.D. Searle & Co. (Celebrex). Atarax was an older generation antihistamine that provided unparalleled allergy relief with also unparalleled somnolence. Due to the latter, most physicians stopped using it. However, a female researcher at UCB figured out how to maintain Atarax's allergy-symptom relief while minimizing its sedation rate, thus prompting Pfizer's interest. At the Zyrtec launch, the "Mother of Zyrtec" charmed the general assembly by telling us, "Many men think they are the Father of Zyrtec, but only *I* know who the father is."

In launching Zyrtec, Pfizer jumped into one of the more cutthroat arenas in pharmaceutical sales. In drug categories where no one agent had data demonstrating its superiority to its competitors, sales reps were forced to dig deep into the minutia to tout advantages. Such nitpicking often led to bad blood between salespeople. The antihistamine market was no exception.

Things got nasty in a hurry, especially with the Claritin reps. Weeks prior to the FDA's approval of Zyrtec, the Schering-Plough people began warning doctors about "Atarax, Jr.," which would still cause drowsiness in all of their patients. These aggressive efforts proved extremely successful, since my customers were asking me about Zyrtec's sedation rate before hearing anything about its superior efficacy. Anticipating such tactics, Pfizer trained us on how to respond positively and forcefully. Despite those efforts, I found myself knocked back on my heels from the start. For the first time, I began to doubt the brainwashing that my drug was the best one in history. In desperate need of a success story proving Zyrtec's merit, I found one in the most unexpected place: my living room. (Considering the amount of dust balls and moldy pizza crusts under the couch, perhaps this should not have been such a surprise.)

My roommates Steve and Michael and I sat around one Saturday afternoon, drinking beer and watching college hoops. Aside from the occasional clapping for action on the court and the more frequent protesting of flatulence, the room's main activity came from Michael's chocolate Lab, Chauncey, and her endless pursuit of her blue racquetball. That is, until Ed showed up.

A fairly cantankerous guy, Ed trudged in and plopped down on the couch with a grunt. Following our grunted responses, the activity returned to its previous level and stayed there for approximately three minutes. Then Ed started sneezing as if he had just snorted a line of pepper. Uncontrollable eye watering followed. Steve thought the stream of snot pouring from Ed's nose was faster than the riptide from his eyes, but Michael and I disagreed. Of course, the three of us mocked his incapacitation, and I got up to get us a round of beers in celebration of this exciting development.

As I headed to the kitchen, Ed managed to catch his breath and spit out, "It's the dog! I'm freakin' allergic to the dog!" It took a moment for the lightbulb to come on: Give Ed a Zyrtec.

One of Zyrtec's advantages over other antihistamines was its rapid onset of action; 95 percent of patients who were going to respond to the drug would do so in fifty minutes, whereas Claritin often took close to two hours. This was the perfect opportunity to put my brainwashing to the test.

"Take a Zyrtec," I sang, delirious from my brainstorm. "You'll be good as new in fifty minutes."

I quickly grabbed a sleeve of samples and, after popping out a tablet for myself, threw a packet to Ed, who missed it since he could no longer see. I didn't need a Zyrtec at that point—my allergies wouldn't start for another month—but I took one anyway. Hey, they were there.

"Can you drink and take Zyrtec at the same time, Jamie?" Ed asked worriedly. I could not answer right away, as my mouth was filled with Bud Light. Having swallowed, I answered, "Yep," which was not the Pfizer approved response to this frequent question. Based on my personal experience, though, I found imbibing while medicating to be perfectly safe.

At one o'clock, Ed wiped his nose again and swallowed the tablet, and so began one of the longest hours of my life. It had not occurred to me that the drug might not work. I mean, I knew it didn't help every allergy patient ("There's no panacea, Doctor" was a common drug rep refrain), but the idea of failure had not entered my brain when I came up with this great idea. Ten minutes post-dose, however, I began to get nervous.

"Hey, Jamo!" Ed barked, using a nickname for my nickname. "I'm still sneezing over here. This drug sucks." The sneezing had gotten so bad that the guys stopped saying "Bless you." His eyes continued to water, and the pile of snotty Kleenex grew to resemble a papier-mâché ottoman in front of which Chauncey, oblivious to her role in this commotion, had dropped her ball so Ed could throw it to her. He did not feel like playing.

At one-twenty, he mocked me again. "Does this shit work for anybody?" I wanted to laugh at his pathetic sniffling or make a crack about his red eyes, but I couldn't. Instead, I sat frozen on the couch, struck dumb by the realization that I would hear about this for the rest of my life. Because that was what it really came down to. In the big picture, I didn't care about Ed's allergies; he could have simply gone home (locking Chauncey in the basement was *not* an option) and felt better in an hour. No, in the big picture I had made a personal guarantee, a declaration of belief. There was nothing guys liked better than to remind a friend about a failed declaration of belief.

"Hey, Ed," Steve snapped, rushing to my defense. "He said it'd take fifty minutes. You've got another half an hour, dipshit." Ed hocked a loogie in response.

Ten minutes later, Steve challenged him. "Eddie, I don't hear so much sniffling over there anymore." Ed barely acknowledged the comment. At the forty-minute mark, he conceded defeat.

"Okay, Jamo, you win. I'm all dried up." Sure enough, Ed sat symptom free with dry eyes and a dry nose. He was crushed. "Man, I was really hoping that stuff wouldn't work," he admitted, revealing more about men in that one sentiment than any book about Venus and Mars ever did. "You would've heard about it forever."

"Never a doubt, Eddie," I said with a smile, hoping its radiance would compensate for the relief in my voice. "Never a doubt." We sent Ed out for beers after that.

Instant access to samples didn't end with Pfizer's products, however. In fact, a drug rep's options expanded infinitely upon arriving at an office. Sample closets were like receptionists; although they ranged in size and accessibility from practice to practice, every office had at least one, containing tens of thousands of dollars' worth of samples of every product from Aricept to Zoloft. These closets served as a pharmaceutical filling station for salespeople in need.

Managers were notorious for grabbing samples while their reps, the people the managers were supposed to be evaluating, detailed doctors. It was straight out of a movie; one bad guy created a diversion while the other heisted the jewels. A rep really found out a lot about his boss's extended family by watching what he lifted from a sample closet: Aunt Becky had acid reflux (Prilosec), Uncle Tony had herpes (Famvir), brother Phil wouldn't leave the house (Paxil), sister Cindy couldn't sleep (Ambien). Ten-year-olds gave their parents less detailed Christmas lists than some Pfizer managers brought on their field rides.

Not all offices had samples of the drugs that reps needed, so creativity increased at a rate directly proportional to desperation. A friend of mine called on a dermatologist late one afternoon. Nothing out of the ordinary there, except for the fact that she was a urology and ob-gyn rep. Seemed she had broken out in a near-fatal case of acne (three pimples for this beauty was a crisis) and needed some dermatological products stat! So, this very ballsy Pfizer woman waltzed into the waiting room as if she had been there before (she hadn't), smiled at the receptionist as if she knew her (she didn't), and headed through the door leading to the back office, saying, "I just need to check samples." The receptionist returned the smile and waved her back, just the way she did for the regular reps. With $100 of prescription drugs hidden in her detail bag, my friend sauntered out. "That was fast," the receptionist said. Without missing a beat, our heroine replied, "Oh, you guys didn't need anything of mine today. See you in two weeks."

Having access and taking advantage of it, though, were two completely different things, at least for me.

In my defense, let me state (at the risk of being redundant) that I was a dumb guy. There was no doubt that a woman would have jumped on this gold mine immediately. As a possessor of the Y chromosome, however, it simply never occurred to me. As you can guess, I can only be speaking of birth control.

The birth control reps, most notably those from Ortho-McNeil, were a constant presence in ob-gyn offices, and they used their "Pill" samples to leverage their other products. Consequently, it was impossible to miss the cases upon cases of birth control boxes that spilled out of ob-gyn sample closets.

About six months into my Pfizer career, my girlfriend visited her gynecologist, and at dinner that weekend, she complained about the cost of the Ortho Tricyclen the doctor had prescribed.

"I couldn't believe it when the pharmacist told me the price went up again," she said with disgust. "What a racket."

"They cost money?" I asked.

"Of course they cost money, Jamie. How do you think I get them?"

And that cut right to the root of the issue. I didn't think about how she got them. I had never thought about how she got them. Like most guys—and, believe me, I have checked with a lot of my equally challenged friends—I had let the woman worry about "that stuff." Fortunately, I came back with a solid answer.

"Uh . . . you don't get samples?"

Her anger receded a bit. "Well, yeah, you get samples when he first puts you on it and maybe once or twice more after that, but then he gives you a prescription."

"That's crazy!" I blurted, about to reveal my own insanity. "They have thousands of samples just sitting there. . . . " I trailed off as soon as I realized what I'd said, but the damage was done. I risked a glance to see if she had been paying attention. She had.

"You mean to tell me that for all these months you've been working for Pfizer, you could've been getting me the Pill for free?"

I nodded, wincing with the knowledge that the money she had (unnecessarily) spent on birth control would be wasted that weekend.

On a positive note, at least I had $20,000 worth of Zoloft in the trunk of the Lumina to help treat my impending depression.

"What exactly is it that you *do?*"

My mother's question hung in the air a long time, possibly because I didn't quite know how to answer it. I had just finished regaling family members with stories of circumcisions and drug samples (though I made sure to pawn off the birth control pill debacle on another guy), when my mom stumped me. Clearly, she was asking me to justify my existence. I wasn't sure if I could. Mistaking my hesitation for confusion, she continued.

"I mean, why do they *need* drug reps?"

An official job description for a pharmaceutical salesperson would read: Provide health-care professionals with product information, answer their questions on the use of products, and deliver product samples. The general public could probably accept that as a useful role. An unofficial, and more accurate, description would have been: Change the prescribing habits of physicians.

And that is why drug reps exist: to get docs to stop writing scripts for Drug X and start writing them for Drug Y, thereby boosting the bottom line of the corporation that makes Drug Y. I didn't give my mom the real deal, since patients rarely want to hear about their doctors making decisions based on what some sales guy tells them, rather than scientific wisdom. Accordingly, I chose to share the official definition.

"But can't they just get all that information themselves?" Uh, no, they can't.

In a perfect world, there would be no need for drug reps. Physicians would receive sufficient pharmaceutical training in medical school and residency, and this training would last them indefinitely. Doctors would have sufficient time to update this training, if necessary, by reading the latest medical journals throughout their forty-year careers. Finally, pharmaceutical companies would bring to market only those drugs that provided marked benefits over products already in use.

Alas, the medical world is a few light-years from perfect. Physicians begin their careers with a solid foundation of pharmaceutical knowledge. Most medical schools require a second-year pharmacology class lasting one or two semesters, in which students are instructed on the mechanisms of action and pharmacokinetics of the products in the major drug classes. Microbiology classes cover some of the same area regarding infectious disease drugs, such as antibiotics, giving the majority of students a thorough review. In the third and fourth years of medical school, part of the internal medicine rotations again deal with the pharmacokinetics of drugs. Then, after selecting a particular field of medicine, the residents are educated about drugs specific to their field, so rheumatologists learn about pain medications while allergists focus on antihistamines. Thus, it is fair to say that most doctors exit their residencies with a solid knowledge of pharmaceuticals. "The problem," a pediatric ICU specialist and friend from Notre Dame explained to me, "is that most MDs in private practice lose their source of education about drugs and don't have time to either refresh themselves with what they previously learned or, more important, educate themselves about new drugs."

This is a familiar refrain among physicians: lack of time. Doctors have a tough gig. In addition to seeing thirty to fifty patients a day, physicians are expected to do dictations for each patient visit, make hospital rounds, explain treatment options to family members, call HMOs to fight for prescription coverage, and speak to pharmacists who like to double-check dosages on prescriptions. After all that in a day's work, a doctor can choose to play with his three-year-old daughter or pick up the *New England Journal of Medicine.* What would you do? They won't miss the earth-shattering breakthroughs like Viagra, but the subtler advances like modifications in dosing or the addition of a second agent do get past them. Without the time to do all of the professional reading necessary in order to stay current, physicians are forced to rely on drug reps for updates.

Of the three duties listed in the official job description, sales reps could be replaced for two of them: Free drug samples could be mailed to physicians, and specific product questions could be answered via twenty-four-hour doctors-access-only Web sites. It is an unavoidable feature of the system, however, that physicians need reps to keep them up to speed. A salesperson has to provide helpful information only a few times before establishing himself as an asset. Once "in," a rep can take advantage of his trusted position and begin influencing the decision-making process.

Things would be a lot easier for doctors if the drugs in each class were radically different from one another. However, there are very few "Michael Jordans" in the pharmaceutical world, best-in-class products that have repeatedly proven far superior to their competition. Such drugs would be used first by every physician every time; if a new agent proved itself more effective than M.J. with an equal safety profile, everyone would obviously hear the news and change their treatments accordingly. Unfortunately, that scenario occurs about as often as an heir apparent to Air Jordan bursts onto the scene and continues flying high—Kobe Bryants are rare in the pharma market.

Instead, the industry has a glut of "me-too" drugs—products with similar efficacy rates but whose slight differences in insurance coverage, dosing, side effects, and cost only muddy a physician's decision-making process. Is it Drug X or Drug Y that is covered by Blue Shield? I know Drug X has a warning against usage in diabetics and patients with liver problems, but does Drug Y have the same ones? In that European study where they doubled the dose of Drug

X, did they cut the number of days in half? Drug reps know *all* that information about their own drugs and the competing products because we get paid to know. For the physician fifteen years removed from residency who is running an hour behind schedule before lunchtime, a drug rep can be a beacon in a storm, the one person able to tell her if Drug Y is on the formulary and safe for use in a mid-fifties Hispanic female with high blood pressure. Helping out in that kind of a situation creates a bond between salesperson and physician, although such trust can lead to problems.

A pediatrician in western Michigan once accused me of lying to him, saying that Zithromax was not the least-expensive brand-name antibiotic on the market, as I had boasted, but the *most* expensive. Fully aware that a course of Zithromax cost under $40, while all of my competitors ran at least $50, I asked him where he got his information. He smiled victoriously as he reached into his desk drawer and pulled out a laminated color chart given to him by a competitor. Though initially panicked, I quickly recognized the problem.

"Doctor, this ranks drugs by cost *per day*," I explained. He failed to see my point.

"Yeah, Jamie, and it says Zithromax costs eight dollars per day, whereas Vantin costs only six dollars per day! You lied to me." The Upjohn Pharmaceuticals marketing guy who dreamed up that cost sheet deserved a promotion. I could not believe that this physician, a very smart man, had been fooled. It was Enron math before anyone had even heard of Enron.

"Doctor, how many days is Vantin dosed for?" Ten, he answered. "And Zithromax?" Five. I looked at him, waiting. He still didn't get it.

"Okay, so Vantin costs six dollars per day times ten days, which equals . . . " He finished my math. Sixty bucks.

"And Zithromax costs eight dollars per day times *five* days, which equals . . . " He didn't finish my math this time. Instead, his face turned bright red. After a long pause, he turned toward me. *"Damn you, drug reps!"* he screamed before storming away. After a few steps, he stopped, walked back toward me, and tossed the laminated sheet back into the drawer. I didn't envy the Vantin guy on his next call with that pediatrician.

I can hear it now: *Ban the pharmaceutical salespeople!* Without drug reps, though, who would bring free lunch to the receptionists and nurses every day?

Five

WORKING FOR A LIVING

PFIZER MANAGEMENT PROVIDED us with numerous weapons to ensure sales success, and none was more important than the expense account. It was made very clear to us, however, that these funds were to be used *only* to build rapport and improve access into offices. Several pharmaceutical companies had gotten in trouble with the FDA, thanks to their reps' attempts to use trips, dinners, and Super Bowl tickets to barter for sales with doctors.

Pfizer was extremely concerned about these violations regarding quid pro quo, a Latin phrase meaning "I will take you to play golf at Pebble Beach if you will then write five thousand prescriptions for Zyrtec." It was absolutely, positively forbidden to enter into such agreements with medical professionals. Unfortunately, Monsieurs Quid, Pro, and Quo were old friends of mine, dating back to my army days when I'd buy beers for soldiers who kept me out of the colonel's doghouse. Some habits were hard to break.

I received a Travel and Entertainment (T&E) budget averaging $800 every two weeks. This money covered the basic day-to-day costs of doing business: gas for my company car, supplies, hotels and meals while on the road, and food for doctors and staff members.

74

The importance of food in pharmaceutical sales can*not* be over-stated. The way to a man's heart may be through his stomach, but the way to a doctor's heart went straight through his office staff's collective stomach. Whether morning (cinnamon rolls, Danishes, bagels, doughnuts) or afternoon (candy, cake, ice cream), medical office personnel ate as if winter hibernation was two days away and they had gotten a late start. Drug reps did everything they could to aid their cause. Some offices grew so accustomed to receiving free goodies they refused entry to reps arriving empty-handed, prompting salespeople to establish an identity by bringing the same treat every time.

One colleague from my training class handed out Blow Pops to every medical employee he saw, while another gave out cookies decorated with purple "Zithromax" stripes. Branding oneself was not limited to Pfizer personnel, however; my arch-nemesis the Biaxin guy *baked* cookies for all his pediatric offices. As much as I hate to admit it, homemade treats from a man in his mid-forties proved to be a formidable obstacle to my efforts to buy the love of those women. Cattily, I'd tell nurses, "No matter how yummy they are, those cookies can't get rid of Biaxin's metallic taste!" My research found chocolate to be the best motivator for female office staff members. Consequently, I became the "M&M's Guy."

I brought M&M's into every office I called on, every time I called on it. Averaging twenty bags per week, I quickly learned through informal polling that the peanut kind made way more friends than the plain, which just so happened to mirror my own preference. My dad had gotten me hooked on the former as a kid, when he showed me how it was possible to inhale an entire bag on the way home from the supermarket "without Mommy ever knowing." Before assuming my role of chocolate candy sommelier, I did not know that Mars, Inc., produced M&M's in colors appropriate for every holiday—the mint green, red, and white ones that came out only during Christmastime were a personal favorite—but it gradually became second nature to look for pink and red ones in early February and red, white, and blue in late June. (Unfortunately, I didn't think of saving proofs of purchase until years later, when I would have accumulated more than three thousand.)

My M&M's mania had its downside because it forced me to acknowledge a mania common among medical employees, aka "kleptos." In selling antibiotics for young children, flavor played an important role, since no parent wanted to fight with a squirming kid to get the medicine down. Consequently, if a company's drug tasted good or just not too bad, its marketing team hyped that advantage nonstop. After the cherry-flavored Zithromax oral suspension won taste tests against every other *brand-name* antibiotic—nobody could touch amoxicillin, "the pink stuff"—Pfizer's marketing geniuses wanted to drive home that point. To this end, we received cases of cherry-flavored tongue depressors and clear, plastic containers stamped with ZITHROMAX in—naturally—purple lettering to distribute to each office.

Well, like most ideas from the marketing teams, this one was only half successful. The tongue depressors came *separate* from the containers, meaning *somebody* had to assemble the package. Not bloody likely. I threw out an ark's worth of cherry tongue depressors, as did most of my colleagues. However, the containers could hold two and a half pounds of M&M's; left on the nurses' counters, I could simply refill them every time I visited an office. That is, if they were still there.

Shortly after launching my container concept, I noticed they had vanished from the countertops in one of my bigger offices and in three other practices I called on that day. The mystery of the missing M&M's containers gnawed at me until I finally asked the nearest staff member, "What happened to the M&M's thingies?" I have yet to get over my shock at her answer.

"Oh, *those.* You know, they make great Q-tip holders."

I was stunned by the thought of my beloved containers held captive in bathrooms throughout northern Indiana. It turned out that their worth was not limited to ear-cleaning products; they also made great cotton-ball holders. I began taping big DO NOT REMOVE labels onto the containers, but some still disappeared.

I considered ceasing my M&M's purchases in protest, but that proved impossible. Unintentionally, I had created a confectionary conundrum for myself: These ladies equated me with the plain and peanut treats. They may not have known what drugs I sold, but they damn well knew I was the M&M's guy.

"Hi," I'd say pleasantly as I approached the check-in window.

"Where are they?" the receptionist would say, holding out one hand while unconsciously wiping away the saliva dribbling in Pavlovian fashion with the other. I became a literal sugar daddy. The rattle of a bag of my colorful little "office keys" brought women running. The M&M's guy usually got back to see a doctor, making that money well spent.

The biggest chunk of my expense account was spent on office lunches. As a new Pfizer rep, I pictured myself aiding the fight against disease by providing doctors and nurses with important information that would help save lives. Little did I know that three months later I'd be running a de facto catering company and that one of my most well-received pearls would be that the Olive Garden's black-and-white cheesecake was available for takeout.

Lunches proved to be the most frustrating facet of pharmaceutical sales because they almost never turned out as planned. While colleagues in major cities utilized caterers, there were few of those in northern Indiana, so I had to pick up the food myself. This presented logistical problems since the restaurants rarely had the meals ready on time, and trays often spilled during transport. On more than one occasion, a woman with whom I was on a blind date glanced into my backseat, noticed the food stains, and remarked, "They didn't mention that you had kids!" I also ruined suits when marinara sauce leaked from the tray I was carrying on two separate occasions, and one of my coworkers told me I was lucky the number wasn't higher.

Inside the office, I'd often find the staff members knee-deep in yet-to-be completed paperwork and phone calls, unable to get the lunch area ready. Having finally schlepped the food in, I'd discover a lunch table covered with three feet of crap, including old Cheetos bags, issues of *People,* and patient charts. Since bigger offices worked through the lunch hour, the women would take their breaks in shifts, with the least-important personnel often eating first. Unfortunately, there seemed to be an inversely proportional ratio between a woman's job importance and her appetite, so the food would occasionally be gone by the time the doctors rolled in.

Perhaps I shouldn't throw stones, however, since I, too, once forced a physician to go hungry. For my first lunch ever, I wowed the staff with an impressive array from Subway. The rolled eyes and barely suppressed groans quickly alerted me to the preference for food that was hot and good, not necessarily in that order. Painfully aware of my brand-new status, the ladies gave me the benefit of the doubt, and things seemed to go smoothly after that. Except, of course, for the absence of either pediatrician, both of whom were "totally swamped." Earlier, the first nurse on break told me, while less than enthusiastically choosing between a BMT or tuna on wheat, she hoped Dr. Blank would be able to pop in for a minute. After sitting down, she urged me to grab a sub. I politely declined, explaining that I had eaten a big breakfast and still wasn't hungry. In truth, I was merely following a basic tenet of army leadership: Troops eat first. The last thing I wanted was to run out of food before the doctors arrived.

Twenty minutes later, the third nurse on break reported that there was no way Dr. Blank was going to have time to say hello, let alone eat. This prompted several more calls for me to dig in, but I continued to resist. Finally, at one o'clock the office manager pointed toward the lone remaining sub and said, "Really, Jamie, he isn't going to stop back here. Go ahead and eat." I relented and helped myself. No sooner had I shoved the six-inch Subway Club into my hasty mouth than a man in his early forties wearing a Mickey Mouse tie—male pediatricians often sported cartoon ties in order to make little kids laugh—glided through the door. Rubbing his hands together with gusto, Dr. Blank headed straight to the table.

"I'm starving! Anything good left?" he asked with a smile. Unable to speak with my mouth full, I shook my head no as the office manager ducked her head and bolted out of the room. After watching his employee leave, he looked again to the table, and then turned his full attention to me. Seeing me with a practically whole sandwich in my hand, Dr. Blank quickly deduced what had happened. I started to offer an apology, but he cut me off with a bigger smile and a wave of his hand before grabbing a handful of Oreos and a Diet Coke. "Don't worry about it, man. It's not like I'm important around here or anything." With a loud clap on my shoulder, he headed down the hall to see more patients. I never ate before a physician again.

Interestingly enough, the purpose of these lunches was not to feed the office staff or inflict mental trauma on drug reps. From the pharmaceutical companies' perspective, these lunches provided salespeople with their best low-cost opportunity to interact with their most important customers, the doctors.

At an ideal lunch, three things would happen:

1. The rep would get the opportunity to sit down with a physician for twenty to thirty minutes, during which the doctor would eat her lunch while listening to the rep's sales pitch.

2. The doctor would be interested enough to ask a few relevant questions such as, "How does Drug X compare to Drug Y side effects–wise?"

3. The physician would agree that Drug X had some clinical advantages and commit to using it in a few patients later that day.

If things went really well, the doc would hang around after the presentation to shoot the breeze. Some guys wanted to talk Pfizer stock, others wanted to talk Notre Dame football, and some—usually married men—just wanted to hear the latest escapades in the life of a single guy. Once I had identified who liked to discuss what, I'd plan accordingly. For the stock savvy, I would call my father the financial planner to get the latest Pfizer price just before pulling into the office parking lot, and for the gridiron gurus, I'd read the current *Irish Sports Report* the night before to catch up on the latest news regarding Lou Holtz's boys. To entertain the husbands living vicariously through a bachelor, I'd call "active" friends for memorable shenanigans when mine were lacking. Regardless of the topic, these BS sessions were important because they could spark friendships while giving a rep a hot button to push the next time he saw the physician.

Unfortunately, most lunches did not end this way. Fairly often, reps barely got the opportunity to speak to a doctor, many of whom preferred to pop in, grab a plate of food, and dash out mumbling through a mouthful of pasta, "Sorry. Way behind today."

Considering the actual price of the lunch plus the time value of the cost of having a rep out of the field for up to an hour (in addition to picking up food at a restaurant, a stop at a supermarket was standard to acquire sodas and desserts) without getting a solid selling opportunity, such an experience was extremely expensive to Pfizer, not to mention very discouraging to a rep. The only saving grace in that situation was the leftovers.

I stumbled upon the miracle of leftovers by accident. Scheduling a lunch for a pediatric office, I mistakenly wrote down twenty-two people instead of twelve. Wearing differing sizes of the same baby-decorated scrub top, ten women (the two docs no-showed) did their best to remove any evidence that I had brought Olive Garden, but an entire tray of chicken parmigiana and a half tray of lasagna sat untouched along with several salads and countless bread sticks. The staff thanked me for bringing in lunch, and I replied, sincerely, that it was I who should do the thanking because getting a free, hot meal was the best part of my job. This statement was met with confused looks.

I explained that I was a bachelor for whom Tater Tots often served as the main course, not the side dish. This prompted a chorus of "You poor thing!" and "We need to get you a wife!" As I tried to alleviate their maternal concerns, an angel disguised as a receptionist stood up and pointed to the leftover food. "Jamie, why don't you take it home?" *Oh, I could never do that.* "You have to!" they cried. *That wouldn't be right.* "Pack it up for him, girls." Not wanting to offend a group of customers, I grudgingly accepted their kind offer. And did cartwheels in the parking lot.

On the way home, I called my friend Lou, another bachelor with limited skills in the kitchen. "We're eating Olive Garden tonight. Bring the beer." Lou was stunned when he saw the spread on my kitchen counter. "And they just gave it to you?" he asked, incredulous. "This is amazing." Indeed.

Soon, I was accidentally over-ordering a few times per week. Buddies were calling to see if they could "stop by with beer around dinnertime." I started scheduling lunches not to create more sales opportunities with doctors, but for the leftovers. My boss noticed my increase in spending and told me to keep up the good work. "Gotta spend it to make it, Jamie." That quickly became a mantra. Whereas I originally mentioned my bachelorhood by chance, I now brought it up routinely, shamelessly inserting "For a single guy, this is the best part of my job" into the first five minutes of every lunch. Maternal instincts kicking into overdrive, nurses practically fought over who got to pack up my leftovers. Turns out I wasn't alone.

Over cocktails one night at a sales meeting, I cautiously revealed my scam to several people. I couldn't wait to see the awe in their eyes as they secretly wished they were me. "You mean you just started doing that?" one guy cackled. "That was, like, the first thing I figured out." The others nodded in agreement, and I realized I was more than a bit behind the learning curve. It wouldn't be the last time.

There was another area in which I tried to exploit cracks in the system, and that involved my work activity. Or lack thereof. Back in July 1995 when I emerged from the interview room with job in hand, Brandon-the-HR-guy, Class of '68, sat me down for a heart-to-heart. "I've taken Notre Dame guys to the top, and I've kicked Notre Dame guys out on their ass!" he said in a threatening voice. "Don't think you're going to get any special treatment." I shook my head, signifying that was the furthest thing from my mind.

He laid out the ground rules for working at Pfizer. In the field by seven-thirty. Making sales calls until five-thirty. Maybe even calling on pharmacies after that. When he told me more specifically that leaving South Bend for Chicago before five o'clock on Friday was not an option, I nodded my head. I mean, what job let you quit work before five? Brandon-the-HR-guy and I were in complete agreement that I would not be leaving for Chicago at five. Of course, neither one of us realized I'd be leaving every Friday at three.

My total abandonment of anything resembling a work ethic did not start right away. Rather, I began my Pfizer career by working fairly hard. I got up on time and usually started my day by Pfizer's appointed seven-thirty. Okay, that's not really true, but it felt pretty good to write it. For the first three days I got up on time. On the morning of Day Four, I hit "snooze" a few more times than normal, prompting a great deal of guilt. The next day, I turned off the alarm immediately—so much for being wracked by guilt—and fell back to sleep till nine A.M., when I awoke in a panic. *Oh my God! I'm going to get fired!*

Out of the shower and back in my bedroom, I noticed the quiet in my apartment. Looking out the window, I saw an empty parking lot. All my neighbors had left for work. Yet, no one had phoned to find out why Lieutenant Reidy wasn't at headquarters or why Jamie Reidy hadn't called on Dr. Sweeney by nine o'clock. Gradually, I figured out that no one at Pfizer—more specifically, Bruce—knew where I was, let alone when I had gotten up. This realization marked the beginning of the end. Pfizer hired ex-military officers like me expressly because we were already self-starters who did not need someone monitoring our work efforts at all times.

"You gotta be shitting me!" That was how my former army boss, Major Curt Croom, reacted upon learning that my new boss lived in Detroit, four hours from South Bend. "That is a *big* mistake on their part," he guffawed. Displaying an amazing lack of self-awareness, I asked him why. "Because you need constant adult supervision, Jamie," he said, continuing to laugh. His assessment quickly proved accurate.

I hadn't always been a slacker. Up until tenth grade, I studied hard in school. Then I experienced an epiphany, only in reverse. I say reverse because most epiphanies concern positive changes in life, whereas mine had negative connotations. At least that's what my parents said.

In high school I realized I could study hard and get an A, or I could coast and get an A–. At Notre Dame, the coasting continued, but the grades declined. An English major, I skipped the assigned reading more often than not, and my class attendance was less than exemplary, but I managed to get Bs. Lots and lots of Bs. I was perfectly happy with those marks, although—once again—my parents did not share my satisfaction. Postgraduation, the U.S. Army provided me with unlimited opportunities to refine my "zero-effort" technique.

Similar to Pfizer's Initial Training, the Officer Basic Course (OBC) required only an 80 on each exam. At the end of the course, an honor graduate was recognized, but there were no other good reasons for doing more than the minimum. The tests covered the material presented in class, often highlighted by the instructor stomping his foot like a mule as he winked, "This might be on the exam."

My OBC advisers were troubled by my lack of effort, and they urged me to take advantage of my "tools and talents." *Why would I want to do that?* I wondered. I mean, when you did well in the army, they gave you "better" jobs, and their idea of better and my idea of better were not remotely related. Better jobs in the army meant an increased chance of getting muddy or shot. Thanks to my poor performance, I got assigned to one of the worst (read: wimpiest) duty stations in the entire army: Camp Zama, Japan. It would have been impossible to have a *less-army* army existence than mine. The dirtiest I ever got resulted not from diving into a foxhole, but slicing into a sand trap. We never stayed at work past five o'clock. At least *I* never did.

The first time I pulled my white Chevy Lumina onto I-80 heading west toward Chicago on a Friday at three o'clock, I felt a little guilty, for some strange reason. For about ten seconds. Then I thought, *This job rocks!*

As usual, my friends had already beaten me to that conclusion.

About three weeks into my sales career, a classmate from training called. A happy-go-lucky guy nicknamed "The Mayor," he had once responded to my question, "How are you doing?" with "You know me; I'm always good." If there was a silver lining to be found, Matt could do it. He and I shot the breeze for a few minutes before he floored me with a verbal left hook.

"Are ya working?" he asked in his East Coast accent. *Oh my God! He knows I'm sleeping late!* I expected Bruce to knock on the door any second and ask for the keys to the Lumina.

"Uh, er . . . what are you talking about, man?" My voice cracked just the way it did in seventh grade when my dad asked me if I was smoking cigarettes with the ninth-graders at the bus stop.

"Ah, c'mon, dude, *nobody* is working." Matt responded like a cool guy, sounding very much like the aforementioned ninth-graders who had encouraged me to smoke in the first place. "I didn't work at all last week," he added.

This confused me. "How could you already have saved up five vacation days when we've only been working three weeks?"

"I didn't *take* vacation, man."

"What, were you sick?"

Matt laughed. "No, I wasn't sick! I just didn't feel like working." I started to relax a bit.

"Soooo, you just didn't go to work for a few days?"

Matt was getting impatient. "*Nooo,* I didn't go to work for all five days." This was way too much for me.

"You didn't go to work for *five days!*" His laugh confirmed this. "What . . . what . . . how did you cover yourself?" His wife would have *killed* him had she discovered his high jinks.

"Well, I got up every morning, showered, and ate breakfast like a normal day, and then I kissed my wife good-bye and headed out the door."

"And then what?"

Matt snickered. "And then I went to the gym, worked out for a few hours, got a steam or whatever."

"Yeah, but . . . "

"And then I'd buy the paper and eat lunch before catching a matinee or two. Hey, dude, if there's anything you want to see, just ask me; I've seen every movie that's out."

There was something I still didn't get.

"Yeah, but *how* did you cover yourself work-wise? I mean, how are you going to show that you called on doctors and dropped off samples and everything?"

Again with the snicker. "I keep forgetting you're new to pharma sales," he said, his words dripping with condescension. Matt came from a long line of pharmaceutical salesmen and had obviously picked up a trick or two. "You just have to work your ass off and see a ton of docs the next week. Or just get a nurse to sign her doc's name; they do it all the time anyway." *They do?*

We chatted for a few more minutes, but I didn't pay too much attention to the conversation. My head was swimming with the possibilities. Matt had opened my eyes to an unforeseen world of laziness and deception, and having taken a bite of the apple, I was dying to catch the first Lumina out of Eden.

After we hung up, I quickly called a few more friends from training, just to see if Matt was an anomaly. He wasn't.

"Why do you think people are dying to get into pharmaceutical sales, dude?" one clued-in southern guy asked me. "I can't believe you didn't know about this before you interviewed." More of the same out west. "Are you kidding?" a woman in southern California screamed. "Please tell me you didn't get into this because you want to *help* sick people." *Uh, no, of course not. I got into this because my daddy made me.*

Apparently, every other pharmaceutical salesperson in the United States knew going in that being a drug rep was the greatest gig going. I needed no further encouraging; I was ready to milk the system for all it was worth.

Clearly, a drug rep could not just play hooky from work. A number of precautions had to be taken to ensure that one was not caught slacking off. In fact, it was a lot of work to make it look as if I was working. Exhausting, practically.

There were basically two types of people in pharmaceutical sales: those who focused on exceeding sales goals and those who concentrated on getting enough sleep. Members of the former group prided themselves on being organized and making lists for *everything*: things to do, sales goals, deadlines, and so on. These people prayed to Stephen Covey every night. Those of us in the latter category, while perhaps lacking our colleagues' zeal for organization, had our own list of daily do's and don'ts. In hindsight, the undetected completion of a work-free workday may have required more planning and foresight than any successful sales month.

Not that there was a *Slacking for Dummies* handbook, but having thoroughly researched this, I think we all followed the same basic tenets that we tailored to our and our sales managers' individual styles. If *Slacking for Dummies* had existed, it would have contained the following three chapters:

Voice Mail: Friend *and* Foe

Perception Is Reality

The Paper Chase

Six

VOICE MAIL: FRIEND *AND* FOE

Nothing a savvy slacker did during a typical day was more important than the first thing: check voice mail. It took me two months to learn this.

Pfizer's requirement to be on the road by seven-thirty provided us with a clear starting point. Obviously, if you were driving around town before eight o'clock, you had already had plenty of time to pick up the phone and check messages. Bruce expected his reps to check voice mail a minimum of three times per day: in the morning, at lunch, and at the end of the day (meaning five P.M.). Not coincidentally, he left us voice mails every morning at six o'clock. I did not give this much thought and, as a result, routinely answered those early-morning messages when I woke up. At ten A.M. Fortunately, dumb luck stepped in and saved me from a very brief career.

Two hours into our second field ride together, Bruce pulled out his cell phone and dialed into the voice-mail system. He then asked me for a piece of scrap paper. After about thirty seconds, I looked down to see what he was writing, and I almost crashed the car.

Scribbled one under the other were the names of the ten reps in our district, and next to each name was a time, for example, "Craig—6:50" and "Sean—8:15," denoting when each person had listened to Bruce's six A.M. voice mail. He was checking up on us, and there was no way of knowing how long he had been doing so! *Of all the low-down, dirty tricks. I mean, if a boss couldn't trust his people to get up on time and work hard, what kind of relationship was that?* Miraculously, I had checked voice mail early that morning—I had *had* to do so to find out where I was supposed to meet Bruce—so my time read "6:30." For the time being I was in the clear, but I grew nervous about how often the voice-mail lady had spoken my time ending in "P.M."

Initially wary of opening Pandora's box, I eventually chose to see exactly how deep the doo-doo was in which I was standing.

"What are you doing, boss?" I asked meekly.

Bruce shrugged disarmingly. "Ah, just something I picked up from another manager. One of the capabilities of this new voice-mail system is that anybody can punch a few buttons and code their message so that when the recipient listens to it, the system sends the originator a message informing him of when they got it." (Keep in mind that this was 1995, and voice mail was not as common-place as it is today.) "So, I'm using it to see when everybody is checking messages."

His blank face revealed nothing. My eyelid began to twitch.

"How long have you been doing that?"

He smiled like a proud papa. "First day!" he said, enthusiastically. "Your six-thirty was the earliest! Is that an everyday thing?"

Not only was I not in trouble, I was being praised! Trying to act nonchalant, I shrugged.

"Nah, it's usually a little later, but I didn't go for my run today." Bruce nodded approvingly, and I sat a little taller in the Lumina, basking in my increased credibility with my boss. I should have been making the sign of the cross to ward off the lightning strike.

The first thing I did after dropping Bruce off that evening was voice mail all my friends. *"They can tell when we're checking messages! They're on to us!"* For once, I knew something they didn't. *"Holy shit,*

Reidy!" was the response du jour, and I was promised hundreds of free beers for my intelligence report on enemy activity. Instantly, longtime habits were changed as reps across the nation set alarm clocks for seven A.M., leaving ample time to wake up, clear sleep from voices, and respond to inevitable messages from managers. After which, they would return to bed danger—and guilt—free.

Having neutralized a powerful weapon in Evil Management's arsenal, I spent the next two months swimming in a sleep-induced sea of mediocrity. During a conversation with two veteran Pfizer reps, however, a storm blew in and rocked my boat.

Walking across a snowy hospital parking lot in Fort Wayne, I spotted Pat and Tom standing in front of the lobby. A combined ten years of Pfizer experience between them, they had already given me several pearls of advice in my short time with the company. I was always receptive to anything they had to offer, and on this occasion, they did not disappoint.

"Hey, you know about voice mail, right?" Pat asked. Finally, a chance to demonstrate that I was not so wet behind the ears, after all.

"Yeah, I know all about it," I said, going on to detail the managers' plan. I allowed myself a brief, proud smile.

"No, that's not what I'm talking about," Pat answered, rolling his eyes at Tom. Pat had my complete attention. "I'm talking about how they can trace the call."

"Trace *what* call?" I asked, hairs standing up on the back of my neck.

"Your call into the voice-mail system!" Tom answered, sharing Pat's impatience.

"How can they do that?" My voice had risen several octaves.

"Don't ask *me,* man. I don't know," Pat said. "But I do know that it doesn't matter how they do it. All that matters is that they *can."* Gulp.

For the rest of the day, my mind was overwhelmed by the likelihood that Pfizer was hip to my check-voice-mail-from-bed trick.

Even worse, as my fear of getting caught had diminished and my laziness had increased, I had begun calling voice mail from home throughout the day, after naps, before *Oprah,* and so on. Now, the gig was up. That night as I sent a message informing my friends of this new development, a thought occurred to me: *Do you have to list a company on your résumé if you got fired?*

The next morning, seven-fifteen did not find me snuggled in my warm bed as I gargled and sang, "Do, re, mi" in an effort to loosen up my voice. I was shivering in my car as I drove to the nearest gas station, a mile from my apartment. Purpose: to use its pay phone to check voice mail. Standing in the freezing wind, I realized I was looking at a very long winter.

Based on the evidence presented so far, voice mail seemed to be a nasty cog in Darth Vader's employee-control machinery. For those of us in whom the Force was strong, however, voice mail proved itself a most capable light saber, one that helped us would-be Skywalkers continue flying our half-assed operations beneath Empire radar.

This reverse strategy was a lot easier than I ever imagined. Picture the Allied forces sending hundreds of false messages in the weeks leading up to the D-day invasion of Normandy, attempting to convince the Germans the attack would occur elsewhere. We sort of did that. Just as Pfizer managers used our listening to messages as a means of keeping tabs on us, we sent messages to make them think we were actually working.

The staple of this deception was the "Success Story." Managers were forever forwarding on messages saying, "Hey, team, check out this success story from Kelly." Unless the originator was a friend (in which case, you would want to listen to the message so you could make fun of him later for being such a kiss-ass), such forwards were immediately deleted, since most sales reps, including me, were too egotistical to admit that another rep could teach them something. What your teammates did with your success story didn't matter, though. As long as your manager noted, "Jamie voice mailed at four-thirty on Thursday," everything was kosher.

For the true artistes of slacking, however, there was a lot more to the successful leaving of success-story voice mails than merely checking in with the boss.

"En*thus*iasm sells!" Bruce repeatedly told us, referring to our delivery when speaking to physicians. He meant that our attitudes were contagious; if we were upbeat when discussing our products, customers were more likely to share that feeling and vice versa. I took that lesson and applied it to other areas. Like ditching work.

How enthusiastic? Suffice to say, I wouldn't press the # key, aka the Send button, until I was certain I sounded as though I had just won my second Oscar of the evening. After all, if the call had truly been successful, wouldn't I be pumped up about it? For starters, I liked to make it sound like I had *just gotten* into my car following a good call, and I *just had to* voice mail my boss right away. Pretending to be a bit out of breath, I'd stammer a bit as if all the excitement made it difficult for me to get my thoughts together.

Giddy laugh. "Hey, boss, it's Jamie!" Gasp. "Man, I just *had* to tell you about an *awesome* call I had with . . . "

Naming the physician was not an every-time thing. If the success story had actually taken place, I would give the doc's name, list his sales potential ranking (*any* customer mentioned in a success story always ranked among my Top 10 biggest), and then relate the details of the call. The next time my manager spent the day with me, I'd remind him about the successful call prior to seeing the doctor again, thus setting myself up to demonstrate my ability to build on a previous encounter.

However, if any or all of the success story just happened to be fictional, I'd omit the doctor's name, thereby removing any chance of getting caught in a lie somewhere down the road. Rather than give the physician's name, I'd say, "A pediatrician in Fort Wayne"; that way, if Bruce ever met a pediatrician in Fort Wayne and asked,

"Is this the guy from that great success story?" I could say, "No. That guy's in Tibet on a month-long trek."

Whenever possible, it helped to leave such a message while driving, since the sound of the road added to the sense that I had *just gotten* into my car following a good call, and I *just had to* voice mail my boss right away.

While enthusiasm and road noise were important factors, nothing played a bigger role than the timing of such a message. Ideally, success stories were sent after four-thirty on Friday afternoon, hopefully giving my manager the impression that I was a model rep who routinely called on docs till the final horn at the end of the week. Aiming for this time of day proved both convenient and productive for me, since I undoubtedly sounded enthusiastic (at the thought of skipping out of work early on Fridays) while speaking with the sound of the road in the background (as I headed out of town for the weekend).

It was a bit risky to leave success stories all the time, though, *especially* for a guy whose sales numbers were fairly mediocre. After all, a manager just might stop and ask himself, "Reidy leaves at least one success story per week, yet he never rises above the middle of the pack. What gives?" In order to combat such curiosity, I'd mix in the occasional Competitive Activity Story or Failure Story or Objection Story.

The Competitive Activity Story simply described the competition's latest bad-guy behaviors, such as taking doctors golfing at Pebble Beach or using a previously unknown trial to discredit one of our drugs or tout theirs. "Hey, Bruce, just got out of a call with an allergist in Elkhart who told me he and the Claritin rep were drinking Cristal in the nineteenth hole when the rep showed him some data suggesting Claritin works better in Irish women. . . . "

The Failure Story simply took the success story and turned it on its head. Rather than speaking quickly with excitement dripping from my voice, I'd slow down my speech and sigh a few times.

Enthusiasm was MIA, replaced by a glum my-dog-just-died-and-there-is-no-Santa-Claus tone. "Uh, hey, boss." Sigh. "Jeez, did I just blow it with an allergist in Ft. Wayne. . . . " This type of message may have been more believable than its happy counterpart; no one wanted to admit failing, so who would ever make that up? But I learned the hard way not to lay it on too thick.

One Friday evening, I received a call from Bruce, who was checking on my confidence level after a particularly rough "failure." Though it was a nice gesture and a great leadership move, this call troubled me because I was in a bar in Chicago when I received it at five-ten P.M. Fortunately, I dodged the bullet because he assumed I was in a bar in South Bend ("Man, I really needed a drink after that ENT ripped me a new one"), but the near miss taught me a good lesson: Sound bowed, not broken.

The Objection Story removed any risks associated with the Failure Story, while adding to my reputation as a team player who shared problems and issues I encountered in the field. As I mentioned earlier, an objection was anything negative a physician said in response to a point made by a rep. Whether in statement ("Zithromax gives all my patients rashes on their eyelids") or question ("Will Zithromax give my patients rashes on their eyelids?") form, we were supposed to report it to our manager, who would then forward it to the rest of the team. Regardless of when I had actually been faced with the question or negative response, I'd wait to send the voice mail till late Friday afternoon, preferably from the road. *I'm a worker, boss.*

On one memorable occasion, I took the phrase "from the road" to new dimensions. Europe, to be exact.

My brother, Patrick, spent the fall semester of his junior year in London, just as I had eight years earlier. My parents invited me to join them on a vacation there, Mom reminding me that during my four-month stint I had somehow managed to avoid visiting a few inconsequential tourist traps like St. Paul's Cathedral and the

National Gallery. I didn't think I could make it. Ten months into the year, I had already burned through most of my days off, with the remainder saved for Christmastime, when it would have been fairly difficult to pretend I was working when I wasn't. I tried to explain the situation to her, but one solid dose of maternal guilt later ("Remember that time you came home from Japan to party with your friends on the Jersey Shore, three hours from home, but failed to tell your parents you were in America?") I was on the phone with British Airways.

A plane ticket did not alleviate my shortage of vacation time, however. I had four days left for the holidays, but had booked a trip to London that would leave the States on a Wednesday, thereby burning three days. I was in quite a pickle: disappoint Mom by either missing the family trip or making said trip but going home for only one day at Christmas *or* get fired for being out of the country when supposed to be selling antibiotics. I decided to solve this problem the old-fashioned way: I blamed someone else. It isn't my fault that I'm out of vacation, I reasoned. It's Pfizer's!

During my three years in the army, I grew accustomed to its generous "leave," aka vacation, allotment. Each soldier, whether five-star general or brand-new private, earned thirty days paid vacation per year. Even though this included weekends (army personnel were technically on the clock 24/7), it still amounted to a lot of time off for yours truly. Imagine my shock when informed that Pfizer employees of less than five years received only two weeks of vacation per year! Faced with a family and career crisis, I decided Pfizer owed me more time off, conveniently overlooking all the days I had already taken without Bruce knowing it.

Which was how my brother and I came to be standing outside one of London's famous red telephone booths on the Friday evening of my trip. Knowing Indiana was six hours behind England, I waited till seven-thirty P.M. to place a transatlantic call to Pfizer's voice-mail system. Patrick and I were on our way to meet our parents for a show, but I would have plenty of time to check messages and leave one of my own. After pumping numerous British-pound coins into the phone, I got through and heard, "You have seven voice-mail messages."

Unfortunately, I would have to listen to every one, because Bruce ingeniously liked to plant "surprises" within his lengthier messages to see which members of his district actually listened all the way through. For example, in the midst of droning on about increasing our number of sales calls per day, he'd casually mention, "Anyone who voice mails me back before five can treat themselves to lunch tomorrow." Those reps who did not respond by the designated time received a call at home from Bruce that night seeking an explanation for their failure to execute. Considering that I would not be home to answer that call, or any others over the next three days, I *had* to make sure no surprises awaited me.

Watching my nineteen-year-old brother, who looked like the ultimate American college kid in his never-been-washed baseball cap with the perfectly molded brim pulled low over his eyes, make suicidal gestures expressing his boredom as he stood outside the booth, I got through the seven surprise-free voice mails. Immediately after, I began recording an objection message for Bruce. About thirty seconds into it, I heard a loud beeping noise, like a garbage truck backing up. Peeking out the door to identify the source of the annoying sound, I saw no vehicles. Patrick looked at me quizzically, and I continued speaking into the phone, tugging on my ear and opening my hands to question, What's that noise? (Ever security conscious, I didn't want to trigger Bruce's spider senses by having a conversation with someone outside a pay phone.) He shrugged his shoulders: What noise?

Then it hit me: The beeping was coming from the phone! I was running out of money! Panicked, I started talking faster as I feverishly wiggled my hands for Patrick to pull out more change. Sensing the seriousness of the situation, he thrust his hand into his pocket and ripped out a handful of . . . stuff: keys; Kleenex, both used and unused; crumpled balls of money; and, at last, coins filled his hand. As I continued talking above the incessant beeping, which had grown louder as my money depleted, I pulled him into the booth to insert the necessary funds. Fumbling with coins like a horror-movie victim trying to get his key in the door as the killer approaches, Patrick achieved a success/failure ratio of 1:1, good enough to keep the connection but not sufficient to stop the beeping. Out of time and options, I took a deep breath before yelling into the phone: "Sorry about that gasoline truck, Bruce! He's been backing up forever!" I hit the # key, entered Bruce's mailbox number, and sent it. As my brother and I ran off toward a taxi stand, he told me, "You owe me fifteen pounds."

I dialed into Pfizer's system again the next day, just to make sure my efforts had been successful. The first message I heard said, "Hey team, this is Bruce. Listen to the following message from Jamie. He's sharing a new objection he got from an ob-gyn in Fort Wayne. Thanks for being a team player, Jamie." *Yeah, that was worth fifteen pounds.*

Seven

PERCEPTION IS REALITY

IT TURNS OUT THAT BEING A TEAM PLAYER wasn't nearly as important as *seeming* to be a team player. Obviously, everyone in pharmaceutical sales knew how easy it was to blow off work, and people routinely gossiped as to which reps were "workers" and which were slugs. So it was important for me to make sure my colleagues did not suspect me of being the good-for-nothing slacker I had worked hard to become. I had to create an image of Jamie Reidy: Worker.

Most people thought maintaining a good appearance was a critical component of sales success, but I found that such behavior was often detrimental to successfully maintaining the appearance of being a hardworking sales guy. This probably seems counterintuitive, but it's important to remember that normal employees woke up before ten A.M. and probably started their workday before lunch. Consequently, their shirts wrinkled, bags under their eyes shrank, and hair gel wore off throughout the morning. In order to blend in with these do-gooders, I had to alter my appearance to mimic theirs.

Preparation started prior to showering. If I knew I'd be leaving the house shortly after waking up (as opposed to catching the last *SportsCenter* first), I'd grab two ice cubes from the freezer and lie down on the floor with a towel under my head. Methodically, I'd rub the ice on my bags, hoping to reduce the swelling so I'd look as if I had been up for a long while.

Having iced sufficiently, I'd head to the bathroom. The last thing I wanted at noon was to smell as though I had just gotten out of the shower, which would have been a dead giveaway. Cologne was not an option. Shaving took considerably longer than normal, as I had to use extra caution to not cut myself. After all, very few nicks continue bleeding past lunchtime. Hair presentation was another area of grave importance. Rather than merely patting my head with a towel to soak up dripping water, I'd vigorously dry my hair completely. I'd use little to no gel, thereby making it seem as if I had groomed hours before.

When meeting with coworkers at lunch, I'd choose a dress shirt in need of pressing. Then at an appropriate moment in the conversation, I'd ask if anyone knew of a good dry cleaner. "I mean, they call this 'heavy starch'? I've had it on for only four hours, and it looks like I slept in the damn thing!" If I knew that I would be seeing colleagues after lunchtime, I'd grab a bottle of salsa or ketchup from the fridge and splash a bit on the front of my shirt before leaving the house. When inevitably asked what happened, I'd sheepishly shrug and say, "Had some coordination problems at lunch." Hopefully, this gave the impression that I had, in fact, been out of the house before noon.

Showing up late to such meetings was another good way to plant the "worker" seeds. Rushing into the restaurant at twelve-ten, I'd say with exasperation, "Sorry I'm late, guys, but Dr. Johnson just would *not* shut *up!*" Using the name of a doc well known for her chattiness was key, as everyone could relate and there was no fear of a colleague mentioning to Dr. Johnson, "Oh, I heard you had a great chat with Jamie last week." If I had gotten greedy and referenced a tough-to-see physician, he might respond to such a statement with, "Who's Jamie?"

On the other hand, when attending district or national meetings I operated on the opposite end of the spectrum, looking sharp and arriving early. Since Pfizer's corporate culture defined late as "not fifteen minutes early," you had to show up *really* early for anyone important to notice. Depending on the level of my hangover, I tried to show up thirty minutes early. Sometimes I got there early enough to help my boss carry stuff in from his car or hang motivational signs and sales charts on the walls, simultaneously allowing me to score some brownie points while cementing the impression that I was a hardworking employee who could be trusted to get out of bed before eight every morning when no one was around to monitor his behavior. *Wow, Reidy sure is dependable, but I wonder why he always has six Altoids in his mouth first thing in the morning?*

Another neat little trick at big meetings was to find out which of the Big Bosses worked out in the mornings. I'd muster all my resolve and wake up at six in order to stumble down to the gym, where I'd hop on a stationary bike or treadmill near the Big Boss. Once we had exchanged greetings, I'd focus on my "workout," as I didn't want to seem like some sneaky ass-kisser who was only working out to make a good impression. Approximately two minutes after the Big Boss had completed his workout, I'd complete mine and try to head back to bed for a few more desperately needed z's. Without fail, the Big Boss commented to my boss that he saw me in the gym bright and early. *Wow, that Reidy really has it together, but I don't know how he can run on a treadmill with a mouthful of Altoids.*

Receipts Are Better Than a Note from Your Mom

While I was able to fool my boss and coworkers with some fancy voice-mail and hairstyling tricks, I still had to navigate the minefield of objective measures Pfizer had laid down to safeguard against such abuses.

Pfizer relied on a paper trail of receipts for both business expenses and drug samples to keep tabs on its flock. Fortunately for me, the limits of the system allowed the company to get fleeced.

Each rep received an American Express card, and we were expected to use it whenever possible. AmEx provided the company with a printed record of every transaction, meaning Big Brother knew if I overtipped a hot waitress or bought a bottle of water in addition to a tank of gas.

Obviously, not all situations were credit card friendly, and in these instances, Pfizer made us submit receipts for *every* little thing, including a 25-cent toll or a 50-cent parking fee. In addition to protecting against fraud, such stringent documentation helped verify that people were working when they said they were. For the savvy slacker, however, this requirement allowed us to verify we were working when we were *not* working.

Dissatisfied with my measly ten days of vacation, I developed a habit of tacking an extra day on the front or back end of any trips I took. As long as I left Bruce a voice mail touting my success or bemoaning my failure, I had nothing to worry about. Eventually, though, one extra day became two. On my annual trip to visit friends down the Jersey Shore, I pushed the envelope to three unauthorized vacation days.

My prom date Maureen and I had remained close friends despite the fact that she may (everyone else thinks so) or may not (as she claims) have kissed another guy that memorable May evening in 1988. She and a large group of her pals from the University of Delaware rented a beach house every summer in Sea Girt, New Jersey. Every night was Saturday night, and they knew which bars had what drink specials when. On a Friday morning, we lounged on their front porch treating Parker House happy hour–related side effects with cold hair of the dog. As beach-bound families pulling carts filled with chairs, pails, shovels, and towels passed by, little children gleaming with sunblock and wearing "swimmies" paused to gawk at the strangely pale, red-eyed creatures sitting in the shade, their mothers quickly urging them to move on. Kicking his way through the sea of empty cans toward the front door, one of Maureen's housemates asked why another of the regulars hadn't come down on Thursday night as usual. "He couldn't get off work today," came the answer.

This stirred a memory in Maureen's clouded brain. "Do you guys know that Jamie didn't even take vacation to come here? His boss never knows where he is. Does he have a great job or what?" Unanimously, the group agreed with her assessment. The conversation shifted to a more important topic when the winner of the previous night's hook-up contest (competitors kicked in $5 and the first person to kiss a member of the opposite sex collected the purse) shuffled home in familiar clothes, eleven hours after the rest of us. As the inquisition raged, I sat back to consider the employment risk I had taken to enjoy this classy visit. Unauthorized absence from the sales territory was grounds for immediate dismissal. I had just tripled my odds of getting canned.

On my second beer of the morning, it occurred to me that there would be very little monetary activity on my next expense report. Specifically, there would be *no* activity for Wednesday through Friday, a surefire red flag. Reps routinely went a day or two without incurring an expense—we didn't bring lunch in every day, and there were plenty of offices that didn't charge for parking—but it was rare to go three straight days without spending cash someplace. The fact that I had been in New Jersey for two days was not helping my spending in Indiana.

Eventually, our energy level revived and we began multitasking, eating lunch and playing whiffle ball while drinking. I left the obligatory success story voice mail, probably sounding happier than ever, at two P.M., and before I could say "two-for-one long necks" it was four. Suddenly, I realized that I needed something concrete to establish that I had, in fact, been in Indiana. I needed a receipt, and it was pretty tough to get a receipt in Indiana when sitting in New Jersey at four o'clock on a Friday afternoon. Who in South Bend could get one for me? After several minutes of casing my mental Rolodex, I thought of Brian, the only person I knew in Indiana who had nothing to do at three in the afternoon Central time.

A friend from Notre Dame, Brian had recently been cut as a linebacker by the Indianapolis Colts and moved back to South Bend to be with his fiancée, a law student. Since he was a dinnertime waiter at a local restaurant, he had a schedule conducive to helping me out of my jam. I called just as he was leaving for the gym. "Dude, I need a little favor." Brian listened silently and paused before responding with a laugh. I could almost see him shaking his head in disbelief.

"Fucking Reidy. Are you serious?" I assured him that I was and that several adult beverages with his name on them would be served upon my return.

"I only need to drive to Elkhart and back?" he asked, referring to a town twenty miles and three highway exits east of South Bend.

"That's it, man," I said, accepting a congratulatory beer from Maureen. "Thanks!"

When I got home and checked my mailbox, two scraps of white paper imprinted with INDIANA TOLL ROAD sat atop the bills and magazines. Worth just 75 cents each, to me they were priceless. I submitted the receipts with my next expense report, careful to omit another charge for the same amount in order to avoid profiting from my scheme. *What do you mean I wasn't working? You have the toll receipts, don't you?*

That little journey cost me $20 in beer, but it was money well spent. From there, I began to refine my skills. Computer experts will tell you that in order to build a successful security system you must ask yourself, "If I were a hacker, how would I get in?" Looking at it from that point of view, I asked myself a similar question: "If I were Sheriff Roscoe P. Coltrane and it was my job to catch lazy, sneaky guys like me, what would I look for to clue me in?"

Answer: easy-to-get, impossible-to-dispute receipts, like those worth less than a dollar with time stamps from parking lots or tollbooths. *Yikes.*

I had to find ways to get receipts with higher charges. This posed a problem, not in terms of the purchases themselves, but the means of payment. For example, if I submitted a cash receipt for $50 worth of whatever to my boss, his spider senses would've begun tingling like crazy. "Why didn't you use your credit card?" And if Bruce approved such an expense, the watchdogs in HQ certainly would ask questions.

Clearly, the most airtight way to document expenses incurred while I was not working was for someone else to use my AmEx corporate card in Indiana. Unfortunately, this was potentially hazardous; even if Brian or another friend agreed to purchase something with my card, a store clerk might ask for ID. The possibility of jail time, my accomplices explained, was a slight deterrent to their assisting me.

Back at the drawing board, I wracked my brain for a way of using the AmEx card to cover my shady tracks without endangering the anal virginity of my friends. To do so, I needed an establishment that was above reproach (someplace a sales rep would normally make a purchase), that accepted American Express, *and* that didn't ask for an ID to compare to the name on the credit card. I came up with nothing.

Shortly after returning from New Jersey, I was leaning against my car while getting gas, and I watched people insert their credit cards into the gas pumps, fill their tanks, accept or decline a receipt, and drive away. Done pumping, I grabbed my receipt and drove off. About three days later, I realized, "Some of those other drivers got *receipts,* and *I* got a receipt. Gas stations give receipts!" All I had to do was find someone to get my gas while I was out of town. This person would have to fill up my car instead of his own, since Pfizer matched company car mileage to the amount of gas purchased.

Receipts turned in with zero miles added to the previous total would smell fishy.

I asked all my buddies, but got no takers. In this case, it wasn't the fear of prison showers that limited their interest, but the location of my apartment. I was the only member of my crowd to live in Mishawaka, a town twenty minutes from central South Bend, and no one wanted to "drive all the way out there, park my car, get into your freaking *company car*, pump your gas, return your car, and then get back into my car to drive all the freaking way back to South Bend." I could see their point. Additionally, since only spouses were insured while driving company cars, I was liable for any damages incurred with a friend behind the wheel, although I would have gladly rolled the dice on a $500 deductible for the thrill of enjoying a cold beer après ski in Vail while supposedly working in the Hoosier state.

When offers of unlimited beer failed to recruit any small-time crooks, though, I resigned myself to cutting back on "days off." Thankfully, a new world of opportunities presented itself. Dr. Wacky, a young, single, female physician, gave me a hard time from the start. While routinely ignoring my sales pitches, she'd roll her eyes and make derogatory comments like, "Shush, everybody, so we can hear Jamie's spiel." For drug reps, the word *spiel* ranks just below *peddle*—as in, "What are you peddling today?"—on the DCSs, or Doctor's Condescension Scale. She made fun of my ties and picked on me incessantly. If we had been in the fourth grade, she would have kicked me in the shins. It became clear that she *liked me* liked me.

Because she worked in one of my more important practices, I saw her often. Over time, Dr. Wacky realized I wasn't a typical drug rep looking to push product; on the contrary, I rarely *mentioned* Zithromax. Eventually, she started asking me about my weekends and what bars I frequented, sharing her own tips for nighttime fun. Phone calls at home became commonplace. Before

I knew it, she had invited me out for drinks a few times, but we couldn't get our schedules together.

This behavior was not lost on my colleagues, who worked under the assumption that my having sex with a doctor would be good for our Zithromax sales and begged me to date her. Sales success, however, was not the only driving force behind these requests. Every male drug rep had at least one story about losing business to a female competitor who dated a doctor, so it was every guy's fantasy to turn the tables on the lady competition. Thus, my dating Dr. Wacky was a no-brainer. I disagreed.

For starters, she was already using a ton of Zithromax. Dr. Wacky had gone from prescribing no Zithromax at all to using it in 45 percent of her patients who got antibiotic prescriptions (according to the sales data Pfizer purchased from the third-party company that got it from the pharmacy chains), making her our second-biggest writer in town. If we started sleeping together, sure, sales would probably soar to 70 or 80 percent for a month or two, but when it ended—and it always ended—she would immediately return to her zero usage days. To me, twelve months at 45 percent were better than two months of 80 percent followed by ten months of nothing.

I thought we could just be friends, get drinks, maybe see a movie once in a while. Friends. She had other plans.

We finally went out for drinks on a Wednesday night. I wore shorts and a golf shirt, while she had on a black skirt and an expensive top and wore more makeup than I had ever seen on her. Dr. Wacky ordered a gin and tonic, and I got a large draft beer. Before I was a quarter of the way done, she tilted her head back, milking the glass for the last drops. She ordered another, and finished that one before I finished my beer. "Nervous?" I asked. She laughed—nervously—and quickly looked for the waitress. In short, she got loaded. I couldn't let her drive home in that condition, and since I lived much closer to the bar than she did, I brought her back to my place. Unbeknownst to me, this was all part of her plan.

I was hoping she'd sober up in an hour or two, but she could not or would not. Dr. Wacky chased me in circles around my apartment like the crazy, love-struck witch chased Bugs in the cartoons. I hadn't run that much in years. At one point, I sought refuge in the bathroom, emerging only when I heard a male voice call, "Jamie?" Returning cautiously to my living room—*Can she morph into another human form and change her voice to suit her evil needs like the Terminator?*— I found my future roommate, Steve, standing in the doorway and my inebriated physician sprawled on the floor, skirt hiked up her legs.

"Uh, I'll, uh, call you tomorrow," Steve said, as he dashed out the door. I chased after him, yelling for him to *please* hang out for a while, but my protests echoed off the stairwell walls, unanswered. Trudging back inside, I slumped against the closed door. Dr. Wacky was no longer lying on the floor, though. Thankfully, she was also not a member of the Terminator class. Finally exhausted from chasing me around my apartment, she had moved herself to my hand-me-down couch, where she had passed out. After covering her with a blanket, I locked my bedroom door and fell asleep. She was gone by the time I woke up in the morning. I figured it'd be a while before I saw her again.

The next evening I was packing for my second trip of the summer to the Jersey Shore when my doorbell rang. *Dr. Wacky! What a nice surprise.* Very sober and very contrite, she apologized for her behavior the previous evening and asked if there was anything she could do to make it up to me. I shook my head no and told her to forget it.

"Please!" she said. "I'd really like to." Feeling uncomfortable, I rubbed my neck and looked around the room to avoid her persistent eye contact. After spying my half-packed bag, I turned back to her.

"Seriously," she said. "Let me make it up to you." Not wanting to be rude, I gave in.

"Well, there is one *little* thing. . . . "

And that was how it came to be that at five-thirty on a Friday night, while drinking beers at a poolside bar in Sea Girt, New Jersey, I actually filled up my gas tank in Indiana.

After leaving her office, Dr. Wacky drove to my apartment, where she got out of her car and into my unlocked Lumina. She found the keys under the mat, then drove to a gas station a few blocks away. Once there, she took my American Express corporate card out of the glove box and, as if she were Jamie Reidy, Pfizer employee, inserted it into the machine and filled up my tank with regular unleaded. After which she took the receipt, placed it— along with the AmEx card—in the glove box, drove back to my apartment, and parked my car. *What do you mean I wasn't working? You have the gas receipt, don't you?*

Eight

THE PAPER CHASE

IN ADDITION TO REQUIRING RECEIPTS FOR EXPENSES, the system of checks and balances had another mechanism to ensure that reps were actually working. Let's say I had left Bruce my standard Competitive Activity Story voice mail and had submitted an American Express receipt for gas. There still existed a way for me to get caught playing hooky: the sample sheet signature.

By law, all pharmaceutical samples had to be accounted for, meaning physicians had to sign a sheet of paper acknowledging receipt of ten cases of Drug X. This requirement was fairly new, borne out of necessity. In the 1980s, a number of physicians and reps got busted for selling samples on the black market. With no system in place to provide a paper trail tracking who had what drug when, it was fairly easy for a rep to say he had dropped off two cases of Drug X to Dr. Smith, when in fact those cases were actually sold to Mr. Slimy Sam in a back alley. Likewise, a physician could remove two cases of Drug X from his sample closet and sell them to the aforementioned Mr. Sam. If asked about the missing samples, Dr. Smith could say, "I never got those. Prove that I did."

The government accepted the challenge and, voila, physicians had to sign in order to receive drug samples. Instantly, shady characters had a large window of opportunity slammed shut. This legislation's impact stretched far beyond the black market, though, as it gave pharmaceutical companies—for the first time—a concrete means of monitoring their reps' activity. By doing so, it spawned the very culture of the industry today. *How many signatures did you get today?*

With the new law in place, each company printed up its own personalized sample sheets. Basically, these were a receipt of a different nature, proving not that the rep had purchased gas on Tuesday, May 6, but that he had actually seen a doctor on Tuesday, May 6.

Members of Pfizer's Pediatric Division were required to make a minimum of eight calls per day, meaning we had to "detail" at least eight physicians. Under the old system, a rep would enter these calls into her computer with appropriate notes ("Discussed Zyrtec with Dr. Potts; he wasn't sure about the dose"). It didn't take Lex Luthor to figure out that there was no way to tell if the rep had actually seen Dr. Potts, let alone discussed Zyrtec's dosing with him, or simply typed that information into her computer. A friend of mine liked to say he made a "BTSA call," meaning he had visited a physician's office and failed to talk with him, but had Breathed the Same Air as the doc had breathed sometime that day. The law requiring sample sheet transactions gave the pharmaceutical companies a tangible way to monitor work activity, and to be sure their employees weren't illegally selling drugs.

For those of us who were brand-new to the pharma game, it took awhile to catch on to this cultural paradigm shift, and we were in for a rude awakening. The dose of reality was injected at a district meeting outside Detroit in January 1996. Bruce began innocuously, walking around the conference table with a nonchalant air.

"Do you guys ever have a day when you don't leave any samples?" he asked. Ten heads shook left and right.

"So, there's never a day when not even *one* office needs *one* sample of something?" he probed, leading us closer to the slaughter. Again, universal head shaking. *No way. We have great drugs; somebody* always *needs something.*

"You would never leave samples without getting a signature, would you?" *Are you crazy? Isn't that illegal?* Bump, set, spike. Bruce went for the kill, handing each of us a single sheet of paper displaying a table of some sort.

"Then, can somebody please explain all the zeroes next to your names under the column 'Physician Signatures'?" *Cricket, cricket, cricket.*

Apparently, somebody at HQ (undoubtedly a former rep who had forgotten where he came from and decided to foil all our tricks for getting out of work) had thrown together a little spreadsheet, outlining the frequency with which the reps in our division sampled physicians. Judging from Bruce's reaction, zero was not the frequency for which he was striving. The source of his anger and disappointment was predictable: His fellow district managers had made fun of him. As happens with anything in the sales world, a contest between the DMs had developed concerning the number of signatures per day. Once this happened, life as we knew it was over.

A manager would rather have made $20,000 less in bonus than lose to a peer in *anything.* If I only had a nickel for every one of these voice mails: "Hey, team, I know you're all working as hard as you possibly can and we've made huge strides in the number of signatures you're getting, I mean, *physicians you're seeing* each day," he corrected himself, since the priority was actually selling our drugs, not just calling on docs who are easy to see and will give signatures. "So, I'm not going to ask you for any more effort." Pause. "The Pittsburgh team just pushed their average to thirteen-point-two per day, and I just *know* we can top that. So, I'm asking for a little more effort. I know you can do it."

I could not. More accurately, I would not. Thirteen calls per day? During my most productive week with Pfizer, I averaged nine calls per day, and that was only because Bruce bribed me.

At the end of a field visit, he initiated a conversation that seemed innocent enough. "How many doctors did we see today,

Jamie?" A cardinal rule in pharmaceutical sales was to work your boss till he dropped, thereby making him think you were a "worker" while also making him think twice before coming out to work with you again. *Oh, no, Jamie again? I don't know if I feel like making calls till five-thirty. Maybe I'll skip him this time.* Being a religious zealot when it came to cardinal rules, I knew exactly how many docs we had seen that day.

"Eleven," I sang, oblivious to the trap being set.

"Eleven," Bruce repeated. "If you did that every day, that'd be fifty-five signatures in a week." We both kind of scoffed at that.

"Dude," I said professionally, "there's no way I could get fifty-five sigs in a week."

He nodded in agreement. "Carl gets forty-five, at least forty-five, every week. You couldn't get forty-five, do you think?"

Carl in Toledo. A former navy pilot, Carl carried himself with a lot of swagger. Appealing to my unhealthy competitiveness over all things pointless was a smart move on Bruce's part. There was no way I was going to let Carl beat me.

"Forty-five? Oh, yeah, I could," I nodded, my eyebrows scrunched to show how easy that would be.

Even though he had me, Bruce decided to go over the top. "I tell you what. If you get forty-five signatures next week, I'll let you expense a pair of Revos." Until that morning, I hadn't actually seen a pair of Revo sunglasses on someone I knew. Driving directly into the sunshine, Bruce and I reached for our shades simultaneously; he smoothly pulled out a pair of cool, stylish black ones, while I fumbled for my latest $8.99 discount-rack specials. The unique font in which the brand name "Revo" was written on the arm of the glasses mocked me every time I looked to my right for the rest of the day. When Bruce challenged me to get as many signatures as Toledo Carl, I would have done it for pride alone, but a new pair of shades clinched the deal.

I got forty-five signatures the next week and headed straight to the Sunglass Hut in the mall on Friday afternoon, where I spent seventy-five agonizing minutes trying on every pair of Revos the store had to offer. Finally, a friend from my undergrad days who had kindly accompanied me to provide guidance said her husband needed her home to cook dinner, so I picked a sleek, gray pair of metal rectangular shades. I wore them out of the store, just like I did with new basketball shoes in grammar school. I could not believe I had just purchased *sunglasses* that cost $189. Neither could Bruce.

"Uh, Jamie, didn't we say you had a limit of seventy-five bucks!" he stated more than asked. I had called him that night to thank him for upgrading my cool factor exponentially, though it had been tough to see the numbers on the phone while sitting on my couch wearing my prized possessions. I informed him that, no, there had been no mention of money at all, or I would never have exceeded the limit and spent my own money on something I would certainly lose or break within the next ninety days. Bruce exhaled in a long sigh and explained that "we" were going to need to do some serious expense account manipulation to cover this disaster. He also reminded me not to say anything about this to any of my teammates, who probably would not have understood why I earned a pair of pricey shades for, um, doing my job. I apologized, insincerely, for the miscommunication over the cost and hung up. Immediately, I felt a headache coming on, the pain emanating symbolically from the points at which the metal arms made contact above my ears.

This pain resurfaced every time I wore the glasses, which seemed a little much for a guy who rarely felt guilty about anything. I thought maybe I needed to suffer for my newfound materialism and looked no further for a cause of my increasing discomfort. Two weeks into the Revo Era, I pulled into an office parking lot and, unable to bear it any longer, ripped them from my head. Looking into the rearview mirror, I noticed for the first time two straight lines pressed into my head. My sleek shades were a little too sleek and had been pressing my head like a vise every time I put them on. They had to go. The clerk was less than happy to see me back at the Sunglass Hut, so I didn't even ask to try on other Revos. I exchanged the pain-focals for a $115 pair of comfy Ray-Bans. I lost them three weeks later.

The trials and tribulations of the sunglasses saga were fitting in light of the tremendous struggle I had coming up with the forty-five signatures necessary to initiate the saga in the first place. In addition to overcoming seemingly insurmountable obstacles like waking up before nine and *then* working for five or six hours for all five workdays, the fact that I didn't know more than sixty doctors (in a territory of 250 customers) really put me behind the eight ball. Throw in a number of customers on summer vacation, and I was screwed. Consequently, as time grew short on Friday afternoon, I had to cajole one pediatrician into signing two of his partners' names. Which, much to my chagrin, supported management's claim that sales reps really had to be out there *every day* in order to meet their daily quota of calls. Unfortunately, there existed other evidence backing this harebrained idea—*living* evidence: the Pfizer Masters.

In order to don the green jacket worn only by the Masters, a rep had to meet two criteria: first, the sum of his Pfizer service time plus his age had to equal at least sixty-five years, and, second, he had to have a history of tremendous sales success. A salesperson also had to be invited back every year, meaning this was no flash-in-the-pan award. Unlike Augusta National, this club had female members, though I recall seeing very few women on tape. Most of the Masters still combed their hair the way they did when they first saw *Rebel Without a Cause* in the movie theater. They were all filthy freaking rich, thanks to their stock options that had soared and split several times from the late 1980s through the mid-1990s. What was more annoying, though, was how hard these old guys worked *despite* being millionaires. They just loved to sell; it was what got them out of bed in the morning. I could not relate.

Once a year, the Masters flew at company expense to a luxurious location for a few days of "meetings." Afterward, the rest of the Pfizer sales force would be forced to watch a video featuring the Masters' sales advice. Unfortunately, this thirty-minute piece of media torture always included pearls like "See more doctors" and other suggestions that were not applicable in my territory. Then the moderator would go around the room and ask each guy how many sales calls he had made the day before the meeting—a time when most reps stayed home to pack—and the answers would be "twenty-seven," "twenty-two," and so on. Occasionally, an octogenarian would say, "fourteen," prompting guffaws and grief from his colleagues.

"Slacker!"

"What are you, a part-timer?"

The poor guy would quickly try to defend himself—"I had my prostate removed that morning!"—but there was no relief in sight. These hard-core guys were largely unfamiliar with the term "sick day."

"Call activity," aka the number of sales calls made per day, was a prominent topic of discussion at every sales meeting I ever attended, and a manager couldn't preach call activity without mentioning my nemeses in the green jackets. "The Masters average nineteen calls per day, and you tell me you guys can't do ten?" What management failed to see were the generational differences that prevented us, or maybe just me, from achieving such lofty work activity. For instance, one Master on video suggested skipping lunch because "most docs sit down in their offices to do their dictations over the lunch hour, and it's a perfect time to catch them." When asked by the moderator what they did for a meal during this time, a trim, gray-haired gentleman replied, "Pack an apple." *Pack an apple?* If I skipped lunch, when was I supposed to read the sports section or take a nap?

Indifferent to any inconveniences in my lifestyle, Pfizer management pressed on with the new signatures-per-day quotas. Sales reps

whose sales numbers were below par *and* whose signature average was also substandard were encouraged to get their résumés in
order. Left with just two options—work hard or quit—I looked for
ways to cheat the system. Thankfully, it had more cracks than an
old sidewalk.

The "California girls" showed me the first one, and it remained
an arrow in my cheating quiver until my last day as a drug rep. Ah,
the California girls. They were something else. Among the 150 of
us who trained together, four stood out. Not just because they were
smart and attractive and in their mid-twenties, but because of their
skirts. Through its devotion to military and Mormon hires, Pfizer
had filled its ranks with opinionated people who felt Pat Buchanan
could have been more conservative. Their dusty views on appropriate dress in the workplace hadn't been updated since Eisenhower
left office. The California girls dropped into this bastion of free
thought and expression with an unapologetic splash. "These skirts
are considered *long* in California." *Note to self: Move to California.*
God bless 'em, those ladies had spunk and flair and an aversion to
hard work. We became good friends.

Talking on the phone to Stephanie one Thursday night, I
complained about the number of signatures I had to get the next
day to cover myself for a lazy week.

"Just double up," Stephanie said, as though it was the most
elementary idea ever. Feeling like Watson, I asked Sherlock what
she was talking about.

"Go to the docs who like you the most and ask them to sign
two or three sheets. Tell them that the extras are for 'a rainy day.' If
they're halfway cool, they'll just laugh and sign away. Then spread
out the samples over the three sheets so you don't lose track of
inventory."

I sat in my chair thinking that Indiana was a lot farther than
two thousand miles from Los Angeles. Immediately running down
my list of doctors, I identified at least ten who would likely help me

bend the rules in such a benign manner. Although Stephanie's tip did nothing to alleviate the stress I was under to see thirteen physicians the next day, she did provide me with the means never to get myself stuck in such a position again. Using her trick, I could see ten docs in the first week of the month, but in "reality," I had seen twenty, twenty-five, or thirty over the next three weeks, depending upon how many extra sheets I asked them to sign.

Getting a doctor to sign his partner's name was another successful ploy, albeit on a smaller scale. Even more so than the previous trick, this required a physician who *really* liked me. I'd start out playfully while watching a guy sign my sheet. "Now, *that* would be a tough John Hancock to copy." He'd normally laugh and agree, at which point I'd get the ball rolling. "Dr. Partner's signature looks pretty easy, though." Another laugh, but inevitably he would share that sometime in the past he had been forced to forge Dr. Partner's signature in his absence as part of everyday business or whatever. That was Go Time. "Listen, Dr. Pal, I am in *such* a jam. I'm trying to cut out early to get a head start on my vacation, but I haven't seen *nearly* enough guys today, do you think you could help me out?" He would always want to help me out. "Do you think you could sign for Dr. Partner?" No one ever said no. Thanks to me, one orthopedic surgeon became so adept at signing his partners' signatures that he joked he could have emptied their bank accounts. Ha-ha-ha.

Getting docs to sign extra sample sheets or their partners' names garnered me thirty to forty extra signatures per month, but those tricks required my actually visiting offices, even sometimes in the morning. This was unacceptable. I needed a big score, one that would nab me twenty sigs at a time. Who would have guessed that a yeast infection would lead me to the buried treasure?

"Jamie's here!" the receptionist announced before I had finished crossing the waiting room. Unusually excited to see me, she even opened the door to the back. Incorrectly thinking that *I* had something to do with this greeting, I strolled down the hall and stopped in front of the sample closet, where I began to check their Pfizer inventory. I needn't have bothered, though, as a nurse quickly asked, "You brought Diflucan, didn't you?" Nodding, I placed a few boxes of the antifungal agent on one of the shelves. "Which doctor is going to sign, ladies?" I asked, pulling a sample sheet out of my detail bag.

Uh, none of them? Thanks to a few inconsiderate newborns that apparently did not get the e-mail specifying their ETAs, none of the members of this four-doctor ob-gyn practice were in the office. After explaining to the staff that I couldn't leave samples without a physician's signature, and I'd return a few days later, I turned to leave. However, the women wouldn't let me. They were in dire need of the world's only one-pill cure for yeast infections, and simply would not take no for an answer.

"Jeez, I've never seen an office in such a craze for Diflucan!" I said. "How many patients with yeast infections are coming in this afternoon?"

My question was met with silence and lots of staring at feet. Finally, one of the receptionists whispered, "One of the girls in back could really use some." Pity the poor girls in the back. In the history of medicine, no front office worker had *ever* had a yeast infection—or any other medical problem, for that matter—but the "girls in the back" were forever plagued with maladies requiring thousands of dollars' worth of free samples. Somebody really should've done a study just to see what it was about back-office work that made those women so susceptible to illness.

I explained that the woman would have to wait until the next day because I was not allowed to leave samples sans signature, making me feel like the dorky kid who had just informed his teenage friends that they could not raid his parents' liquor cabinet. The pall cast over the room by my declaration lasted several uncomfortable moments before one of the RNs asked, "Can Dr. Jones sign at Pizza-n-Dash?" *Pizza-n-Dash!*

As usual, I had completely forgotten about a dinner program we were having that very night. Normally, we held our physician-education programs at restaurants and provided an expert speaker to discuss a specific disease state in which one of our drugs was very effective. A new breed of sales rep, however, had ushered in a creative era in "programming," one in which boring eateries and expert speakers were replaced by irresistible draws. For instance, Pfizer reps hosted "Christmas-Tree-n-Dash" (docs swung by a Christmas tree lot and picked out a tree paid for by Pfizer), "Flowers-n-Dash" (docs swung by a florist and picked up a bouquet for their better halves), and a "Movies-n-Dash" (docs would bring up to three kids to a movie theater Pfizer had rented out for a Saturday morning). In return, the physicians were expected to pay close attention to an extended sales pitch while waiting for the tree to be tied to the roof, the flowers to be arranged, or the movie to start. (Pfizer was not the only company to run these events. Other companies hosted "Gas-n-Dash" at gas stations and "Turkey-n-Dash" during the holidays.) Amazingly, the doctors usually did pay attention, and these "outside-the-box" programs always drew our best attendance. Unfortunately, because there existed a directly proportional relationship between "rep creativity" and the speed with which Pfizer headquarters declared an event illegal, these events were normally banned shortly after word reached New York.

Thankfully, headquarters took awhile to figure out that it had to ban all such programs at the *same time* or else reps would invent other ones that had yet to be outlawed. First, "Movies-n-Dash" had its run ended. Next, "Christmas-Tree-n-Dash" was axed. They had yet to burn "Pizza-n-Dash," so we had hastily scheduled one before it, too, was deemed illegal.

As the clever name suggested, Pizza-n-Dash involved doctors swinging by a pizza parlor to order pies for their families' dinners. While they waited the customary fifteen to twenty minutes for the pies to be ready, four to five reps detailed them on all of Pfizer's products.

So when the nurse told me I could get Dr. Jones's sample signature at Pizza-n-Dash, I made the command decision to bend the rules and leave the Diflucan. For the girls in the back. Upon arriving at the pizza place, the ob-gyn immediately said, "Hey, the girls think you're a rock star! They told me I needed to sign something right away." As Dr. Jones signed the top sheet on my pad, a *second* doctor approached, slapped me on the shoulder, and signed a sample sheet, too. Something was happening here, but I didn't know what. When a third physician blindly followed the second guy, I *really* knew something was happening. Finally, when a doc who had never deemed me worthy of his time walked up and said, "Where do I sign?" even I could recognize the jackpot. By the time we left, I had twelve signatures, and Dr. Jones hadn't started the signing frenzy until halfway through the evening! After realizing what I had accomplished, a colleague turned to me and said, "You, sir, are a genius." I didn't correct him.

On the drive home, I brainstormed on how to expand this scam into our dinner programs, which we held much more frequently than Pizza-n-Dashes. The main obstacle to a smooth transition was the simple fact that I wasn't giving out samples; I was just collecting signatures for later use. It had been risky to let other docs sign the sample sheet when they hadn't gotten samples that day. Recognizing that I wouldn't always be able to count on physicians acting like sheep, I knew I had to come up with a legitimate reason for docs to sign a sample sheet while at a restaurant without receiving samples. On my own, I came up with nothing.

Standing around in the private room of a restaurant where we were holding a dinner program, a group of us were discussing ways to make the night more entertaining. A counterpart asked what we thought about raffling off a bottle or two of wine. *Sure, what the hell.* Someone else suggested that after picking the winner's name out of a hat, we make the physician answer a question from the lecture. *Hey, that's a good idea.* Another rep said we should rig the raffle so that the docs with whom we need to improve our relation-ship the most get the bottles. *Promote that woman immediately!* However, someone pointed out that we needed something on which to write the physicians' names. This was not a problem, as our drug rep cars in the parking lot contained approximately 40,000 note pads imprinted with product names. So I had to act quickly. "Uh, guys," I said, "I think I can handle this."

During the cocktail portion of the evening, each physician was invited to sign up for a raffle to be held after the lecture. A *free* raffle? People couldn't wait to sign up. Curious as to what the prize would be, the docs didn't seem to notice they were signing a sample sheet. After dinner, I drew two names out of a bowl, and—what were the odds?—the two biggest orthopedic surgeons in town walked out with bottles of wine.

We were required to hold at least one dinner program per month, and these usually averaged ten physicians. In two hours of "work" that consisted of drinking free wine, eating free filet mignon, schmoozing with customers, and trying to stay awake during a one-hour lecture I had trimmed—at the very least—two workdays off my monthly schedule. *Hello, United Airlines?*

Basically, I implemented what, unbeknownst to me, was commonly known as the "T to T" work schedule. A friend of mine from a competing company explained that "T to T" stood for "Tuesday to Thursday, ten to two." Although I was a bit disappointed that my routine was so commonplace it had a catchy name, I was psyched to know that there were others like me. Moreover, like Tom Cruise in *Interview with the Vampire,* I needed a protégé with whom I could share my secrets, not of raping and blood sucking, per se, but of slacking. The search didn't take very long; he lived in my house.

Michael had been trying to get into pharmaceutical sales for quite some time when he landed a job with G.D. Searle & Co. in late summer. Fresh off three weeks of brainwashing, er, training, he couldn't wait to barge into cardiology offices throughout northern

Indiana on his first day of work, which happened to be a Monday. It was a dark, nasty, hungover Monday that followed a Notre Dame home football game weekend.

Though he had gotten up early to pack his car with all the drug paraphernalia and samples his company had sent him, the process took much longer than he anticipated and he didn't finish till lunchtime. Having just gotten out of bed, I told him to give me twenty minutes to shower and put my suit on and then I'd take him to lunch at our roommate Steve's establishment to celebrate Michael's first day in the industry. After toasting his future success, we left Lula's Café, a hip coffeehouse and sandwich place near Notre Dame's campus, and headed home. Strangely, Steve came with us, complaining of "flulike" symptoms. As the three of us sat on the couches—"just for a minute"—I flipped to the movie section of the local paper. Nothing looked good.

"Anybody want to see a movie?" I asked, noting that the weather had somehow gotten worse in the short time we had been home. Steve shook his head, saying he had to do the café's books. Michael didn't say anything at all. *Blood in the water.*

"Man," I said, hoping to sound empathetic, "what a shitty day to start your career." Pause. "You get out there in a day like this, get rained on, stain your suit pants, that could ruin a sales guy forever." The living room fell silent just in time for us to hear the first drops of rain hit the roof. Hard.

"What's playing?" Michael asked.

Steve cracked up. "You are so weak."

Michael, God bless him, simply shrugged and grabbed his keys.

That night, after we tried to convince Steve that Bill Murray's *The Man Who Knew Too Little* actually had been pretty funny, Steve told us he had given my work ethic, or lack thereof, some thought.

"How many times, Jamo, do you think you've gotten up and gotten ready for work just in time to go to lunch, only to go back home after eating without actually seeing any doctors?"

That was a doozy of a question, and both guys knew it. Steve watched me closely, his eyes sparkling in anticipation, and even Michael folded down the newspaper to see my face. I started to count, but the exercise proved taxing, like asking Wilt Chamberlain to name every woman he's ever slept with. The guys eventually grew bored and told me to stop before I came up with the answer. Steve shook his head in a mixture of awe and disgust. "You and Michael Jordan get paid more per minute of work than anybody in America," he said.

"Wow!" I replied, wondering if we had an abacus. "I am really embarrassed."

So embarrassed, in fact, that I had to play hooky the next day, too, because I couldn't bear to face my customers.

As it turned out, those ominous clouds brought more than rain that day; they foretold a thunderous storm approaching in my life. Ironically, my days of putting on a suit only to go to lunch were nearly ended by Michael's company and its evil, newfangled method of monitoring its reps.

Michael sat on the couch during *SportsCenter* one night, pecking at a computerized gizmo that looked like the thing a UPS driver had you sign to get a package. "What the hell is that?" I asked, during a commercial break.

"Sample tracker," he hissed, without missing a peck. *Sample tracker?*

They say that people with life-threatening food allergies feel a sense of dread as soon as they have swallowed something they are allergic to, as if the body's self-defense system can *instantly* identify the presence of a lethal intruder. That is how I felt when Michael uttered the words "sample tracker." I did not know what they meant, but I instinctively knew that they were not good for me and could even be fatal.

Looking to "cut down on paper usage," G.D. Searle & Co. spent a ton of money on an electronic sample-tracking system. Brandishing handheld computers, reps had physicians sign their names on the screen—just like the brown-clad deliverymen did. As a side "benefit," this new system time-stamped each signature, meaning management knew the exact date and time when Dr. Smith signed for samples.

This was truly a sign of the apocalypse. How was a sales guy supposed to wake up at ten-thirty A.M., not see any docs all day, and still enter eight calls at eleven P.M.? After a few moments of breathing into a paper bag, I had the answer.

"Just change the time on the, uh, the thingy," I said, as if it was the most elementary idea in the world. Apparently, it was.

"They already thought of that," Michael responded, glumly. "The time is controlled via satellite." Bastards! Genius bastards!

I could hear the proverbial bell tolling. If a little company like G.D. Searle & Co. had ponied up the cash to adopt this new technology, then Pfizer, Inc., industry titan, would not be far behind. I grew nauseous at the thought of updating my résumé.

So the wait began. I flinched every time I heard my boss's boss's voice on voice mail and soon turned into a nervous wreck. Days turned into weeks, and it finally dawned on me that there was nothing to worry about. Maybe Pfizer actually trusted us!

More realistically, perhaps management resisted the urge to implement a system of which Big Brother would have been proud. I once asked Bruce how often he drove past his reps' homes in the morning to see what time they left for work. He looked at me as if I had suggested selling company secrets to Abbott Labs.

"Can't do it!" he said, face reddening. "That would be considered harassment. We could get sued for that."

I shook my head as though I didn't hear him correctly. "You can get sued for checking up on your people to make sure they're doing their job?" He nodded.

I'd finally found a difference between the army and Pfizer!

An army captain who commands a company has three or four platoons of forty soldiers each. This guy works for a lieutenant colonel, who runs a battalion, which consists of three to five companies. Throughout the week, the lieutenant colonel will check the battalion training schedule to see where his Alpha, Bravo, Charlie, and Delta Companies are conducting their M-16 marksmanship or orienteering or bivouacking, and then jump in his vehicle and drive out unannounced to observe. Brigade commanders (colonels who have three to four battalions under them) and division commanders (generals who have five brigades reporting to them) do the same. How else can a boss know if his people are truly exhibiting the behaviors necessary to succeed? Checking up does not reflect a lack of trust, just a desire to ensure that standards continue to be met. Any leader can get his people to look good when he knows the Old Man is in the area, but what about the 99 percent of the time when he and his soldiers are not being observed? Every boss likes to make sure his people are doing things correctly; if they are not, the commander will "suggest" ways to improve.

I can only imagine the scene if a company commander told his battalion commander, "Sir, I cannot work like this. I do not appreciate your showing up to monitor my efforts without any notice. It is nothing short of harassment. Cease such behaviors immediately, or I will sue." That young captain would spend the rest of his (short) career trying to remove his boss's combat boot from his rear end. Yet, that was the situation within Pfizer. I could park my Lumina on the street all day long and not worry about Bruce driving by and busting me. Even if he did cruise through my neighborhood and spot my car at two P.M., the evidence was inadmissible in pharmaceutical court.

Bruce developed his own system for keeping me in line, though. Without fail, he would schedule a ride-along with me on Friday (preventing me both from going out Thursday night and leaving early for the weekend), or the day after my birthday, or the Super Bowl, or a Game 7.

After one particularly brutal day when Bruce had hit the Daily Double by working with me the day after the NCAA championship basketball game fell on my birthday, I collapsed on the sofa at six. At night. My back and feet ached; my stomach was still doing somersaults thanks to a hangover combined with a daylong case of the nerves from walking into offices and being terrified doctors would ask, "Who are you?"

"Jesus, that was a long day!" I announced to my roommates. "I don't know how people do that."

"How long was it?" Steve asked.

"Eight to *five-thirty*," I whispered, barely able to summon the energy to speak.

Steve and Michael exchanged looks. "Welcome to the real world," Steve said without a trace of sympathy. *The real world?*

We've gotta have a drug for that, right?

Nine

IT'S THE SALES, STUPID

DESPITE BEING PRESENT for all my nonworking working hours, I was stunned to discover that my sales stank. I thought that doctors would find me as likable as I found myself and would proceed to write prescriptions hand over fist for all my drugs. Instead, I was ranked in the lower half of my team and the lower quadrant nationally. This shocked Bruce, as well.

"I don't get it, Jamie," he said, over an extended lunch at Lula's Café. (I gave Steve a lot of business.) Bruce and I were reviewing my sales performance. More accurately, he was doing the reviewing while I was doing the hemming and hawing. "Do you realize you're only going to make two grand in bonus for the first half of the year?" he asked, incredulous. At this, I looked up from my standard turkey and provolone on sourdough and met his hard stare.

"You mean they pay me more?" I had forgotten all about the bonus thing.

Bruce's bug eyes nearly exploded from their sockets. This was not the answer he expected, and he began massaging his temples the way my dad had done in high school when we discussed my C minus in theology. Then he smacked his hands on the table and shook his head repeatedly. "I need to find a way to motivate you,

Jamie, because money obviously isn't it. You *do* realize that most people get into sales because they want to make as much money as they can?" I shrugged. He exhaled loudly and looked around the café as if the answer was somewhere within range of our table. "I just don't understand how you're not blowing out your sales. Whenever I work with you, Jamie, the nurses make sure you get to see the docs, and you always give a solid detail and close them for the business, so I can't figure out why you're not doing better, let alone not number one." Figuring it was safer to say as little as possible, I shrugged. "But this," he said, pointing down at the table, "this is . . . " He couldn't finish the sentence. A manila folder with my name on it rested on the table between us. It contained numerous charts and graphs and reports, none of which put a smile on Bruce's face.

Reps were given sales quotas for each of our four drugs, with each holding a different weighting, or importance, like in a college class where half your grade was determined by the final exam, and the remaining 50 percent was split between papers and class participation. As our division's most vital product, Zithromax impacted our overall quota far more than the others. Doing well with Zithromax could almost guarantee a successful year, while cranking out sales of Diflucan, a drug whose market potential and importance were minimal, didn't mean much.

"This is an embarrassment," he finally managed to summarize. "A guy as smart and as well liked as you should be at the top, Jamie, but you're not even close. Even Jerry is beating you."

Ouch. Telling me Jerry was a better salesman was equivalent to touting Al Gore as more charismatic, Gilbert Gottfried more handsome, Homer Simpson more athletic. A moody, weird guy who taught his kids to shoot chipmunks in the backyard for fun (seriously; he told me all about it), Jerry evoked a "Hello, *Newman*" response from every member of our district. On top of that, he couldn't even identify an American bar-food staple.

At dinner during a three-day district meeting, I sat with Bruce and Kristi, the female team member who had married the FedEx stalker, leaving one spot open at our four-top. As we quietly but feverishly waved Jack over to take the last seat, Jerry spotted it and plopped himself down. Within seconds, he was regaling us with stories of farm life in Ohio or wherever he had grown up. Fortunately, his soliloquy was interrupted by the arrival of our appetizers—chicken fingers, chicken wings, and nachos.

As Bruce, Kristi, and I started digging in, Jerry stared quizzically at one of the orders. "What's that?" he asked, pointing at the plate of nachos deliciously covered with cheese, salsa, sour cream, guacamole, olives, and onions.

The three of us Earthlings exchanged looks. *Is he serious?* Then Kristi said, "Jerry, those are *nachos*." He shrugged. "I've never seen those before. I need to tell my wife about them."

"Jerry," I said, "you need to get out of the Ponderosa, man."

So mentioning that Jerry's sales were better than mine was a shrewd move on Bruce's part. I felt like Jon Lovitz playing Michael Dukakis on the *Saturday Night Live* skit parodying his 1988 debate with George H. W. Bush: "I can't believe I'm losing to this guy." It stung, but didn't cause me to leap from my chair, sprint to the car, and call on ten more doctors that day. It was more like a tiny splinter in my skin, a minor irritation that would eventually fester into a raging infection.

Despite dropping the "Jerry Bomb" on me, Bruce refused to relent and continued blistering my sales performance.

"You are right in the middle of the district in Zithromax sales, Zyrtec sales, Zoloft sales, and overall sales. But you're totally *killing it* with Diflucan. What's your secret?" Bruce asked, registering a 10 on the sarcasm scale. I got up to refill our drinks.

In reality—not that I pointed this out to him—I wasn't doing all *that* badly. My performance certainly disappointed Bruce, but it wasn't like I was in danger of getting fired or placed on a "development program," which was the first step toward getting fired. The ultimate goal in sales was to make quota, meaning that you achieved 100 percent of the sales target the company gave you at the start of the year. That number was calculated using the weightings given to a division's different drugs; my middle-of-the-road sales for Zithromax, Zyrtec, and Zoloft plus my high-achiever number for Diflucan added up to more than 100 percent, meaning I'd done my job. Not very well, but well enough for me. Bruce wanted me to be Abe Froman, Sausage King of Chicago; I saw myself as more of a Ferris.

When I returned, Bruce picked up where he had left off. "Not to mention, you're *last* in the district in calls per day and signatures per day." I refused to meet his gaze. "You can forget about getting promoted to the training department with stats like this, guy."

He looked deeper into the folder and flipped through several pages until he found one he wanted. "I guess it's not all negative, though," he said. I stopped examining the tabletop for microscopic crumbs and looked up to meet his gaze. *Really?*

"Yeah, it's not fair to say you're not number one in anything. You're actually leading the district in one category." I sat up a little straighter and thrust my chest out to its normal capacity. You're damn right I'm leading the district in a category!

"Which one?" I asked, trying to suppress a smile.

Bruce took another pull on his soda. "Sick days. You've taken three times more than anyone else."

Fortunately, this was not my fault. It was his.

If you recall, one of Bruce's mantras was "Enthusiasm sells!" Conversely, he added a corollary to this rule stating that an ill sales rep who insisted on toughing it out and working rather than staying home in bed could actually do more harm than good. "When you're sick, you have less energy. And when you have less energy, you have less en*thu*siasm," Bruce reasoned. "When you have less enthusiasm in general, you'll have less enthusiasm about our products, and when you have less enthusiasm about our products"—he changed his voice to sound sick and sleepy—"*Doctor, Zithromax is a fairly okay drug, really,*' you're going to have the opposite effect of what you want, you're going to turn docs off. So stay home when you're sick." A devoted student of this philosophy, I chose to stay in bed rather than put sales at risk whenever I felt less than 100 percent. Apparently, my short-sighted teammates did not see the potential disasters awaiting them. Yet I got chided for being number one in something. What a crock.

Staring at mediocre sales and undesirable number-one rankings didn't deter me from thinking I deserved to get promoted, however. After all, I was Jamie Reidy; people loved me wherever I went, and northern Indiana had proven no different. Also, I was getting pretty tired of the Lumina, and promoted reps received a car upgrade. Hence, I should be climbing the corporate ladder faster than the one hundred reps who were kicking my ass numbers-wise. Bruce did an impressive job of not laughing in my face when I shared this view with him.

Fortunately, Pfizer shared another similarity with the U.S. Army when it came to promotions. As a lieutenant I saw several people who should have been *de*moted due to their incompetence, but they were inexplicably elevated to the next rank. This phenomenon was succinctly explained: "Fuck up, move up."

Let's say a commander had grown tired of dealing with a nitwit who wasn't due to change duty stations for another two years. Since U.S. Army HQ managed all personnel assignments, a commander could not unilaterally decide to transfer a soldier out of his unit. Quite often, however, a promotion prompted a reassignment to another organization, thus removing said headache from the commander's world. While certainly not beneficial to the army in the long run, a promotion like this accomplished a valuable short-term mission: Let him be somebody else's problem.

Considering how many former military officers worked for Pfizer, it wasn't shocking to learn that a variation of the "Fuck up, move up" concept managed to find a home in pharmaceutical sales. Reps were rarely fired at Pfizer, as termination proceedings required reams of evidence documenting repeated shortcomings and counseling sessions concerning those shortcomings. Faced with such hassles, managers preferred to make life miserable for a substandard rep by spending more field days with him, requiring more paperwork, and having him perform other onerous chores, until he quit. Senior management condoned such an approach, as it decreased the odds of lawsuits. What could a manager do about a perfectly mediocre salesperson, someone whose numbers weren't good or bad? If the individual's reputation was good, promote him.

I don't think it ever occurred to Bruce to push for my promotion outside of his district. Looking at my middle-of-the-pack sales ranking, he must have resigned himself to the fact that he was stuck with me until *he* got promoted. However, once I expressed my ridiculous belief that I was upwardly mobile, he made making me someone else's problem a top priority.

My first opportunity for promotion came in September 1997. A position within Pfizer's Neuroscience Division (calling on psychiatrists) opened up in Detroit, and Bruce had convinced district manager Bob Kelley to look no further: Jamie Reidy was the man for the job.

Since managers routinely spent a day in the field with prospective hires, Bob met me in South Bend to check out my sales style and other skills. Accordingly, I scheduled appointments with physicians who liked me and always talked with me for several minutes. The morning went extremely well—though I hoped Bob hadn't noticed several doctors express surprise at my actually discussing drugs as opposed to Notre Dame's lack of a pass rush— and we went to Chili's to eat lunch and discuss my future. Pfizer taught its managers that past sales history was the best indicator of a rep's future sales success, so when he asked for a copy of my sales numbers from each year with the company, I could see my future with Bob dimming.

I tried nonchalantly to eat chips and salsa while he read, his brow growing more furrowed by the page. He shook his head upon finishing. "You know, Jamie," he began, sounding annoyed, "I told Bruce I'd come down here to see you because he said you're a top rep. I think I'm going to have to have a little conversation with him when I get back." Bob, I discovered over lunch, had been a military officer, too. Undoubtedly, he had sniffed out Bruce's plan.

Having nothing to lose, I explained to Bob that I had certainly dogged it my first year out of the army, taking it easy in the civilian world. However, I explained, I was now "on fire," a rep who had seen the errors of his ways and taken giant steps to overcome them. I pointed out that I had finished among the top two in my district in calls per day for the past two months, and that my sales numbers had trended positively for the past three. I assured Bob that I was a new man, a reenergized selling machine, and he started to buy it. He shared with me his concept of leadership, explaining that he borrowed heavily from Phil Jackson's book *Sacred Hoops*, which chronicled his attempts to get supertalented players, i.e., Michael Jordan, to focus on improving the team. I had played team sports my whole life, and I related a few examples of my ability to thrive within a team atmosphere.

The more I talked, the more Bob's eyes brightened, the more he leaned across the table toward me. He believed me; more important, he *wanted* to believe me. Then without warning, his face clouded over and he picked up one of the pages listing my sales numbers. Grimacing, he shook his head. Then he listened to more of "I know what it takes to be great, now," and the gleam returned to his eye. Back and forth his facial expressions battled, as though the angel and the devil from *Animal House* were sitting on either shoulder, prodding him. Finally, it was over.

"Jamie, I think you'd do great in this job, and I'd like you to work for me," he said, nodding. "But there's just no way my boss [a regional manager, like the former Marine with whom I originally interviewed] would let you in the room, let alone interview you, with these lousy numbers." Bob urged me to "stay on fire" and said he'd have no problem promoting me once I put up some decent sales numbers. As I drove him back to his car, he saw a Borders Bookstore and asked me to pull in. He returned a few minutes later with a new copy of *Sacred Hoops*. "Read this," Bob said, "and we'll talk about it the next time I interview you." Fortunately, we did not run into each other again, since I left the book in the seat pocket in front of me on a flight a few weeks later and never bought another copy.

Overall, I thought the day had gone extremely well. For starters, I hadn't really wanted to get promoted to *Detroit* so much as I wanted to get promoted *in general*. It would have been interesting to see how I would have reacted if I had gotten the job and had to move to the Motor City. Also, I learned that there was no getting around my boss's theory on work activity and the credibility it gave a rep in lean sales years.

Bruce had explained, "Good numbers absolve a multitude of sins. When you're number one, nobody cares how many signatures you get per day. *But*, when you're dead freaking last, you need to show that you are working your tail off! You can always blame bad sales on things out of your control—like the biggest HMO in the state doesn't cover your drugs—but you need to make sure the things *within* your control—signatures per day, the number of dinner programs you hold—are at the top."

Bob had wanted to believe I was on fire, that I was getting more signatures than anyone else, but sixty days of evidence wasn't nearly enough; I needed to sustain that for at least a semester. Last, and most important, I saw firsthand that people wanted to hire someone they liked, and the more they liked you the more willing they were to take a chance on you.

That was where my best opportunity lay. In order to get a promotion interview, a rep's boss and his boss's boss had to officially support it, thus providing a filtering system; not just any loser could interview for any job. Because of this, the managers conducting the interviews operated under the assumption that all candidates were solid ones. The fact that I was interviewing in the first place meant that someone thought I was promotable. Bob refused to send me on in the interview process because he knew his regional manager would chew him out for recommending a candidate with horrible sales and work activity. As long as my stats were passable, then, all I needed to do was get the interviewers to like me.

I didn't have to wait long for my next opportunity. In December 1997, rumors began circulating that "they" were interviewing for the new Urology Division, the one that would sell Viagra. I hadn't heard much about the drug for erectile dysfunction, but that didn't matter. All I cared about was getting promoted, and the creation of a new division improved my chances dramatically. I called Bruce.

"I haven't heard anything, Jamie," he told me, sounding a bit alarmed. *A chance to get rid of this guy, and I'm asleep at the switch?* An hour later, he called back to say he'd made contact with an HR person. "You're willing to go anywhere, right?"

Originally, I had been completely mobile, but something changed when I interviewed with Bob in September. Even though I hadn't gotten the job, hadn't even gotten an offer, I felt emboldened, as though I were a terrific candidate who held all the cards rather than a lucky-to-even-be-considered slacker.

"No, I'm interested only in Denver or San Francisco," I told Bruce matter-of-factly. He did not attempt to hide his surprise and suggested that, as a guy ranked in the bottom half of the nation, perhaps I should expand my wish list. I refused.

Bruce called back to say interviews were being conducted in Washington, D.C., over the next week and that he had arranged one for me. "Are San Francisco or Denver available?" I asked, sounding like Norma Desmond making demands of Cecil B. DeMille. Bruce sighed with worry; Denver was already filled, but S.F. was still open.

Each candidate was guaranteed interviews with two people: his prospective district manager and the assistant regional manager (a position beneath DM but above sales rep, like an aide-de-camp in the military). If both interviewers gave him the thumbs-up, the candidate met with the regional manager. All three would later convene and decide which reps they wanted and which they did not.

My first interview started at nine with Jackie, the district manager for the Pacific Northwest. Unaccustomed to getting up so early, I had set the alarm for seven and worked out for an hour in order to get the blood pumping. "Enthusiasm sells!" With my sales numbers, I'd need a lot of it to sell these people on Jamie Reidy.

An enthusiastic person herself, Jackie answered the door of the hotel room with a big smile. A single woman in her late thirties, her dark, curly hair bounced in time with our handshake. Once inside the room, she slid behind a table and pointed to a chair for me. Jackie put me at ease immediately. "Well, you certainly are a popular person, Jamie!" she said. "I got several messages from the district managers in your territory, and I have to say I was quite impressed."

During my layover at O'Hare, I had voice mailed three managers with whom I had come into contact over the previous two years, none of whom were Bruce. Basically, these were three guys who loved me: the Managed Care supervisor (it was his job to get Pfizer drugs added to HMO formularies) because I led the charge to get Zyrtec added to Partners Health Plan, the biggest HMO in northern Indiana; the Pfizer Labs district manager because he was a Notre Dame grad, and I used my contacts in the alumni office to get him football tickets; and a Pediatric Division district manager because he had played football at a Division II college and I gave him a tour of the Notre Dame Monogram Room (home to every bit of important Fighting Irish memorabilia, including all seven Heisman Trophies) when he was supposed to be calling on doctors with me.

I gave these three men Jackie's voice-mail number, asking them to tell her what an amazing rep I was. A person didn't get promoted to a management position within Pfizer without being able to sling the bull a little bit, and these guys were no exception.

The Managed Care supervisor told Jackie I made things happen. "I needed a 'go-to' guy, and Jamie was it. He builds great rapport. You're going to love having him work for you." The Labs DM echoed those sentiments. "You're going to love having him work for you. He's a go-getter. What a rapport builder!" The Pediatric Division manager concurred. "He gets things done. Unbelievable rapport." Interestingly, nobody mentioned anything about my ability to sell drugs. She failed to pick up on that omission. She also made a rookie mistake of not calling Bruce to ask about my weaknesses.

Already convinced she had a superstar in front of her, Jackie jumped into the interview. Her questions had a familiar ring to them, possibly because Bruce had thrown a few "hypotheticals" at me prior to my departure, and I breezed through until asked about my less-than-stellar sales numbers. My conversation with Bob several months earlier convinced me that honesty was my best policy—just acknowledge having been a slacker and then provide evidence of my "new man-ness."

"Jackie, I was lazy for the first two years of my career. I did just enough to get by," I admitted, thinking that was probably the first time any prospective job candidate had said that in an interview. The blank look on her face informed me I was correct. I continued.

"When I got out of the army and started with Pfizer, it was a relief to be free from such a restrictive environment [Jackie didn't know anything about Camp Zama's country-club atmosphere, and I felt no need to enlighten her]. I kind of went crazy. But then I got a wake-up call. Reps in my division whom I knew couldn't *spell* rapport were killing me sales-wise, and I got angry with myself that I had totally lost my competitiveness. I knew I had to get it back, and I knew the only way to do that was to start working my tail off." I pointed to my Brag Book, a fancy folder that contained all the lousy reports Bruce had mocked during lunch months earlier. This time, it was filled with positive info. "You can see there that for the past five months, I have been."

She quickly flipped through the pages, eager to find data that would allow her to defend her hiring me. When she didn't raise an objection, I closed her. "Is there *anything* keeping you from hiring me, Jackie?" She said I got her vote, but she was concerned that she didn't have a territory I would like.

"I was told San Francisco was open," I said. She shook her head. "We filled that spot yesterday with a woman who already lives there." In response, I exhaled loudly, trying to look annoyed that she had wasted my valuable time by making me fly all the way to D.C. to interview for a position that was filled.

"I still have Fresno and Seattle open?" she asked more than stated. I didn't know anything about the former, but having spent a rainy summer of army training at Fort Lewis, Washington, forty minutes outside Seattle, I knew there was no way I'd be moving to the Pacific Northwest. Who needed a hopping mix of good music, good coffee, and plenty of young tech-millionaires anyway? As a guy originally from the East Coast with little knowledge of California, I presumed Fresno was twenty minutes from the beach. Recalling Bruce's advice that a rep ranked in the bottom half of the nation should be happy to take a promotion anywhere, I gleefully bounced out of the room.

The pesky "sales numbers" question came up much earlier in the second interview with Don, the assistant regional manager, but my pat answer seemed to placate him. He asked a few other work-related questions, and then fixated on my having wrestled at Notre Dame. Turned out that he played basketball in college, which surprised me since his body resembled that of a middle linebacker more than a point guard.

"The wrestling room was located just off our gym," he explained. "Every day we'd wonder what they *did* to you guys during practice, 'cause you'd always come out looking like total dog shit." I laughed at the all-too-familiar image.

"Yeah, and I *walked on* the team. [Ru-dy! Ru-dy!] So, I just got *pounded* every day; guys used to fight over who got to wrestle me for the last match in practice when everybody was dead tired."

Don laughed, shaking his head. "Why'd you keep doing it?"

I shrugged casually. "My freshman year I set a goal that I'd walk on and earn a monogram—that's what we called a varsity letter at Notre Dame."

He ate it up. "Guess you accomplished your goal," Don said, smiling. I took that as a good sign and closed him immediately. He laughed again and said, "You get my vote, Jamie, but it's the big guy you need to worry about."

When Gary-the-big-guy opened the door to his suite, I breathed a sigh of relief. He looked exactly like every friend's father I had ever seen at a Notre Dame tailgater: map of Ireland etched across his face, bright eyes, and a head of silvering hair. He smiled as he shook my hand firmly, putting his left hand on my shoulder to lead me inside. Suit jacket nowhere to be seen, his tie was loosened, and his sleeves were rolled up.

Without warning, he barked, "So why should I promote you, Jamie?"

His face had morphed from friend's-fun-father to guy-responsible-for-a-$400-million-quota-who-can't-believe-he-has-to-waste-time-interviewing-this-loser. He sat down with a *whoosh* on the sofa across from me, his two-hundred-plus pounds squeezing all the air out of the cushion. An uncomfortable stillness enveloped us; at least, it was uncomfortable for me. My throat tightened, and I envied Gary's ability—as the big guy—to loosen his tie.

Having already told the story of reclaiming my competitiveness twice that day, I began confidently. He didn't seem to listen and rifled through some papers on the coffee table. When I finished, a few seconds passed before his eyes locked onto mine, staring right through me. "You're competitive, huh? Tell me how you're competitive."

I told him how my competitiveness had damaged my relationships with friends and their girlfriends and the relationships between my friends and their girlfriends. The weekend before the interview, my roommates and I were late for a dinner because I refused to quit playing two-on-two basketball in our driveway. The reason? My team hadn't won a game yet. "Grow up, Jamie!" Steve yelled. "You're twenty-seven years old, for Chrissake." Finally, darkness prevailed. I got those guys back on the court the next day, hangovers notwithstanding, and I won.

I told Gary how my competitiveness had cost me untold dollars in Las Vegas. I took it personally when blackjack dealers beat me, and—despite the protests of friends and, occasionally, the dealers themselves—routinely continued gambling at cold tables much longer than advisable in order to show those dealers I could win.

I told Gary how my competitiveness had proven hazardous to my love life. Playing electronic trivia at a bar, I repeatedly ignored my better half's answers in favor of my correct ones. After she expressed some dissatisfaction with my behavior, I asked, "Do you want to break the record or not?" We did not date much longer after that.

Gary chuckled knowingly and began nodding his head, but he wasn't ready to throw me the keys to the Pontiac Grand Prix just yet.

"Okay, now tell me how you're competitive at work."

I explained how in the spring of 1997 Bruce and the Managed Care supervisor met with Jack Howe, the PharmD (Doctor of Pharmacy) in charge of the formulary for Partners Health Plan, the largest HMO in northern Indiana, to discuss getting Zyrtec added to the list of drugs covered by his plan. "You guys need me a lot more than I need you," Mr. Howe told them arrogantly. "I have Claritin, Claritin D, and now Claritin Syrup as antihistamines on my formulary. Zyrtec will *never* get added to my formulary! No way—"

"Some of these pharmacists are unbelievable," Gary interrupted.

I nodded. "After hearing that story, Gary, it became *totally* personal for me. Who the hell did this guy think he was? *Zyrtec will never get on my formulary!* I'm sorry, Mr. Pharmacist, did you go to med school? What gives you the right to tell doctors what drugs their patients get? So, I made it my mission right then and there to get Zyrtec added to the Partners Health Plan formulary."

Gary moved to the edge of the sofa seat. "What'd you do?"

I explained that over the next two weeks my Zyrtec colleagues and I called in favors and cajoled customers and achieved the impossible: We learned the identities of three members of the Partners Health Plan's P&T Committee. Every health plan and insurance company had a Pharmacy and Therapeutics Committee that voted on which drugs to add to formularies, but the identities of its members were tightly guarded to prevent pharmaceutical reps whose drugs were not on formularies from trying to sway a member's vote. On these three influential physicians we unleashed a barrage of letters and phone calls from some of the biggest allergy and dermatology specialists in northern Indiana (three of whom, I did not mention to Gary, were personal friends I had gone skiing with in Aspen) demanding the addition of Zyrtec to the formulary.

"A month later, Gary, just *three* months after the PharmD declared it would never be added, Partners Health Plan added Zyrtec to its formulary." I left out the part about how it was the Zyrtec *syrup* used for children that got added, not the much more commonly used tablet. Apparently, the pediatrician on the P&T Committee assumed that it was *because* he was a pediatrician that my dermatologist friend had called him in the first place, so he only nominated the formulation he would use most often.

"That's a great story, Jamie. Just the type of competitiveness we're looking for." I tried to close him, but he wouldn't give me the commitment. "I'll leave that up to Jackie and Don. We'll be in touch."

An agonizing three weeks later, Jackie called and offered me the job. Mediocre sales and poor work activity notwithstanding, I had managed to get promoted. Or, looking at it another way, even with an extra three weeks of interviews, they couldn't find anybody else who didn't know that Fresno wasn't twenty minutes from the beach.

Fuck up, move up.

Ten

VITAMIN V

HISTORY IS LITTERED WITH WONDERFUL MISTAKES. Columbus thought he had sailed to Asia. An inventor at 3M discovered an adhesive that would not stick very strongly, and it became Post-it Notes. What if the guy with the chocolate bar hadn't turned the corner and crashed into the girl carrying the open jar of peanut butter?

Medicine, too, has benefited from fortunate errors. Lifesaving developments such as the smallpox vaccine, penicillin, and the Pap smear were all discovered by accident or dumb luck. Viagra was also a mistake, although in terms of medical importance, it probably falls closer to the Reese's Peanut Butter Cup than penicillin.

Dr. Ian Osterloh and his Pfizer research colleagues developed sildenafil citrate as a treatment for angina, a painful condition caused by the reduced supply of oxygenated blood to the heart. By inhibiting the enzyme phosphodiesterase 4 (PDE 4), the drug was supposed to relax cardiac blood vessels and increase blood flow, thereby relieving angina-caused chest pain. Unfortunately, clinical trials failed to demonstrate pain relief, and, by the end of 1992, Pfizer was ready to cut its losses and discontinue research on the compound.

When several male patients refused to return leftover pills after completing their participation in the trials, however, Pfizer scientists reexamined their data. Researchers were surprised by the number of times "erections" had been mentioned as a common side effect. Patients enrolled in clinical trials were required to report *any* physical changes that occurred while taking an experimental drug, even one as innocuous as "itchy left ear." Test subjects for any product normally listed headache, nausea, rash, or diarrhea; *erections* got Pfizer's attention.

Viagra's failure to relieve chest pain proved only that it failed to relax *cardiac* blood vessels and increase blood flow to the *heart;* increased erections indicated that the drug succeeded in relaxing nontargeted blood vessels, resulting in increased blood flow to a surprising and soon to be profitable area. Researchers quickly deduced that while Sildenafil had a weak affinity for PDE 4, it had a much stronger affinity for PDE 5, an enzyme in the penis that suppresses the flow of nitric oxide, the key ingredient in causing an erection. From heart to hard-on, Viagra was reborn.

Acknowledging the uniqueness of the drug, the FDA agreed to review Viagra under its fast track, six-month process reserved for compounds that present a best-in-class therapeutic option. The agency's subsequent approval of Viagra on March 27, 1998, set off an unprecedented media frenzy and left doctors and patients clamoring for the drug. They'd have to wait awhile.

Pfizer had not yet packaged any Viagra for sampling or sale. Had someone fallen asleep at the switch in a case of corporate carelessness? Not even close. Call it calculated caution. Pharmaceutical companies anticipating FDA approval of a product adopted either a conservative or aggressive approach to drug-launch preparedness, with the fear of looming competition normally the deciding factor.

In addition to determining whether a drug could be brought to market, the FDA retained final approval of the wording on the product's label and package insert (PI). FDA committee members often asked for changes in wording in either document. For companies that took a conservative approach, these minor alterations were nothing more than a small annoyance, since the finalized product labeling and PI had yet to be printed and the product had not been packaged or shipped. On the other hand, a mistake of overaggression could cost millions of dollars, because every bit of the drug would have to be recalled and thrown out, and replaced by drug with the proper labeling. Under certain circumstances, for example if a similar, competing product would be launched only weeks after approval of Drug X, the latter's company might take the risk of labeling and packaging Drug X prior to FDA approval in order to maximize the amount of time it would be alone in the market. With no real competition to Viagra, Pfizer wisely waited for government approval before setting the wheels of production in motion.

The FDA approved Viagra on a Friday, and by Monday afternoon I had received thirteen phone calls from urology offices demanding samples. I don't know what I found more surprising, that thirteen urology offices even knew who I *was* or that now *I* was being solicited as opposed to soliciting doctors. People were less than thrilled when I explained that I would not be delivering samples for at least a few weeks, since it was bad business for reps to distribute a drug about which they knew nothing.

On April 7, Pfizer flew the 120 members of its Urology Division to the Doral Golf Resort and Spa in Miami for a thirty-six-hour crash course on Viagra. We tore apart the hot-off-the-presses PI (the package insert contains every piece of information the FDA wants physicians and consumers to know about the drug), memorizing success rates and side-effect percentages. We rehearsed our sales pitches until we knew them cold. We were ready for war.

And nobody would listen to us. Not only had Viagra reversed the traditional doctor-rep relationship, it altered the way urologists approached new treatments.

Under normal circumstances, most doctors cautiously refused to try a new drug for at least a few months following FDA approval. There were always a few "cowboys" who wanted to practice cutting-edge medicine, and those guys, God bless 'em, would jump at the chance to try something new. For the most part, however, physicians liked to wait to see what the *New England Journal of Medicine* stated or what a partner in their practice said. Although I hated that attitude from the perspective of a sales rep, I appreciated it from the patient's perspective. "Better safe than sorry" was certainly not a bad credo for a doctor to follow; just ask the patients who got Fen-Phen.

Physicians wanted proof that a drug worked, and then they wanted proof to back up the proof. They would then question the validity of the efficacy data, or they would argue that the study parameters were not strict enough or that there were not enough patients enrolled in the study or that the data had been collected in Europe, not the United States. Doctors wanted safety data showing that their patients were not going to grow a third eye or, worse yet, call them in the middle of the night to complain about gas.

Physicians also wanted to know if the drug was "covered" by insurance yet. This was an important point in terms of cash flow; both the patient's and the doctor's. Take Mrs. Jones, for instance. She did not like finding out from the pharmacist that the new drug prescribed for her was not covered by her insurance, and, as the result, she would have to pay $90 instead of her normal $5 copay. Mrs. Jones would probably call her physician in this case to express her displeasure, which made for a disgruntled medical professional.

Additionally, every HMO cut deals with drug companies to lower their acquisition costs for pharmaceuticals; these agreements normally involved the HMO guaranteeing the company a certain amount of volume in exchange for a price break on that drug or another commonly used one. In order to hit that guaranteed number, however, the HMOs had to make sure the doctors participating in their health plans used Drug X exclusively over Drug Y. To ensure that, the HMOs did one of two things: withheld money from physicians throughout the year to be paid out only if the doctors met the required usage targets or paid doctors higher year-end bonuses based on their having met said goals. Faced with such incentives, many physicians wouldn't even listen to a new product detail, saying, "Come talk to me when it's covered."

The urologists of America did none of the normal things American doctors typically did post–FDA approval. They didn't want to see studies showing Viagra's efficacy. They didn't want detailed safety data. They didn't even care whether the HMOs were covering it or not. We were stunned. We were bursting with information, and nobody would let us talk. As one insightful urologist explained to me, "We've been waiting years for this fucking drug." The pun was not intended.

They wanted to know, in this order:

1. How do I dose it?

2. Who *can't* I give it to?

3. How high can I go? (What's the maximum dose?)

4. What are the side effects?

5. Can I use it in women?

Despite these seemingly simple questions, debate raged within Pfizer as to the correct answers.

Big shots in the company couldn't even agree on the recommended dose. Pfizer produced tablets of 25 milligrams, 50 milligrams, and 100 milligrams. According to the FDA approved labeling, Viagra's recommended starting dose was 50 milligrams to be taken an hour before sex. Twenty-five milligrams was recommended for elderly patients or those with renal dysfunction, while the 100 milligram dose was intended for men who had moderate or no response to 50. Pretty simple, right?

Although it was common industry practice to charge more money for a larger dose of a drug, Pfizer chose to charge the same amount for both the 50-milligram and 100-milligram tablets. This decision had nothing to do with corporate philanthropy and everything to do with keeping the sales representatives from pushing the higher dose.

Each rep had a quota that she was expected to meet each year. Let's say Sally's Viagra sales target was $1 million. Let's also say the 50-milligram tablet and the 100-milligram tablet cost $7 and $8.50, respectively. To make her quota, Sally could have sold 14,285 50-milligram tablets or 11,764 of the 100-milligram tablets. Considering that the average Viagra prescription written was for six tablets, making quota by selling the 100-milligram tablet would have required four hundred *fewer* scripts. For a sales rep, the choice would have been a no-brainer: Push the higher dose.

While that decision would be profitable for the sales force, it could be costly to Pfizer. With practically every pharmaceutical product, there existed a directly proportional ratio between the amount of drug given and the frequency and severity of side effects. Viagra was no exception; clinical trials demonstrated a higher side-effect profile with the 100-milligram dose. From a corporate standpoint, Pfizer couldn't risk the physician negativity and possible negative publicity that accompany a high number of adverse events. Hence, HQ made it clear that the 50-milligram dose was the right one.

As a headquarters decision, it was not well received in the field. From the start, savvy sales managers realized that patients would ask their doctors to write prescriptions for the 100-milligram tablet, which the men would then cut in half, thereby saving half the money while slicing our profits in half. Some physicians didn't wait for the men to ask; they instructed the patients to cut the pills from the start. Nothing makes pharmaceutical sales people crazier than news of "tab cutting."

The members of the Viagra sales and marketing team thought they had nipped this in the bud through the revolutionary design of the pill. In addition to being aesthetically pleasing, Viagra's unique diamond shape was intended to make it impossible to fit the tablet inside a pill cutter, and, at the very least, extremely difficult to cut it manually with a knife. Regardless, pill cutting commonly occurred throughout the country.

Faced with a potential sales crisis, several regional managers got together and directed their reps to push the 100-milligram tablet as the more efficacious dose. This was spun to physicians by focusing on the apprehensive patient. "Doctor, I can understand your concern about cost, but what about that patient who tries 'fifty' and it *doesn't work?* How much courage did that guy summon to come in here the first time and admit he had problems *down there?* Do you really think he is going to come back a *second* time, and basically tell your female receptionist and female nurses that even with *help,* he still can't perform? There's no way. Doc, go with the 'one hundred' and be sure." If the physicians prescribed the 100-milligram dose, the patients wouldn't be allowed to cut it in half, and our sales would not suffer. Unfortunately, teamwork between divisions suffered, as people gave doctors conflicting messages.

We were all united, however, in our efforts to halt the evil tab cutting. Predictably, the reasons we provided physicians for doing so varied dramatically. At first I pretty much told the truth when asked what would happen if a patient took a split Viagra. "We really don't know, Doctor," I'd answer, hoping to strike fear into his control freak heart. Physicians don't like surprises any more than they enjoy phone calls from angry patients. An unsuccessful try with a split tab Viagra could cause both things to happen.

Later on, I picked up a better response—one based on "science"—from Dr. Glove, a nationally renowned urologist and Viagra speaker. After he earned yet another $1,500 for touting the wonders of vitamin V to a dinner crowd of community physicians, I drove him to the airport for the next stop on the Dr. Glove West Coast Speaking Tour. We were having a drink in the bar while he waited for his flight, and I asked him how he would handle the tab-splitting problem.

Swirling the ice in his glass of scotch, he pondered my question for a moment. "Tell them that Viagra is covered in a thin film coating"—which was true—"and that the thin film coating is key to the absorption," meaning the rate at which the drug is absorbed into the bloodstream. "Tell them that we don't know what can happen to the rate of absorption when the film coating has been *compromised*." What a great word, I thought, as he finished his drink.

"If it would normally take sixty minutes for Viagra to start working in a particular patient, maybe it'll only take fifteen after the tab has been split, or maybe two hours. That could really throw off our man's timing, so to speak, and maybe it won't work." I asked him if that was really true.

"Hell if I know," he laughed, and signaled the bartender for another round. "But it sure sounds good, don't it?"

So that's what I went with—the film-coating crisis. It had been working fairly well until I strolled into a urology office south of Fresno one afternoon. Right away, the nurse revealed that the doctor was now telling all of his patients *not* to split their tabs "because of what Jack said." I raised my eyebrows at this. Jack was a dinosaur—close to twenty years with the company—as well as a Bible thumper, two things that made him a wild card in my eyes.

"That's great. What exactly did Jack tell you?" I asked with a nervous smile. At this point, the urologist came out of an exam room.

"He said the Viagra is actually found on only *one side* of the tablet, and there's no way to tell which side. So anybody who splits it may not get the actual drug, just blue filler powder." *Blue filler powder!* Maybe I had overlooked a sense of humor in good ol' Jack.

I started to laugh. "That's a good one," I admitted, winking at the doctor to show him I was in on the joke. Only, no one else was laughing.

"You mean that's not true?" he asked, annoyed.

"Uh, you know, Doctor, Jack has been with Pfizer a lot longer than I have. He knows a million people at headquarters in New York City—scientists, researchers, and everything—so it would not surprise me *at all* to find out that Jack knows something I don't. In fact, I am going to call him to find out about that, because that's the kind of thing I need to be telling the rest of my physicians!"

He nodded. "Makes sense to me," he confirmed. Oh boy. Was it a lie? Yes. Did it accomplish the mission? Yes. *Hello, Machiavelli.*

Having fumbled the recommended starting dose, the geniuses at HQ blundered again in answering the second of the urologists' questions: To whom *can't* I give Viagra? Looking back, it seemed like an easy question. History has shown us that the answer should have been: guys on nitrates, guys who have had heart attacks, and guys who *look* like they are going to have heart attacks. Adding "fat guys" to the list would not have been a bad idea, either.

Of course, there was no such answer. The only men who were specifically ruled out from getting Viagra were those "who have a history of complications with Viagra." I always get a kick out of that line, which can be found in the package insert of every drug on the market. I mean, how can someone have a history of complications with a drug if he has never taken it before?

There was a warning in the package insert, however, that made it crystal clear that men taking nitrates (a class of drugs commonly taken to prevent second heart attacks; many people have cylinders of nitroglycerin on their key chains) ran a significant risk of cardiac side effects. In most patients, Viagra caused a drop in blood pressure. In patients taking nitrates, however, a synergistic effect between the two drugs caused sudden and significant drops in BP, often resulting in major medical crises. The warning was very clear in its wording, but it largely went unheeded. Unfortunately, a package insert warning resembled a yellow traffic light at an intersection; they were both easy to ignore, and most people did just that.

And guys started dying. As the media gleefully reported more deaths, I incorrectly thought I was going to get crucified by my urologists. Which is not to say that the urologists were unconcerned. Rather, they understood why it was happening.

During an initial office visit, most specialty physicians thoroughly review a patient's medical history. Urologists are no exception. These consults take a great deal of time, but they provide the doctor with an essential view of all the disease states and lifestyle issues facing them in the treatment of the patient. Consequently, specialists often know a patient better than his primary care physician. This close relationship allows many specialists, especially urologists, to avoid prescribing Viagra to men who do not meet the guidelines.

Family practitioners, also known as primary care physicians (PCPs), faced a difficult task. Given fifteen minutes to see each patient, they do not have enough time to complete a thorough medical history. This played right into the hands of desperate men who *lied* about their usage of nitroglycerin. Additionally, many patients went in to see the doctor for treatment of allergies or arthritis, only to ask for Viagra at the end of the visit. Short on time and badgered by men eager to revive their dormant sex lives, PCPs occasionally chose poorly and wrote prescriptions for bad candidates. The recipe for disaster was not lost on urologists.

"*Of course* they're having heart attacks and dying," an exasperated urologist barked at me. Dr. Charming, as my colleague referred to him, had a great sense of humor and rarely got upset about anything. "If you wouldn't let a guy carry a suitcase up a flight of stairs, then he shouldn't be fucking!"

Common sense not withstanding, the suits against Pfizer piled up. Yet Pfizer never settled a case, and Pfizer never lost a case. Our stance was simple, yet correct. Viagra did not kill those men; sex did.

Nobody took Viagra and then, boom, had a heart attack. Rather, they took Viagra, *had sex,* and then had a heart attack. The activity killed them, not the drug. Echoing the aforementioned "suitcase" logic, a rule of thumb heard in cold-weather areas said, "If you wouldn't allow a patient to shovel the driveway, then you shouldn't allow him to have sex." After all, hundreds of men suffer heart attacks while clearing snow each winter. Yet Ralph Nader and his merry band of consumer advocates have never campaigned to ban snow shovels, have they?

The deaths did serve as a powerful wake-up call. Pfizer sent a "Dear Doctor" letter to every physician in the United States, warning them of the danger of giving Viagra to patients in poor physical condition and those with access to nitrates. Likewise, the company sent another letter to every hospital emergency room and every paramedic unit in America, urging them to ask heart attack victims if they had taken Viagra that day. (The standard treatment for heart attack victims is to place nitro under the tongue, which would be the *worst* thing to give a man who had already had a cardiac episode while on Viagra.) Additionally, Pfizer approached the FDA to change the package insert's guidance from a "warning" that Viagra and nitrates are bad to a "contraindication," a statement forbidding such concomitant usage. Having put the message out to all involved parties, Pfizer had to wait for the media to finish getting the word out to the public. And the word was not good for us: Viagra kills.

Still, guys kept pouring into offices telling docs, "Dying in the saddle; what a way to go."

chapter Eleven

VIAGRA PLANET

APART FROM POSSIBLE DEATH, the other side effects didn't look too bad. Headache (16 percent), flushing (9 percent), and nausea (6 percent) were the most commonly reported adverse events, none of which interested anyone. The side effect all the urologists wanted to hear about was the blue-green visual haze that affected 3 percent of patients. Researchers deduced that Viagra had a weak affinity for PDE 6, an enzyme found in the retina. Once again, we anticipated a barrage of objections, mostly concerning drivers mistaking red traffic lights for green and causing accidents.

The urologists thought this was the coolest side effect ever. "Trippy," exclaimed one doctor who attended college in the 1960s, and that word was repeated in urology offices throughout my territory. "It'll be a big hit with your Grateful Dead fans," I told a group of skeptical nurses, and their physician cracked up. Docs *never* wanted to hear from patients, but drug-related side effects often prompted such calls. So adverse events could be showstoppers because physicians would be more likely to prescribe a drug that made patient phone calls less likely. In the case of Viagra, however, all of the urologists wanted to *see* a patient who was seeing with a blue-green tint.

Three months after launch, I checked voice mail and heard, "Jamie! I got a guy! I got a guy who sees green. This is so neat!" That had never happened with diarrhea.

The blue-green haze wasn't the only side effect to spark a surprising conversation. On my first call one day, I pulled into my favorite practice. Offices generally prefer not to see reps first thing in the morning because such visits disrupt preparations for that day's patients. (Given my previously stated aversion to waking prior to ten A.M., I normally respected such wishes. On this occasion, however, I had tickets to a San Francisco Giants day game and needed to make a few calls in order to get there in time for the 1:05 P.M. start.) That same absence of patients made the early morning an ideal time to drop by, since docs and nurses were not yet bogged down in exam rooms. Finding a handful of practices that allowed an unannounced visit was difficult, but this group gave me free rein. I knew they'd be happy to see me and chat.

As I opened the door, voices and laughter from the office bounced off the walls of the empty waiting room. The staff members stopped talking immediately upon seeing me and began busying themselves with suddenly important paperwork. I tried to make eye contact with the receptionist, who avoided my gaze. The girls usually greeted me like I was Norm on *Cheers*. Something was going on.

In an overly suspicious voice I asked, "What are you ladies up to?" Unable to keep it in any longer, the three nurses and the receptionist burst into laughter. All of them turned red from giggling, but Carly in particular looked as though she had a Christmas stocking covering her face and neck. Strangely, her hue did not fade after several minutes of conversation. Confused, I finally inquired about the source of her newfound coloring. "You should know, Jamie!" one of them blurted, triggering an avalanche of hysteria. When I finally figured it out, the shock triggered my best Macaulay Culkin in *Home Alone* impersonation. Carly had taken Viagra.

Prompted by work frustrations, three of these medical professionals had decided to conduct their own little drug study. Purely for the sake of medical research, of course. During the previous days the nurses had refused numerous requests for Viagra prescriptions from female patients. Nurses become nurses because they have a natural desire to help people, and saying no over and over again didn't fulfill that need. After a while, they got annoyed. "Why *can't* women try it?" one of the RNs asked, echoing a frustration commonly heard across America. "It just increases blood flow. That could help *us,* too." The staff members shared a look, and a plan was quickly hatched. Each of them would go home, pop a Viagra obtained from the sample closet, and then seduce their husbands as guinea pigs. The following morning they would return to work and hopefully swap stories about the greatest orgasms of their lives. I happened to walk in just as story time concluded.

The results of this strictly regimented study? Nada. None of the three women experienced any heightened sensations, let alone memorable orgasms. In fact, Carly was the only one to notice any difference whatsoever—the modern-day equivalent of Hester Prynne's scarlet "V" was the red flush on her face and neck, which occurred in 9 percent of patients.

The nurses' curiosity about Viagra gave me some inspiration, since women were an untapped source of sales. Because the FDA had approved Viagra only for men, our sales quotas were based solely on male patients. Therefore, any female patients we picked up were gravy. Not surprisingly, every rep was scrambling to find a doctor or two who wanted to write prescriptions for women. On the other hand, Pfizer was not enthusiastic about this very real possibility.

The FDA had made it very clear to HQ that any—repeat, *any*—efforts by Pfizer salespeople to market Viagra for women would be met with a swift kick in the corporate pants. Understandably, the FDA was extremely nervous about the misuse and abuse of a novelty drug like Viagra, and they were ready to knock Pfizer to pharmaceutical Pluto if they caught any of us doing anything but walking the straight and narrow. This was a smart move by the government agency, because the company, in turn, put the fear of God into its sales force regarding this no-no. Studies of Viagra in women had already begun, and Pfizer did not want to upset the FDA in any way. Companies that ticked off the agency, coincidentally, seemed to take a lot longer to bring their new drugs to market. The scare tactics worked. Common knowledge held that the government paid physicians to monitor the sales practices of pharmaceutical salespeople and report any illegal activity. I, for one, was scared shitless, certain that I would be the moron nabbed by FDA spies for promoting female usage of Viagra.

For the first two months postlaunch, I managed to avoid any illegal conversations. Whenever the topic was raised—approximately forty-seven times per day—I would simply shake my head and say, "Sorry, Doctor, Viagra is not FDA approved for women. But let me tell you what is FDA approved for your female patients: Diflucan for yeast infections!" Despite my best intentions, a seemingly harmless conversation with Dr. Charming would soon send me down the slippery slope.

A smooth-talking, well-dressed, and savvy businessman, this urologist always gave me at least five minutes of his time, thereby guaranteeing himself a visit whenever a manager spent the day with me. Upon meeting Jackie, my first boss in the Urology Division, he ushered us into his private office where he dazzled her for fifteen minutes with self-deprecating humor and shameless compliments. Prior to our arrival, Jackie had expressed some displeasure with my sales performance, making me seem more Willy Loman than Donald Trump. After the call, however, she seemed ready to nominate me for the Sales Hall of Fame. Hearing my description of this surprising turnaround, one of my teammates said, "Thank you, Dr. Charming!" and the nickname was born.

A month later on a fateful day, he had some time to kill because one of his patients had canceled an appointment. A large Pfizer shareholder interested in the company's bottom line, Dr.

Charming asked if I knew how the Viagra studies in women were going. I explained that the company would never share that kind of information with us, fearing that reps like me would blab it in conversations like this. *However*, the evil voice inside my head reasoned, *no one ever said I wasn't allowed to ask a physician about the biological processes that would result from vitamin V in this patient population.* "What would happen anyway, if a woman took Viagra?" I asked, my curiosity overriding the alarms going off in my head. His face took on a professorial look as he began to theorize.

"Well, the body parts are pretty much the same. I mean, the clitoris is basically a really small penis. They both contain hundreds of highly sensitive nerve endings and both fill with blood when the brain sends signals that it is stimulated. So if a woman took Viagra, you might be looking at an increase in lubrication and some clitoral engorgement." I thanked him for the biology lesson and headed to my next appointment, pleased to have learned this valuable information and certain I would not share it with any physicians. I managed to keep quiet for twenty minutes.

In addition to urologists, I called on ob-gyns. Predictably, it was this group of specialists who badgered me the most about Viagra's use in women. The call following my discussion with Dr. Charming was no different.

"So when are you guys going to let me give Viagra to my patients?" Dr. OB asked immediately. A sharp, quick-witted African American woman, she regularly listened to my sales pitches, never hesitating to call bullshit on me. In fact, she liked to challenge salespeople. The threat of her posturing with hands set sternly on her hips intimidated a lot of reps, myself included.

I began to respond to her question, but Dr. OB was not about to suffer through my canned response again. "Oh, don't even bother, Jamie," she interrupted with her head shaking violently back and forth. "It's a male-dominated world, and those boys that run Pfizer and the FDA and the insurance companies don't care about keeping us girls happy." To protest would have been futile. "How else can you explain that HMOs are starting to cover Viagra, but they have never paid for birth control pills?"

I could not explain it. I just wanted to crawl away. Surprisingly, she softened her tone and dropped her hands from her hips. "Theoretically, what would Viagra do for a woman, anyway?" Maybe her change in delivery caught me off guard, or maybe I was just happy she stopped yelling at me. Whatever the reason, I regurgitated the information Dr. Charming had just given me.

"Well, Dr. OB," I began, trying to sound professorial, "what you are basically looking at is, uh, is, ahem . . . " That's when it hit me: She was a *woman. How the hell could I talk to a woman about woman parts?* My heart pounded as my face flushed and beads of sweat burst onto my forehead. She raised her eyebrows, signaling that she was waiting for me to continue. I took a deep breath and, avoiding eye contact, started talking as fast as I could. "What you are basically looking at, Doctor, is an increase in lubrication and some clitoral engorgement." *There.* I had done it without too much embarrassment. However, I could not stop talking. Referring to the clitoral engorgement, I added, "And, you know, Doctor, ha-ha, anything that helps us guys find it has *gotta* be a good thing."

Dr. OB stared at me for a long moment before she started to laugh. Shaking her finger at me knowingly, she told her nurse, "He's cool. I'll always see Jamie." Dr. OB began writing prescriptions for Viagra.

And it worked. Not for most women she gave it to, but for some, mostly postmenopausal patients. I looked at it like a baseball player views hitting: three out of ten is pretty damn good. Of course, some women hit grand slams with Viagra, and one of them happened to be married to a urologist.

A coworker in Sacramento called me several months later, laughing and screaming as though he had lost his mind. A veteran drug rep with a been there, done that nonchalance, Joe rarely worked himself into a lather over industry happenings. "You are not going to fucking believe this!" he exclaimed. He was right.

Earlier that day, he called on a urologist with whom he had no rapport whatsoever. Accordingly, he planned on scheduling a lunch appointment for the next month and, at best, speaking with a nurse. After handing the receptionist his card, she waved him in and led him straight back to Dr. Romeo's private office, where she instructed him to make himself comfortable. Joe thought that odd. After a few minutes, the physician walked in and shook Joe's hand as if they were old army buddies. Joe had entered the Twilight Zone.

Dr. Romeo sat down behind his desk and asked Joe if he needed help with anything. Physicians rarely asked reps if we needed anything; normally, they asked if we could get them something. Thrown off balance, Joe said no. "Are you sure?" the urologist asked. "Don't you have any other drugs besides Viagra that I should be using?" Shocked, Joe stuttered a bit before mentioning our two other urology drugs, which the guy immediately offered to start prescribing. "At that point," Joe told me, "I thought he was going to ask to see me naked. It was weird, man." It would get weirder.

Dr. Romeo leaned forward in his chair and looked my nervous colleague in the eye. "Joe, I need a favor." *Here we go,* Joe thought. Before proceeding, the doctor shot a quick glance at the door as if to ensure it was still closed. Joe tensed in his seat. "I need Viagra samples. Lots of them."

Thoroughly relieved that he would be keeping his pants on, Joe sat back in his chair with a smile. "That's not a problem at all. I just got a huge shipment of samples," he said, rising to walk out to his car and grab a case of little blue pills. With a horrified look, Dr. Romeo motioned frantically for Joe to sit back down. "No, no, no. Not for the clinic, for *personal* use."

Joe thought things were getting weird again. "But, Doctor, you're a *urologist.* If you need Viagra samples for your own personal use, why not just take them from your sample closet?"

Dr. Romeo leaned forward in his chair to get closer to Joe. "I don't want my staff to know about this. The samples aren't for me," the physician said before pausing. "They're for my wife." *Hello.* Joe tried desperately to keep something resembling a poker face.

"It's like she's a different woman, Joe." The urologist continued speaking as Joe cringed. "We've been married for almost twenty years, and I don't know who this new woman is. Viagra has changed our life! She gets wetter than she ever did, and now she's coming three, four times a night." *Please, God, don't let this woman be the office manager!* Joe prayed. "The sex has never been this good. She was the one who wanted to try the Viagra, but I wasn't too crazy about the idea. Now, neither one of us can get enough. When she's on it, she's a tigress."

I interrupted Joe's story. "What'd you do?"

"What could I do?" he responded. Only one thing. He met Dr. Romeo behind the office, slipped him a case of Viagra, and made a lifelong friend and valuable customer in the process. "You know," Joe said with an awestruck laugh, "Viagra makes people crazy."

Pfizer's Viagra mania hit full speed at the company's official drug-launch meeting in Orlando in early May 1998. It was an industry-wide tradition to hold a three- or four-day meeting to mark the approval of a new drug. Whereas my Urology Division colleagues and I had attended the crash course in Miami in early April, the company wanted to bring together all five divisions that would be selling vitamin V to officially kick off the Viagra era.

Designed to promote product knowledge during the day and morale during nightly activities, each launch meeting was basically a huge party. Held at upscale hotels in desirable locales, and highlighted by seven-hour open bars with enormous shrimp and crab buffets, launches were wildly expensive affairs that reps critiqued closely; the Zoloft launch had been legendary, while Lipitor's disappointed. Reps acquired gift bags filled with giveaways such as golf shirts or pullovers emblazoned with the new drug's name and logo, as well as other necessities like bottled water (hydration proved key) and Visine (a Pfizer product).

The Viagra launch proved notable for its size (over two thousand Pfizer personnel), security (ID tags were required for entrance into any conference room), and seduction (a female urology colleague of mine met her future husband at one of the evening events). It was the civil-treatment training that sparked the most conversation, though.

Extremely concerned that the sensitive subject matter of erections could create awkward moments for reps and medical professionals alike and that "humorous" conversations with office staff could lead to lawsuits against the company, Pfizer put all of us through four hours of civil-treatment training. We were shown videos demonstrating how female reps should handle lewd male physicians and how to extract ourselves from Viagra jokes. "Don't dress slutty and don't tell dick jokes to chicks" was how one teammate, seemingly unaffected by the training, summed up the lengthy session. The training was not unwarranted. During my tenure in Indiana, a cute Cefzil rep had been licked (that is, the guy leaned forward and licked her with his tongue) while detailing a male physician. She had been talking about bronchitis when this happened; imagine what could happen when female reps discussed erections.

Fired up after appearances by Dr. Ian Osterloh—the father of Viagra proved to be a sheepish Brit completely devoid of melanin, who appeared quite embarrassed by the sustained ovation we gave him—and Bill Steere, our adored CEO, who told us how great we were, the Viagra sales team floated away from the launch, high on our company's and our own futures.

Not every Pfizer employee was thrilled about Viagra. The worst job in pharmaceutical sales? Being a Pfizer rep who *didn't* sell the wonder drug. Pfizer was divided into six separate sales forces—Roerig, Pfizer Laboratories, Pratt, Powers Rx, Alta, and Specialty (further broken down into CHR, or Cardiology; Uro/Gyn; and CNS, or Psychiatry)—each with its own business card. No two divisions sold exactly the same product lines, but each force overlapped with at least two others for every drug it sold. Practically speaking, this duplication ensured that products would continue getting detailed regardless of vacation schedules, maternity leaves, and other rep absences. On a more devious level, this overlap allowed reps to continue calling on physicians who, fed up with anywhere from three to six Pfizer salespeople calling on them, had banned "Pfizer reps" from their offices. "Uh, Dr. Johnson, I'm with Alta Pharmaceuticals, not Pfizer."

The majority of doctors and staff members didn't realize that Pfizer's sales force consisted of six separate divisions. Consequently, few medical professionals knew that not all our sales reps sold Viagra. As the result, every person who walked through the door with a Pfizer product was bombarded with questions and comments about the little blue pill. In an unprecedented move, Pfizer made its entire sales force, even the poor Roerig, Powers Rx, and Alta reps who didn't have the little blue pill in their portfolio, study up on Viagra just so they would be able to answer basic questions if asked.

"Jesus, this sucks!" one particularly outspoken Powers Rx saleswoman told me. "All anybody wants to talk about is Viagra, Viagra, Viagra," she said, sounding more like Jan Brady than a sales professional. An Alta colleague admitted, "Nobody wants to hear about bronchitis when they can hear about boners. Even pediatricians!"

Reps from the other pharmaceutical companies ran into a similar problem, but they couldn't even take consolation in the fact that at least their stock price was soaring. "When are you guys going to come out with something like Viagra?" doctors teased them. Most of my colleagues heard complaints from competing reps about the fact that Viagra had thrown them off their game. Even the Merck reps, who generally carried themselves as if their shit didn't stink (or if it did, they had a drug to cure that), couldn't hide their envy. "You guys hit the jackpot, man," a guy admitted to one of our cardiology specialists. "Enjoy it while you can."

Such comments had to be relayed to me, as I heard none first-hand. How could I when I never talked to the bad guys? You were either on my team or you weren't, bled Pfizer blue or didn't. I simply didn't understand the desire to befriend someone who was trying to take money out of my wallet or, even worse, beat me at something. Very few colleagues shared my views on fraternizing with the enemy, and more than a handful of lunchtime meetings were interrupted by someone rolling her eyes to say, "Jamie, you know the Roche rep, don't you? Oh, wait, I forgot. You don't talk to the bad guys." (I did, on occasion, waive this rule if I needed to gain strategic information of vital importance from a competitor who may have been an attractive single woman.)

To my dismay, my coworkers did not restrict their contact with NPP (non-Pfizer personnel) to the accidental crossing of paths in a parking lot or waiting room. Many reps actually hung out socially! In most cities one could find a regular "rep happy hour," where, I was told, discussion of all things pharmaceutical was forbidden in order to force cats and dogs to get to know each other better. This drove me batty. I mean, with the Biaxin rep's asshole-ness already well documented and my hatred of him rising, why humanize him by finding out his wife was a quadriplegic who still managed to raise a family of seven blind kids? In a nutshell, competing reps were cheaters and liars or, at the very least, they were jerks who thought their drugs were better than mine. And I couldn't stand for that.

My hatred of Abbott Laboratories and its Biaxin sales force began in initial training, thanks to a stellar job of brainwashing. Forced to memorize five key advantages Zithromax possessed over Biaxin, an earlier generation agent in a similar class of antibiotics, I could not fathom why any physician would ever use Biaxin. In fact, to this day, I cannot think of a reason. Yet lots of pediatricians prescribed lots of Biaxin because they thought it was more effective in treating ear infections. Where did they get this false impression? The Abbott reps, of course.

With no data to back it up, these parrots simply repeated over and over again, "Biaxin is more powerful! Biaxin is more effective!" It worked. We, on the other hand, kept saying, "Zithromax has a cherry flavor and is only taken once a day!" We learned the hard way that physicians care much more about efficacy than compliance. It irked me to know that Abbott's marketing strategists had been smarter than ours and that I hadn't been smart enough to figure that out. It wasn't hard to take my bitterness toward Pfizer and myself and redirect it toward a common enemy. A legendary story helped cement my hatred forever.

Pharmaceutical salespeople followed a number of unwritten guidelines, more like professional courtesies, intended to maintain a healthy atmosphere for everyone involved, including other reps, docs, and nurses. Number one was, *Reps should never attempt to go back in an office if another salesperson was already back there.* Not far behind was, *Reps should not bad-mouth a competitor's product.*

One story spread swiftly, via voice mail and phone calls. District managers retold it at district meetings, giving it more strength and credibility. I never once doubted its veracity—until researching this book. I guess when you want to believe something badly enough, it is easy to do so.

An internist purportedly in the southeast was sitting at his office desk when a male Biaxin rep dropped by. The doc waved him in. The guy approached and tossed an object onto the desk. The physician picked it up and saw that it was a Kermit the Frog puppet. He asked what that was all about.

"Did you know, Doctor, that Jim Henson was taking Zithromax for his pneumonia when he died?" The physician had not known that. "If you don't want that to happen to your patients, be sure to use Biaxin first line." Offended by this tactic, the internist allegedly threw the rep out and barred him from the office. No matter. A line had been irrevocably crossed. Biaxin guys were dirt.

Checking some "facts" during the writing of *Hard Sell*, I discovered that Mr. Henson had indeed died of pneumonia, in 1990. That bothered me. Zithromax received FDA approval in 1993. The possibility existed that the Muppets' creator had been enrolled in a clinical trial for Zithromax, and had in fact died while on the drug, but that was highly unlikely. So either the Biaxin guy was a moronic prick who decided to make up a story and risk his career to gain business or a Pfizer district manager invented the story to fire up his sales team. Hmmm.

Apocryphal sales tales were not limited to Abbott Labs. The Schering-Plough reps committed equally reprehensible offenses in the name of Claritin, the world's number-one-selling antihistamine and Schering's most important product. Representing more than 30 percent of the company's sales, the allergy medication single-handedly determined stockholders' happiness. Since Pfizer did not play for second place, Claritin immediately became Zyrtec's biggest rival after getting FDA approval in early 1996. The battle for supremacy in the $4 billion antihistamine market centered on one issue: What was more important, efficacy or somnolence? There was no question that Zyrtec relieved allergy symptoms more effectively than Claritin; a head-to-head trial demonstrated this superiority. However, the latter had a sedation rate similar to placebo, whereas the former made 13.7 percent of patients drowsy.

To us, this was not a big deal. We had answers for the disparity, of course. "If I told you there was a 14 percent chance of rain tomorrow," Bruce would ask physicians, "would you cancel the picnic?" No one ever said yes, but many physicians shied away from Zyrtec due to Schering's scare tactics. The atmosphere quickly grew ugly, as the Claritin reps, desperate to maintain market share with their corporation's bellwether product, yapped incessantly about this distinction, making unsubstantiated claims that the Airline Pilot Union had banned its members from taking Zyrtec and that several motorists had been cited for driving under the influence while taking our antihistamine. Tension mounted as Pfizer personnel, feeling personally attacked, vigorously defended our product.

We had been programmed, I mean instructed, to ask wary physicians to put just one or two patients on Zyrtec, confident that they'd see the efficacy advantage. This strategy backfired on me several times, with one *doctor's wife* becoming so drowsy after taking Zyrtec that she fell asleep on the sofa at seven o'clock at night. Another pediatrician found himself unable to get out of bed on a Saturday—at noon. "Daddy, Daddy, get up and play with us," his children pleaded, futilely. In situations like those, I was supposed to ask the physician, "But did Zyrtec alleviate the allergy symptoms?"

Unfortunately for my manager and my sales, I could relate to a doctor's hesitance to try it. A hay fever sufferer my whole life, I had overslept on several occasions thanks to Zyrtec's sedative effect. This became an issue with Bruce when I called to inform him that I would be late for a meeting in Detroit because I had to go to the dermatologist for an incredibly itchy rash that had appeared overnight.

"*Hel-lo!* You have a trunk full of an antihistamine that relieves itching better than anything!" he yelled, annoyed. I hesitated. "Well?"

Seeing no way out, I explained. "Uh, well, it's a long drive, man—maybe four hours—and I don't want to get sleepy—"

"*That's just great, Jamie!* Way to have confidence in your product! No wonder you're ranked last in the district in Zyrtec sales, with passion and faith like that! Why not go work for Schering?" The interruption was not unexpected.

Based on physician anecdotes and personal experience, I did not push doctors on the sedation issue. If an allergist liked to use

Zyrtec, then great. If not, I stopped calling on him. Then I got a voice mail that changed my attitude. That neither my teammates nor I managed to recognize the story as a possible knockoff of the aforementioned Jim Henson tale still baffles me. Regardless, we didn't, and we believed it. A Schering rep walked into an allergist's office and dropped a six-pack of beer on the desk. Similar to the aforementioned internist, he asked what that was all about.

"If you prescribe Zyrtec for your patients, Doctor, you might as well tell them to drink this beer before driving home because that's how impaired they're going to be on Zyrtec." Again, the physician allegedly tossed the rep out of his office, and, again, without any questioning, I instantly hated the company responsible for said story. My Zyrtec focus and effort quickly increased and, combined with the soon-to-follow Partners Health Plan formulary success, my sales ranking improved to number two in the Great Lakes region.

That was all it took: two stories—or should I say, two versions of the same story—for me to write off every Abbott and Schering-Plough rep in America. Of course, the fact that Biaxin and Claritin were my two biggest competitors may have slightly heightened my sensitivity to such pharmaceutical urban legends. I certainly didn't develop a venomous hatred for Ortho-Biotech's birth control reps or Eli Lilly's diabetes reps with whom I did not compete. Similarly, I didn't have an instinctive dislike for the people who sold Muse, the nation's leading treatment for ED at the time of Viagra's launch. After all, the Muse reps may have been competitors, but they were no competition.

As recently as 1990, there were no pharmaceutical solutions for impotent men, their only options being penile implants. Guys weren't exactly lining up to get a Terminator penis.

Prospects brightened considerably with the introduction of Caverject, the first FDA-approved, nonsurgical treatment. Injected directly into the penis, Caverject caused an erection within seconds.

Not surprisingly, the inclusion of the words "injected" and "penis" in the same sentence greatly reduced demand.

Men suffering from ED got another boost of hope in 1997, when a company called Vivus introduced Muse, the first trans-urethral delivery system. In layman's terms, that means a pellet of Muse was delivered through a tube *shoved into the hole* at the top of the penis. In 2005 this may not sound like a tremendous breakthrough, but in 1997 this was great news for ED patients! Sales of Muse skyrocketed as men across America chose sticking a tube inside their penis over sticking a needle into their penis. Unfortunately for Muse users, inserting the tube into their urethra was only the start of the procedure. The following instructions are taken directly from the Vivus Web site. I think my dad had an easier time assembling my first bike.

Administration

- Stand or sit for the administration of MUSE
- Extend the penis in an upright position
- Slowly insert the applicator up to the collar
- Completely depress the button, then keep the MUSE in position, up to the collar, for 5 seconds
- While in position, gently rock the applicator back and forth to dislodge the pellet
- Roll the penis between the hands in the upright position for 10 seconds to distribute the medication
- Stand or walk around for 10 minutes after administration as the erection develops

Roll the penis between the hands? Was he fixing a joint or trying to get an erection? *Walk around for ten minutes?* Uh, baby, why don't you, uh, keep busy while I, uh, do a security sweep of the property?

Given the previous choices of needle or tube, it was not surprising that many men who had resisted seeking treatment for their ED now wanted to try a little blue pill. Muse was about to become the Betamax of the pharmaceutical industry, yet some of their sales reps refused to see the truth.

I was standing in a Fresno parking lot in May 1998 when I met my first Muse rep. He drove a gold Lexus and had slicked back hair; the attitude was palpable.

"Oh, the Viagra guy," he said. "How's it going?" I wanted to respond, *You mean, how's it going selling the most popular drug in the history of the world, jackass?*, but I decided to give him the benefit of the doubt.

I shrugged sheepishly. "It's crazy." He nodded, silently assuring me that he had expected as much.

"Yeah, I think it's only going to help all of us." I asked what was going to help all of us. "The hubbub over Viagra," he replied testily. He might as well have harkened back to fourth grade and said, "No doy." I asked this Pat Riley clone for further clarification.

With a huge sigh, he tried to explain. "It's like this: With more and more people trying Viagra, the law of averages says it isn't going to work for everyone, so there will be more men trying Muse. I think our sales will go up, too." After reaching $130 million in 1997, sales of Muse dipped to $59 million in 1998, eventually falling to $20 million in 2002.

I met a more realistic Muse sales rep a year later. Enjoying cocktail hour at a wedding in San Francisco, I spied a very cute Asian woman in a short dress across the room. I made a mental note to get the scoop on her from Greg, the groom. Later in the evening, I felt someone smack me hard on the arm. Assuming an overserved friend had given me an over-enthusiastic greeting, I turned with a smile to find the very cute Asian woman in the short dress staring at me, no smile in sight. A glass of Chardonnay, certainly not her first, sloshed in her hand. "Thanks for putting me out of a job!"

she spat. *Excuse me?* This turned out to be the groom's cousin. She explained that she sold Muse, or *had* sold it until the Viagra explosion forced her to seek employment elsewhere. She later turned down my dance request.

Twelve

SEX SELLS

HOT GIRLS MOVED PRODUCT. This is a law of nature, like short guys make better jockeys. No amount of sales data or media coverage demonstrated Viagra's market dominance better than Greg's cousin's inability to sell Muse. That an attractive female rep waved the white flag in the face of a superior drug was noteworthy.

In the pharmaceutical world, men and women continuously debated whether it was better to be a man or a woman. The guys argued that given the choice, male doctors would always choose to speak with the salesperson wearing a skirt. While conceding the veracity of that point, the ladies—understandably concerned that their success would be written off as the result of what's on the outside, as opposed to intelligence, personality, and strategy— insisted the boys had a huge advantage in accessing the physicians because the predominantly female receptionists and nurses preferred to talk with male reps rather than attractive women of whom they might be resentful. I could see both sides of the discussion, and with the benefit of hindsight I can objectively state that the women's view was stupid.

Admittedly, nurses liked guys better because we weren't a threat and they could flirt with us. Even if the head RN adored me and granted me access whenever I wanted, though, that did not guarantee the physician would drop everything to speak with me. On the other hand, no matter how much a "gatekeeper" disliked a female rep, if the doctor let it be known that he would always see Tammy, she would always be allowed into the back of the office. People have been fired for less grievous errors than preventing an orthopedic surgeon from his monthly drool over the Celebrex rep. The women had the most basic human response on their side; regardless how behind schedule or how crazy the day, a male doctor would snap to attention at a mere whiff of perfume or a glance at a pretty girl, his instinctive desire to reproduce having kicked into gear.

I witnessed men undergo complete personality makeovers in the presence of female salespeople. Entering a pediatric practice in Goshen, Indiana, I stamped the slush from my shoes with an uncharacteristic frown. The weather was not the cause of my sour mood. The doctor I was attempting to call on, an older stiff well known for being impervious to humor or insightful commentary on Notre Dame's offensive woes, rarely saw reps. So, I'd driven thirty miles in the snow to probably not see the guy, and even if I did get to see him, it would be a less than pleasurable experience.

Deeper inside the waiting room, I found him standing outside the check-in counter, an unusual location for a man normally holed up in his office when not with patients. Stranger still, the doctor—the *Mennonite* (think "Amish with electricity") doctor I'd never seen smile—was laughing heartily. Joining him in joyous laughter was the Cefzil rep, a cute brunette with a rocking body, whose back he was rubbing. The closest I had ever come to receiving a backrub in my career occurred while being shown the door by an annoyed allergist. I exited quickly; no one seemed to notice.

Bristol-Myers Squibb (BMS), a company whose human resources manager must have formerly been in charge of the Hawaiian Tropic annual talent search, marketed Cefzil, an antibiotic no more effective than the other members of its class. The other Cefzil rep in northern Indiana just so happened to be a cute blonde with a rocking body. Seemingly aware of their assets, the "Cefzil girls" dressed up for various holidays; their cavewomen Halloween costumes made Halle Berry's wardrobe from *The Flintstones* movie look conservative. They sold a lot of Cefzil.

There was no need to look solely at my competitors for evidence of the female advantage in the marketplace, for examples aplenty existed within Pfizer. During my initial visit with a physician, I rarely delved too deeply into a sales pitch. To my managers' dismay, I preferred to get to know my customers on a more intimate level, asking about spouses, kids, colleges attended, and other personal data. Speaking for the first time with a younger urologist in Modesto, I instantly connected with this fresh-faced guy from the Midwest who, like me, loved beer and the Yankees. A five-minute appointment had stretched to fifteen when Dr. Hawkeye shared the exciting information that he used "a ton of Cardura," our drug for men who urinate frequently at night.

In initial training, we had been taught to reinforce positive behavior, so I asked a question that would allow me to drive home our message. "What made you such a big Cardura fan, Doctor?" I waited for him to respond, "twenty-four-hour effectiveness" or "rapid onset of action." This married father of four smiled broadly and said simply, "Donna told me to."

I had heard of an attractive rep in her mid-thirties named Donna, but she lived in Fresno, not Modesto. Clearing my throat, I asked, "When did Donna call on you in Modesto?"

He shook his head. "Not in Modesto—Turlock. I used to have a clinic there," he added, referring to a town twenty minutes south. This still didn't clear things up for me, though.

"But that had to be awhile ago," I half stated, half asked. Dr. Hawkeye nodded, eyes sparkling at the memory.

"Yep, four years ago."

Who knows how many times competitors from Merck (Proscar) and Boehringer Ingelheim (Flomax) had called on him in those four years, how many times he had been wooed with free golf and extravagant dinners. Had they only known their efforts had been rendered futile by a rep named Donna he hadn't seen in fourteen hundred days. When I finally met her months later, I immediately shared the story and thanked her for the contribution to my Cardura sales. She beamed at the news saying, "Oh, he's so cute. Tell him I say 'Hi.'"

I agreed, and when I saw Dr. Hawkeye next I added, "Donna said you're cute!" I got twenty minutes with him that day.

In addition to any subjective superficial advantages female reps possessed over their male counterparts, the ladies had an objective edge: Considerably more doctors were men than women. According to the American Medical Association's Web site, females made up 24.6 percent of the physician population in 2001, meaning that three-quarters of prescription writers were male. To me, it was a no-brainer. If I had been promoted to district manager and given hiring authority, people would have mistaken our team picture for a Delta Delta Delta sorority photo.

Unfortunately, the female physicians of the world did not mimic their male colleagues' behavior toward reps of the opposite sex. Aside from trying to set me up with their friends, very few women allowed me more time to talk about my products than they would have given a female rep; it was as though the women were fearful of appearing swayed by industry salespeople and, as a result, held themselves to a more professional standard. This was disappointing, as I needed some assistance in offsetting the impact of Christmastime elf costumes. Admittedly, though, being the center of flirty attention in an exclusively female practice was a total rush. Crazy things occasionally transpired in such conditions.

On Valentine's Day, it became my practice to send a dozen red roses to "my favorite girls"; the florist always looked at me suspiciously as I filled out seven identical cards for seven different addresses. I liked to schedule a Valentine's Day lunch with my truly favorite office, though, a three-specialist group with a staff of six—all women. Toward the end of lunch, the topic of conversation switched from my love life to that of the only unmarried doctor. After taking some ribbing, she asked me a question.

"Jamie, what would a guy rather get for Valentine's Day: candy or clothes?" As I took my time chewing, I reviewed my options: I could play it safe by picking clothes, or I could jeopardize my career by telling the truth. I paused for a moment longer. All nine women stared intently at me.

"Blow-job coupons."

As the single doctor silently turned redder than the sweater she'd worn in honor of February 14, the room erupted in noise.

"I knew it!"

"That's all they care about."

"They should reciprocate once in a while!"

The receptionist nodded knowingly. "I'm not surprised. Pete is always asking me to *swallow*," she said with an expression signifying her lack of enthusiasm for that pastime. "And I'm just like, 'How'd you like me to blow my nose in *your* mouth?'" Things had gotten a bit out of control.

I sat back in my chair as they laughed themselves silly, laughing, undoubtedly, at the knowledge that I'd be fired the next day, possibly even that day. How would I explain to my mother that Pfizer terminated her eldest son's employment after he instructed female medical professionals to provide their significant others with paperwork redeemable for fellatio? A voice snapped me out of my fatalistic daydreaming, but I had no idea what had been said or asked. Recognizing my clueless expression, the speaker repeated her question.

"How many coupons would he get?" the unmarried doctor asked sincerely.

"Excuse me?" My voice cracked with surprise.

"Well, how many coupons would I give him, like, three or twenty?" I could not believe my luck. The women ignored my stunned silence and began a roundtable discussion as to what the proper number of blow-job coupons would be. They settled on five, but the questioning was not yet complete.

"What do the coupons *entail?*" a nurse in her mid-twenties inquired. "I mean, she doesn't have to do it whenever he wants, does she?" Emboldened, I laid down the rules for a deal I had never even tried to implement for myself.

"Listen, ladies, these are a *gift;* you can't put strings on them. These coupons are for a blow job whenever *he* wants. Period. It doesn't matter if you come home from a lousy day at work and the last thing you want to do is *that;* the coupons are redeemable anytime, anyplace."

Lunchtime ended shortly after, and the gift-giving doctor assured me she would follow through with my suggestion. Later reports indicated it had been her beau's best Valentine's Day ever. At the beginning of April, Bruce rode with me the day after my birthday. Again. Having somehow forgotten the conversation from February 14, I strolled into the all-female office, ready to unleash a peerless sales call on one of the physicians (not the single one!) who was always accommodating. Nine women smiling with anticipation greeted us.

They handed me a sealed blue envelope with my name on it, prompting me to turn to Bruce with a cocky look. *How many other reps get birthday cards from offices?* I opened it and two pieces of colored construction paper fell out. Bruce, my Mormon manager, reached down, picked them up, and read one aloud.

"One BJ coupon, redeemable anytime." His head snapped in my direction with a sound like a Michael Jackson video. I held my breath while staring in horror at the staff members, whose giggles indicated they did not know my employment was once again in jeopardy.

"Well, you know," Bruce began after solemnly collecting his thoughts, "Jamie is an up and *coming* rep. He's a really *hard* worker." The women squealed with laughter, and we left shortly thereafter without mentioning any of our drugs, both of us delirious over the conversation that had just taken place. As we walked to the car, Bruce grabbed my arm. "Guy, I have never seen *anybody* who has rapport like you do with the ladies in these offices!"

Alas, establishing such relationships with female physicians did little to help my sales. Despite her willingness to discuss oral sex with me, the single doctor never gave me any time to discuss medications, continuing instead to prescribe Claritin instead of Zyrtec for patients with itchy skin. Conversely, had the Cefzil girls suggested a new cunnilingus technique to a male physician, that guy would single-handedly have written more prescriptions than the rest of Indiana combined.

Not even the Cefzil girls, though, could have successfully sold Muse. Guys were lining up to get their little blue pill rather than a pellet tube. Literally.

Two weeks after Viagra's launch, I pushed open the door to a urology office, only to find it partially blocked. "No room," a man said. The waiting area was jammed with patients. Fortunately, two left shortly, allowing me entrance. Twenty pairs of anxious eyes looked me over as I made my way toward the receptionist. Twenty pairs of anxious *male* eyes. The waiting area was filled entirely with men eager to get help for their ED, yet worried that Viagra might not work for them.

The urologist happened to be standing behind the counter, and he smiled upon seeing me. Instead of waving me back, he opened the door and walked into the crowded room. I was the center of attention as he pointed to me for a moment without saying anything, prompting all of the men to wonder who the hell I was. Finally, he announced with great dramatic flair, "*This* . . . is the Viagra guy." In unison, the patients stood up and began clapping. My first standing ovation, and to think it came as the result of helping strangers get hard-ons.

My parents hoped I'd grow up to be a doctor or lawyer; boner maker never made the list. On paper, it may not have appeared to be an important or dignified job, but I'll bet the men for whom Viagra worked would argue differently. Even the Pope validated what we were doing.

In a brilliant marketing move, Pfizer contacted the Vatican to get its approval—its blessing, if you will—of Viagra. There had been concern within Pfizer that the Catholic Church might oppose Viagra because it would undoubtedly be used by unmarried couples and masturbating men, two church no-nos. Fortunately, the Pope chose to focus on the benefits Viagra would provide married couples. Declaring that Viagra would restore vitality to many marriages, he enthusiastically supported the introduction of the little blue pill.

Viagra may not have resulted in an increase in church attendance, but it certainly caused many parishioners to scream out the Lord's name for the first time in years. I was stunned to see how many older people—older than my parents, even!—still desired sex. On several occasions, I thought I had mistakenly walked into a World War II reunion rather than a urology office.

Not everyone was a fan, however. Often, one half of an older couple wanted to climb back in the saddle, while the other person was perfectly happy to continue walking, not riding. This was a side of the story seldom presented by the media. For many people, Viagra was an unwelcome visitor, knocking on the door to an attic that had long been sealed shut. Suddenly, urologists were forced into the role of marriage counselor and sex therapist, an unexpected development.

"What are we here for today?" a urologist asked the patient and his wife sitting across the desk from him, even though he already knew the answer. Both in their late sixties, the effects of his diabetes had prevented them from having sex for fifteen years. Responding to the question, the woman shrugged and looked away nervously. The husband sat up forcefully and said, "We're here for the Viagra." The physician looked from one to the other.

"And this is something you both want?" he asked. Simultaneously, the man said yes and the woman said no. *Commence counseling.*

Doctors couldn't always assume they knew what to expect. The same urologist walked into his office to find a couple in their early fifties waiting for him. Although he had never examined the man or the woman, he knew from the nurse's notes that they were there to discuss Viagra. "What are we here for today?" the physician began.

Predictably, the husband spoke first. "Beats the hell out of me," he said with annoyance.

Smacking her husband in the arm, his wife said forcibly, "We need Viagra, Doctor." Stunned, the urologist watched the husband shake his head.

"No we don't, Doc," he insisted, though he was unable to make eye contact with his wife. He didn't know it, but he was outvoted.

"Oh, yes we do!" the little missus exclaimed. They left with a prescription. *You go, girl.*

Of course, then you had the standard couple in which both partners wanted to have sex. Both *seventy-five*-year-old partners. "Saw a delightful couple today," a physician told me. "Been married fifty-six years!" He paused. "They thought they might want to try Viagra." Friends at the nursing home had encouraged them. It had been ten years since they had last made love, and both husband and wife were a bit hesitant. The man was worried that the drug might not work and that he would seem less manly to his wife. From her perspective, she was worried, after all the time that had passed, that certain parts would not work properly or that the act itself would simply hurt too much.

"What did you tell them?" I asked, trying not to picture my grandparents sitting across the desk from him discussing erections and vaginal lubrication.

"I just reminded them to be patient with themselves and each other, and to be very gentle because I didn't want the orthopedic surgeon calling me two days later!" The couple laughed and left his office holding hands.

The urologist did receive a phone call two days later, but it wasn't from the hip doctor. The husband—the *irate* husband—was on the line. "It didn't work!" he screamed. "I've taken it twice in two days, and nothing happened. Nothing!" With an idea of what went wrong, the physician asked the man how he had taken it. The answer confirmed the doctor's guess.

An hour before bedtime, the seventy-five-year-old man popped a Viagra and climbed into bed beside his naked wife. And there they remained for the next two hours, waiting for an erection. Since the doctor had warned them that Viagra often doesn't work the first time (thanks to nerves or a poorly timed dose, many patients saw no results with Viagra initially, but succeeded in subsequent attempts), they simply decided to get some sleep and try again the next night. After two fruitless attempts, however, the patient called the doctor.

"Did you engage in any foreplay?" the urologist asked, well aware that this part of the dosing instructions often got overlooked by men who thought they would get an erection immediately after taking the pill. "Remember I said there has to be some *stimulation* in order for the Viagra to work?" (This was a common misconception—that simply swallowing the tablet would cause an erection. After the TV show *Mad About You* aired an episode in which Paul Reiser—coincidentally, a perfect name for a guy on Viagra—ran around New York City with a rod poking out of his pants all day, Pfizer sent a letter to NBC protesting the incorrect portrayal.) Following the urologist's reminder, the gentleman said he recalled the proper advice, thanked the doc, and hung up.

"Can you imagine?" the physician asked me incredulously. "They were probably more nervous last night than they were on their wedding night!" He didn't hear from that patient again.

Until the guy called to get his Viagra prescription renewed. *Giddy up.*

Not everyone could be bothered with such an old-fashioned approach to obtaining a drug. Pesky prescriptions? Pshaw. Some guys decided to remove the middleman—in this case, a physician—from the process of getting their horny little hands on vitamin V. One entrepreneur in Crown Point, Indiana, stole thirty-five hundred tablets from two storage units at the self-storage facility where he worked. (The majority of drug reps rented lockers to hold the hundreds of boxes of samples, pens, and the like we had.) Twice the thief used his master keys to break in and help himself to cases of Viagra, which were never recovered. Fortunately, this particular Pfizer rep paid close attention to his inventory and immediately noticed when his count was off; as a LIFO (Last In, First Out) guy, I never would have detected the loss. We received reports of other attempted thefts in which bad guys tailed Viagra reps from a doctor's office to their storage facility, after which the would-be-robbers were denied entry—probably by facility managers who then got the bright idea to steal the samples themselves.

I would be remiss, however, if I only cast stones at criminals, for pharmaceutical pilferers were plentiful. This should have come as no surprise to Pfizer personnel, most of whom had granted themselves several "five-fingered discounts" on competitive products over the years, like my suddenly-a-dermatology-rep colleague. Office staff members, however, were going through Viagra samples at a faster burn rate than a dot-com through start-up cash.

"Jamie, I think *other reps* are taking the Viagra samples!" one outraged RN told me. I assured her it was no big deal, unfortunately a common practice among some "unprofessionals."

"I'd keep an eye on that Flomax guy," I suggested, mentioning a competitor whose help-men-stop-peeing-during-the-night drug was killing Cardura, my help-men-stop-peeing-during-the-night drug. To address the problem of theft by rep, urology offices universally began treating Viagra as a controlled substance and placed samples of it under lock and key just as they did for Valium. I wondered which was more addicting.

With patients, evildoers, and competitors all clamoring for Viagra, my friends' interest should not have surprised me, but it did. My buddies hadn't been this giddy since somebody brought a whoopee cushion into class in third grade. These guys couldn't wait to talk about the little blue pill; they had to know *everything*. Seemingly overnight, I was transformed from just a guy with a job that let him play hooky all the time to the V-Man; I, like all my Viagra colleagues, became a de facto celebrity.

In planning the Viagra launch, Pfizer had the foresight to realize we would face awkward workplace situations previously not encountered in industry history, and as the result, the company provided us with training to handle said situations. Pfizer did not, however, anticipate the rock star–esque rise our social standing would take among friends and family. A little media training would have been nice.

In hindsight, most of the barroom conversations I had during the six weeks postlaunch have blurred together, partially because of the multitude of refreshments purchased for me in honor of my sudden hipness, but mostly due to the fact that they were all so similar. From my friends' handling of introductions to the listeners' reactions upon meeting me to their questions once the drinks had kicked in, each discussion mirrored the one before and the one after. They say you never forget your first time, though, and the Friday night following Viagra's initial seven days on the market will remain seared into my brain long after the little blue pill's patent has expired.

Walking into happy hour at Bayside Café, a sports bar on Union Street in San Francisco, my friend Mike and I sensed we stood on the cusp of something big. Having witnessed firsthand vitamin V's first week of life, I looked forward to watching the craziness crescendo over the next few months. Mike looked forward to telling everybody he knew that he knew the guy who had witnessed firsthand vitamin V's first week of life. His level of excitement would've led a casual observer to think that I, not Tommy Lee, had been in that sex tape with Pamela Anderson.

Mike and I had plans with friends of his from the consulting and technology industries, people he had specifically invited out to meet me. It was as if he was attending adult kindergarten, and I was his show-and-tell object. Months later, when twenty-somethings began pointing at other partygoers and nonchalantly announcing how many millions their stock options were worth, the Viagra guy was pushed into the background. In April 1998, however, the V-Man held court. Jeff Bezos had nothing on me.

During my first two months in California, Mike introduced me like so: "This is Jamie, an old friend of mine from Notre Dame. He just moved to Modesto, but don't hold that against him." If Mike was not present to introduce me to new people, his friends would say, "This is Mike's friend Jamie. He's an annoying Notre Dame fan, too. He lives in Fresno." A.V. (After Viagra), normal introductions got tossed aside. Mike waved to two guys walking aimlessly through the crowd. They approached, shifting their beers to their left hand and extending their right, but Mike could not contain himself. Before they could even shake his hand, he put his arm around me and blurted, "This is Jamie"—dramatic pause—"HesellsViagra!" He could not get the latter phrase out of his mouth quickly enough.

Judging by their reactions, which were as simultaneous as they were similar, Mike had obviously not told them whom they were meeting. Picture Shaggy and Scooby saying, "Zoinks!" only without sound. That night Mike took great pleasure in watching the facial expressions of the people I met; apparently, it was great fun. I never saw them, since I had no idea how to react myself. My face flushed like the first time in fourth grade a girl asked me to skate at the roller rink; I felt cool, yet embarrassed, and ended up staring at my feet. At Bayside Café eighteen years later, I had matured enough to take a long pull on my beer while staring at my feet.

A brief lull followed, as four guys modeling the latest Gap pullovers stood dumbstruck. Finally, the silence was interrupted by a loud, nervous laugh. His buddies exchanged sideways glances with themselves and then Mike. *Are you serious?* Beaming, Mike replied, "Oh, yeah! He's the Viagra guy." Rather than sparking discussion, his confirmation set us back a step. More drinks appeared, giving the guys some time to absorb the surprise.

Finally, one gushed, "Wow." This broke the ice.

"What a *hard* job!" his buddy commented.

"You mean, a hard *sell!*"

Mike added, "His career must be on the *rise,* huh?" Viagra salespeople would hear those jokes more than once in 1998.

Just when I thought we were grooving, the conversation jumped awkwardly to another, non-sex-related topic. The sudden focus on Viagra proved too much for most people to handle with no warning. One minute John Consultant and Jim Dot-commer were talking about Stanford's Graduate School of Business, and the next thing they knew, they were meeting Mike's friend and talking about blood flow to the penis. These guys demonstrated a need for some preparation time—or three drinks—before being ready to consider hard-ons and the lack thereof. As the hours and beers increased, hesitation about asking questions decreased.

My friend Ron joined us at the bar, and he also proved unable to resist the urge to say, "He sells Viagra!" His buddy Doug had left his wife at home to converse with the V-Man. No one bothered to introduce the other men to one another. Doug gave me a sheepish grin followed by, "Soooo." I smiled back and shrugged as if to say, Crazy, huh?, and we were off to the races.

"How does it work?" he asked, surprising me. I would've thought only science geeks would care about that, but I quickly learned that everybody was interested in Viagra's mechanism of action. No one ever cared how an antihistamine worked. Fortunately, I had come up with a sports metaphor to ensure that the guys would get it.

"Okay, so think of getting an erection like it's a football game. You've got your offense and your defense. You are trying to get your running back into the end zone, but the defense has a great linebacker who has tackled the running back on every play so far. Now, a man gets an erection when the brain sends signals that it is sexually excited. When this happens in a man with erectile function, nitric oxide—the running back—flows into the penis and stimulates the blood flow that causes an erection. In other words, it scores a touchdown. In a man with erectile dysfunction, however, the linebacker, phosphodiesterase 5 [PDE 5], tackles nitric oxide. This is where Viagra comes in. Viagra naturally blocks PDE 5 from interfering with nitric oxide. So, think of Viagra as the fullback who blocks PDE 5 from tackling nitric oxide, thus enabling us to score a touchdown."

Doug, Mike, and Ron—and all their friends—smiled and nodded. Everybody loved an All-American, but one satisfactory answer was not sufficient for the masses. They had more questions—a lot more questions.

That night each of my friends, not to mention *their* friends, asked to take Viagra for a test drive. To each request, I vigorously shook my head. The last thing I needed was to have someone keel over with a heart attack after taking one of my samples or somehow get busted by the cops with one of my samples in their pocket. Neither case would have been good for my career advancement. "No, no, no," I told them. "Viagra isn't for *you*. It's only intended for older guys with erectile *dysfunction*, not twenty-eight-year-olds in good shape."

The fellas who were only looking to take their game to the next level, so to speak, accepted this explanation and moved on to more important topics such as, "Who's that chick in the black?" One guy, however, didn't give up that easy.

With his head on a swivel like a neighborhood snitch about to give up a tip to the cops, he leaned in close to me, and whispered, "Sometimes not everything works the way it should. You know?" *Ever think it might be the thirteen shots of Jagermeister?*

Unfortunately, not everyone omitted the more painful details. Another guy went so far as to reveal, with excruciating specificity, his periodic bouts with erectile dysfunction. I do not recall how we got into the conversation, but I am fairly certain that I did not say, "Hey, why don't you tell me about your penis problems?" I do remember the sincerely worried look on his face. I thought perhaps one of his parents was seriously ill. "Well, man, there was this one month where nothing, I mean . . . nothing." I had no idea where he was going with this, but I deduced it did not involve his dad's colon.

"I mean, we had been doing it twice a night for forever and wham! Nothing. We tried everything. My girlfriend was like, 'I can't believe this is happening!'" *That's two of us*, I thought, resigning myself to a lifetime of impromptu counseling sessions. Apparently, the fact that I spoke to urologists every day gave people the impression I *was* one.

The guys were the least of my worries. Whereas no women had made any comments or asked any questions earlier in the night, their shyness disappeared along with the happy-hour prices. While I may have been annoyed and slightly embarrassed by my discussions with the boys, their innumerable sample requests and personal revelations paled in comparison to the interrogations I faced with the girls, whose feline curiosities proved insatiable. Mike waved over two women, a blonde and a brunette with whom we had had dinner previously. These two roommates gradually steered me away from the group. As the bar's noise level rose, they began to quiz me about the wonder pill.

Lobbing softballs at first (Has it been crazy? How does it work?), the ladies gradually grew more intense, more focused.

"Does it make it longer?" The brunette asked. *No.*

"Does it make it *last* longer?" her roomie wondered, an impressive bridge on her friend's query. *No, but it does decrease what urologists refer to as "the refractory period," which is what we laypeople call recovery time.* Feeling like a suspect grilled by Sipowicz, I searched for relief in the form of Mike and the guys. After spotting them drinking and laughing near the bar, I suggested that we join them. The ladies barely acknowledged my request. These gals had acquired their target and were not about to let me slam on the brakes to watch them fly right by. Without realizing it at the time, this was my first encounter with the Look, the change in a woman's eyes that occurred just before she was about to ask me a doozy.

"Does it burn in your throat?" None of the guys had asked that one.

"Does it burn inside you?" *Uh, we're gonna need another round over here.* And, for the coup de grâce, "Have you tried it?" The brunette's last question hung in the air for an eternity.

Ah, the Million-Dollar Question. Let me start by saying, "Hell yeah, I tried it!" I must shamefully admit, however, that it took me three months to find the nerve. Despite my pals' pleas, the thought of breaking open a sample pack never occurred to me. After all, I was a healthy, twenty-eight-year-old guy, not a middle-aged man with any of the medical issues like hypertension that would cause ED. Hence, I didn't try it. This baffled my friends no end. Even Mike's dad, the late Jack Pearl, questioned my decision.

As Mike drove out to Modesto one night to help me drown the pain after the Woman of My Dreams IV had shattered my fragile heart, he called his parents from the road. His father, a Class of '49

Notre Dame grad whom I had met on a dozen occasions, asked him where he was heading.

"Ah, Jamie's got girl problems, so I'm driving out there to cheer him up." Mr. Pearl had a voice like John Wayne's and his tan, lined face hinted he had seen quite a bit during his seventy years. He replied, "How can a guy who sells Viagra have girl problems?"

Public opinion aside, my failure to take advantage of unsupervised access to the biggest sexual sensation of the twentieth century did not surprise me; missing the V-Train was not out of character. In high school I cut one day of class in four years. I pass out when the blood pressure thingy gets too tight on my arm. I'm afraid of needles, heights, and mice. I took naps on spring break. Living on the edge was not exactly a hallmark of my first three decades on Earth. But then I had a conversation with a comely blonde colleague who possessed some Viagra-like abilities of her own.

"I was talking with this guy I used to work with in my last division," she began benignly enough. "He's in his thirties, married, three kids and all that." I nodded along, having no idea where she was headed but happy to be along for the ride. "Well, he told me it *totally* worked."

Our topic still eluding me, I asked, "What totally worked?" Her sigh indicated a deep sense of disappointment in me, but my crushing depression proved fleeting as she bent toward me to whisper the answer.

"Duh! *Viagra*." With her heavenly aroma wafting around me, feeling stupid never felt so good. I did not get any smarter, though.

"Is he diabetic or something?" I asked.

Her face scrunched as she shook her head.

"So, then why would he need Viagra?" No wrinkled brow this time. She actually smiled, as if she had solved the mystery of what had burdened me my whole life.

With a seductive smile, she said, "He didn't *need* it. He wanted to try it out. He said it's never been so rigid." She breathed the last word in two husky syllables: *rih-gid.* That's when it hit me: Why *wouldn't* somebody try it? Why the hell hadn't *I* tried it? How long will it take me to get to my car's trunk and back?

Let me pose the question like this: If you had the chance to have the greatest orgasm of your life, but you had to take a relatively safe drug to do so, would you do it? That is the hope we all had with Viagra. I spoke with colleagues who said their sex life was already super, so they had no reason to try it. The New Jamie said, "Well, why not see if it can be a little better?" That would be a good thing, right?

Think about the Olympics. Remember Ben Johnson, the Canadian sprinter who tested positive for steroids during the 1988 Summer Games? Drug-free, he had been one of the fastest guys *in the world,* but that wasn't good enough for him. He risked permanent physical damage and international scorn to get thatmuch faster, just two-tenths of a second. It's all about pushing the envelope for these athletes, and I, as an amateur bedroom gymnast, was always on the lookout for an edge to improve my game that much more.

So, yeah, I tried Viagra, and let me tell you, that little blue pill was a guy's best friend after the aforementioned thirteen shots of Jagermeister.

"How hard?" was the question I got from guys, their eyes aglow at the thought of secretly calling for a psuedo relief pitcher from the bullpen. I'd answer by flicking my finger against the beer bottle in my hand, prompting envious nodding.

However, the women who asked me if I had tried Viagra didn't necessarily want to hear about that. In fact, it was questionable if they wanted to hear *anything* about my taking it. Leave it to a woman to ask a question to which she didn't want to hear the answer.

Taking Viagra as a healthy, twenty-eight-year-old guy was not exactly like being the cool guy in junior high who brought reefer to the party. "Have you tried it?" the cute seventh-grader with braces would ask. "Sure, babe, and it is some good shit." Then she'd tell her friend, "Oh my God, he *tried* it. I think I want to give him a hand job." No, this was something completely different.

If I said no, she'd probably shrug and think, "Of course not. A healthy guy like that wouldn't need it." No harm, no foul. *Or,* maybe she would look at me like I was a moron, a guy with easy access to a revolutionary sex drug who didn't take advantage of it. Maybe she'd think I was the *geek* in junior high who left the room when the bong got passed around.

If I said yes, though, the obvious question would be "Did it work?" I couldn't just pull the cool-guy routine and say, "Yeah, babe, it did," because she might have deduced from such an admission that I *needed* Viagra. I could not have blamed her for thinking so, since that was exactly what *I* thought after trying it and noticing a difference.

Dr. Charming's staff was more than a little surprised to see me at eight A.M. on a Monday. This was not your normal Monday, however; this was the Monday after the Saturday I had taken Viagra. I practically tackled Dr. Charming when he entered the office from the "secret" entrance in the back of the building. "This'll only take a minute," I assured his confused nurse as I shoved the equally confused doctor into an empty examination room.

"What's up?" he asked, smoothing out any wrinkles I'd caused in his thousand-dollar suit.

I didn't hesitate. "There is something majorly wrong with me."

He opened his hands. "Well, what is it?"

"I tried Viagra this weekend." I paused to see if he was shocked. He wasn't. "And?"

Gulp. "And it . . . *worked,*" I said, whispering the last word.

He was unfazed. "And?"

I could have strangled him! "'And?' What the hell do you mean, 'And?' I'm twenty-eight years old, and I just told you that Viagra *worked* for me, and all you can say is 'And?'"

His laughter did not calm me very much. Ditto for the could-you-be-any-dumber? look on his face.

"Jamie, you have nothing to worry about," he assured me. "Look, *most* guys would notice a difference after taking Viagra. It's a vasodilator! Viagra's job is to increase blood flow, so that is what it's going to do for everybody. Let's say you're operating at ninety-eight percent 'efficiency.' In that situation, Viagra would increase your blood flow two percent, or if a guy is at seventy-five percent, it'd increase it twenty-five percent. But Pfizer can't run around telling every man in the country that Viagra may give them an improved hard-on, because the government would shut you down right away. That's the last thing the FDA needs, you sales guys promising better boners to all the men in America. So the feds required Pfizer to limit Viagra's labeling to only those men with serious erectile dysfunction."

What he said made sense regarding "all the men in America," but they had not tried Viagra that weekend and gotten the surprise of their life. "So, there's nothing wrong with me?"

He shook his head. "No, there isn't. Now, get out of here and let me do some work, Limpy."

It was a good thing I could take a joke.

Thirteen

SALES OR LACK THEREOF

UNFORTUNATELY, THE JOKE WAS ON ME when it came to Viagra sales. Thousands upon thousands of men sought treatment once a noninvasive option was made available. Viagra had literally created the market.

Everywhere, that is, except central California.

It took awhile for me to figure out that my Viagra sales sucked. Everybody in every office wanted to talk about Viagra. "Is that your Cadillac out there in the parking lot?" Dr. Door asked with a wink, alluding to the fact that I would obviously be making a bundle in bonuses. Every urologist I saw told me without prompting that they were writing more prescriptions for Viagra than they had ever written for anything else. So I assumed I was doing well.

I finished the 1998 sales year at approximately 94 percent of quota, good for third to last in *the nation*. The national average for urology reps was somewhere around 120 percent. Many people—my boss being the most curious—attempted unsuccessfully to figure out why my Viagra numbers drooped so far below those of my colleagues. I had the answer all along: The company screwed me.

Sales reps always took full credit for good sales and rarely accepted blame for poor sales. If Joe Rep made it to the top, there was *no way* he would credit random luck, e.g., the new PharmD of his biggest HMO added Zoloft to the formulary, or a hospital pharmacist who feared a price increase after New Year's quadrupled his normal order in December. Sometimes, a rep had no clue as to how he had managed to finish number one. No matter. When asked to share the secret of his success with the group (managers *always* asked the number-one rep to share his secrets with the group, forgetting that the group's members would not pay a lick of attention because they attributed his success entirely to luck), the guy peered down from his lofty perch and credited his own creativity, hard work, perseverance, blah, blah, blah.

When Joe Rep subsequently tumbled *down* the mountain, however, said fall had nothing to do with him. He'd blame HMOs, doctors sleeping with competing reps, or even locusts, but he would never, *ever* take responsibility. Just about out of excuses, a desperate rep would cite the reporting glitch, the infamous claim that he had not gotten credit for all the sales in his territory, as in, "The wholesaler's numbers were off in March!" Often initiated, this theory was rarely substantiated.

What to do when blaming everyone from Jonas Salk to the Democrats didn't work? Blame the company, of course.

"The company screwed me" had to be the most common phrase spoken at any Pfizer meeting. It was as if Billy, the blond kid from *The Family Circus* comic strip, had morphed into a real person and chosen pharmaceutical sales as his career. *Not me.*

The basis for "The company screwed me" plea was simple: The bean counters in New York City had no clue what it was really like in the field, so they simply invented sales quotas, most often utilizing a dart board to do so. Sales reps resented their fate being determined by nameless people seemingly fresh out of business school.

HQ claimed that quotas were based on years of statistical analysis of each territory and how "equal" competitors, i.e., comparable agents in the same class of drug, had fared in each territory postlaunch. For instance, before Pfizer launched Zithromax, the company researched Biaxin's sales for each territory in the country, factoring them into the quotas for each rep. Territories in which Biaxin had been more successful received higher quotas than those in which it had not done as well. To their credit, the Suits presented a solid argument that made it seem like there was no way to screw us.

That being said, reps routinely received sales goals that were completely unrealistic and, therefore, unreachable. If there is one basic rule in sales, one *absolute must*, it is to "reach goal," aka make quota. I did not make quota with Viagra. In two years.

I was ready to blame the company, believe me. I mean, how could some MBAs in *New York City* who couldn't sell condoms to Colin Farrell know how much Viagra would be used in the San Joaquin Valley's farming communities? Well, they couldn't, but it wasn't their fault. Viagra broke the mold. There was no "equal" competitor for Viagra. It was impossible to use the first-year sales of Muse as a barometer for Viagra sales projections, since thousands of men had resisted seeking treatment for their ED until a pill arrived on the marketplace. Accordingly, the bean counters had simply underestimated what some territories would sell, and overestimated the amount in others.

For a time, a female rep in Utah had achieved more than 300 percent of her quota. Jokes flew about the marital habits of Mormons, as people tried to explain the strange phenomenon of her doubling the sales of the next best territory. Finally, someone in HQ determined that most of Viagra's Internet orders from across the nation were being filled in Utah. She subsequently stopped receiving credit for Internet orders, and her sales numbers returned to earth.

A teammate of mine in Seattle benefited from the aforementioned phenomenon of underestimating potential sales and finished the year ranked number one at a whopping 170 percent of quota. We all had a lot of bitter, sarcastic fun asking Dan for his "secret"; the joke being that we were the *urology* reps! We focused on urologists—the docs whose job it was to treat erectile dysfunction—and it wasn't as though some reps were better than others at getting those specialists to prescribe more Viagra. No urologist in America looked back on an appointment with an ED patient and slapped himself in the forehead like he could've had a V8, saying, "I could've given that guy Viagra!" Apparently, this fact managed to escape Dan, who actually talked for ten minutes when asked to stand up and share the secret of his success with the group.

"Maybe some of you can take a lesson from Dan," our boss Jackie suggested, looking in my direction. Bosses did not like it when their reps finished low enough that people could include "to last" in the sentence. Fortunately for me, she stepped down. Unfortunately, her replacement made it his personal mission in life to ensure that I made my Viagra quota in 1999.

I really thought I would do it. Really. I figured HQ now had a year's worth of data to go by, and they'd look at things fairly and give us a fair quota.

Not so much. At the Viagra launch meeting in 1998, Pfizer's VP of Sales—the biggest dog in our sales world—Hank McCrorie stood up in front of us and boasted, "Viagra does not drive our stock price." *Crazy cheers.* "Other companies would kill to have just one billion-dollar drug. We have *four* other billion-dollar drugs [Lipitor, Norvasc, Zoloft, Zithromax]. Viagra is going to be a billion-dollar drug. This is something we are used to at Pfizer." *Crazier cheers.* Fast forward to 1999, when Pfizer stock had been flat for months. The big dog had learned a new trick. "Viagra drives our stock price," Mr. McCrorie announced, without a trace of irony. "We need to sell more Viagra."

I, for one, did not need my boss's boss's boss's boss to tell me I had to sell more of my most heavily weighted product in 1999; I already knew that. You see, for the first time in my pharmaceutical career, I had become embarrassed by my lack of success, but Viagra was not the turning point. Amazingly, vitamin V was not the first drug I failed to launch successfully in 1998.

Drug reps loved launching a new drug for two reasons: One, it gave us something new to talk about with physicians in a job that could become very boring very quickly; two, the company's inability to correctly predict how much of the product would be sold could result in huge moneymaking opportunities (or, in my case with Viagra, not). In February 1998, six weeks before Viagra, Pfizer introduced Trovan, a revolutionary antibiotic the FDA had approved for an eye-popping fourteen bacterial infections. As a member of the new Urology/GYN Division, my Trovan efforts were focused on prostatitis (an inflammation of the prostate) and urinary tract infections. The sales quotas for our division were set *extremely* low, and my colleagues and I could not wait to hit the field and blow out our Trovan numbers.

I had to wait a long time. Fortunately for my colleagues, most of them posted their finest sales numbers ever. One guy in New England reached 1,000 percent of quota at one point during the year, before fading to a paltry 800 percent at year's end. I made it a point to introduce myself to this sales sensei at a meeting, and I had the reaction most fans have when meeting a celebrity: I thought you'd be taller. He was a nice guy—don't get me wrong—but charismatic he was not. "Outgoing" would even have been a stretch. Later, I met another person who surpassed her sales goal by six or seven times, a chatterbox Jewish girl from New York City who could have been the inspiration for Chandler's girlfriend Janice. This mid-twenties mensch offered to fly out to California to work with me and see what I was doing wrong because "this is, like, the *easiest* drug to sell ever!"

In normal years, making quota was sufficient. In Trovan's debut run, however, my 102 percent prompted jokes from my colleagues. "Reidy, you could sell ice to Eskimos, really." Toss in my third to last in the nation Viagra ranking, and 1998 finished up as a complete waste of time for everyone involved with Jamie Reidy.

No longer could I kid myself. For two years, I had ignored the fact that I had finished behind a guy who had never seen nachos. But now that my shitty Trovan performance had prompted offers of assistance from strangers, I finally acknowledged a burning humiliation: That splinter had festered into a full-blown sepsis. Enough was enough.

Sick of getting my ass kicked, I approached 1999 with a new determination. I resolved to sell Trovan with the energy I should have applied in '98, to relaunch the antibiotic in the San Joaquin Valley. This did not mean that I began waking up before nine or working past four—after all, I didn't undergo a brain transplant—but I did begin to target the high prescribers in my territory, in addition to the docs with whom I liked to joke around. I even implemented a radical new strategy in which I'd actually discuss Trovan with physicians when calling on them. And it worked!

With a year's worth of sales data to analyze, Pfizer HQ had zeroed in on the appropriate quotas for everyone; subsequently, no one stood above 200 percent. By the end of May, I ranked seventh in the nation at 160 percent, but this number belied my actual position since my weekly sales were still trending upward while those of the six reps ahead of me were falling, due in large part to competitors' spreading news of Trovan-related liver failures in the first half of that year. Fortunately, no patients in my territory had experienced this tragic adverse event, and my doctors continued prescribing it. I was finally kicking ass! Until June, that is.

After consulting with the FDA, Pfizer voluntarily pulled Trovan from the U.S. market due to the increasing reports of severe liver damage caused by the antibiotic. Looking at the big picture, I was proud of the company for doing the right thing ethically despite the negative financial impact on our bottom line. Sitting in Fresno with my personal blinders squarely on, however, I was crushed. *But I was gonna be number one!*

My new boss Mitch quickly recognized my symptoms of depression and began damage control right away. "Jamie, I know this sucks, but you can still have a great year. Your Trovan ranking won't drop, so you'll have that number seven, albeit weighted less heavily, going for you. And your Celebrex numbers look good, so just focus on Celebrex and Viagra from here on out."

We had launched Celebrex, a new anti-inflammatory drug in February 1999, and for a nice change of pace, I actually managed to not screw up the first year's sales. Sitting comfortably above quota, I still had several docs who had not bought into the advantages of Celebrex, meaning Mitch's plan for focusing on this drug held a lot of promise. Focusing on my nemesis product, Viagra did not look as rosy.

In order to complete my worst-to-first campaign, I'd have to get my urologists to prescribe more of the drug they claimed they could not prescribe any more often. "Of course they can't prescribe any more than they are already doing," came the reply from up above. "That's why we need to get more men into the urology offices."

For once, it seemed as if headquarters and field-based personnel were on the same wavelength. We couldn't wait to see the ad campaign that would make Claritin's in-your-face marketing tactics seem tame. Everyone knew Pfizer had landed a national spokesman, but he had yet to be named publicly. The rumor mill buzzed; maybe even Hugh Hefner? The possibilities were tantalizing.

We got Bob Dole instead of Hef, which is sort of like getting Ralph Malph when you asked for the Fonz. Disappointment gave way to rage when the former senator refused even to mention Viagra in his television ad; like the whole world didn't see your wife raving about the little blue pill on *Larry King Live,* Bob. Not that I didn't appreciate the sincerity of his plea for men to get checked out, but patients across America were not going to burst from their Barcaloungers and run to the urologist just because a ninety-year-old, ex-presidential candidate from *Kansas* urged them to do so.

Imagine how many guys would have been standing in urology waiting rooms the day after a commercial featuring Hugh Hefner and his seven lovelies aired during *Monday Night Football!*

(In mid-December 1999, Pfizer signed a deal to sponsor a NASCAR racing team. At races across the nation, Pfizer set up medical tents in which men could undergo free screening for diabetes and hypertension, two common diseases in a population—white southerners—known for its poor dietary habits. In addition to possibly saving lives, this program identified future Viagra patients, as men suffering from diabetes and hypertension often developed erectile dysfunction. On the track things were not as successful, as Jeff Fuller's number 27 car performed miserably, even failing to complete several races. This prompted painful commentary from *SportsCenter* anchormen: "And the Viagra car *petered out* today at Talladega.")

After it became clear that our spokesman had failed to generate an increase in prescriptions, Pfizer chose another means. Frighteningly, it involved yours truly.

"*You* are going to drive patients into offices," Mitch told us with a straight face. We all got a kick out of that one. He did not return our smiles, however. In fact, he had that "I-am-the-boss-and-even-though-this-is-clearly-a-horseshit-idea-I-have-to-present-it-as-though-I-think-it-is-brilliant" look on his middle-manager face. As a former army officer, he had years of experience at implementing ludicrous ideas that had originated in headquarters. He would need to draw on every ounce of said experience to make it out of this meeting room alive.

"You guys are going to set up community outreach programs, at which local urologists and cardiologists will tell the public how Viagra works and why it's safe." The room fell silent until someone braver than me spoke up. "But we're sales reps. Why are *we* the ones doing this? Our job is to *sell* the drugs to the patients, not *find* the patients." I had to hand it to Mitch, though. Presented with undeniably perfect logic, he stuck to his guns.

"This is going to work out great! See, you'll put some money in your urologist's pocket for the speaking fee, and he'll be your friend forever. Plus, you'll be helping build his practice by getting him new patients from the attendees; how many reps can say that?" There was one major flaw in that theory—a flaw that had been repeatedly communicated to headquarters and repeatedly ignored: Urologists didn't want to treat *more* ED patients. They wanted to treat *fewer*.

Urologists considered themselves surgeons first, clinicians second. Sometime during their internal medicine residencies, they figured out that they liked to cut, but didn't want to do general surgery and didn't want to spend too much time in a lengthy fellowship. They also liked dealing with patients. Urology was a nice compromise for them. The HMO era threw their routine out of whack, however, by severely curtailing their reimbursement for surgery. Thus, urologists were forced to operate more often in order to maintain their income. Result: They had less time to see patients in the office.

Because of the awkward nature of the condition, patients with ED took considerably more time than those with incontinence or bladder infections. One urologist told me, "You can't get these guys to shut up! I just want to say, 'Okay, I understand. This is treatable, and here is what we are going to do.' But they never let you off that easy." Referring to the amount of work required to uncover what truly ailed a patient, Dr. Charming, who had a large number of migrant farmworkers in his practice, revealed, "*Back pain* is Mexican for ED." Hence, urologists wanted to pass the burden of ED patients to their primary care colleagues.

"Viagra has taken the mystery out of treating this. If Viagra doesn't work, *then* patients should see us."

Unmoved by such arguments, Pfizer turned its reps into recruiters. Our original strategy wasn't too aggressive. In fact, it actually made some sense. We contacted local VFWs, Lions Clubs, and other community organizations to see if they had any interest in a Viagra information program. With memberships consisting primarily of men over the age of fifty, most organizations acquiesced. One of my colleagues printed up stamped 3 x 5 cards with the speaker's name and address on the front, and left them in front of every place setting. All an attendee had to do to set up an appointment was fill out the back (name, phone number, "I'd like an appointment in July") and mail it in. In spite of these efforts, the urologists giving the talks failed to gain many, if any, new patients. No new patients meant no new prescriptions for Viagra; not exactly the return on investment for which the higher-ups were looking.

The word came down from above. "We're doing this all wrong." We nodded knowingly, eager to see them eat crow.

"You need to go directly *to the community*." Apparently, we were not thinking on a big enough scale. They wanted us to think on a "Billy Graham–revival" scale. I was beginning to think on a "car-bomb-in-HQ" scale. The Viagra sales team in Visalia, California, a town of ninety thousand famous for its citrus production, found religion and set out to host the nation's biggest Viagra program. And we did.

Not that I had anything to do with it. As *the* urology rep, you'd think I would have been one of the ringleaders, if not Gunther Gabel-Williams. However, I was not involved in any of the planning, coordinating, or doing. Rather, four extremely motivated and organized people—having correctly recognized that I would only get in the way—created the largest undertaking of its kind in the history of pharmaceutical undertakings. They went all out.

You could not go into a doctor's office in Visalia or its neighboring towns without knocking over a flyer. You could not enter a pharmacy without seeing a poster—a poster!—advertising the event. I even picked up a leaflet at a gas station. This was going to be so big that we reserved a conference room at the Holiday Inn with nonalcoholic drinks and finger foods for two hundred people.

When we totaled up the costs, including $500 each for the local urologist and cardiologist, we had spent close to $3,000. Lord knows how many man-hours they spent on this, the Mother of All Programs. Half an hour before the scheduled start time, one of the newer reps looked out at the sea of empty chairs filling the conference room and asked, "What if there aren't enough seats?" Such was our confidence level.

Four people showed up for the program. F-o-u-r. *Cricket. Cricket.* Two older gentlemen arrived separately, sat on opposite sides of the aisle from each other, and spent an awkward ten minutes making small talk. *I'm just covering for a friend who couldn't make it.* I felt so bad for these guys. You could tell they had expected to find comfort in a crowd. Fortunately, the attendance doubled when a married couple in their mid-thirties showed up. See that, the old men seemed to think. It happens to men of all ages!

We finally told the doctors to begin their talk—twenty minutes late—and no more than five minutes had elapsed when the married couple got up and left. One of my colleagues chased after them to ask why they were leaving so early. They had expected a sex-education class designed to restore the spice in a marriage. I walked to the hotel bar and ordered a beer.

At least nobody got yelled at. That's what we expected to happen, that somebody in HQ would start a big ball of shit rolling downhill until it crushed the poor worker bees in Visalia. It didn't happen, though. Mitch explained that it *couldn't* happen, because we had done everything right. It wasn't our fault that nobody showed up. Word of the disaster spread quickly across the country, and talk of community programs vanished. Fifteen hundred dollars per attendee was somewhat more than Pfizer's preferred dollar-to-participant ratio.

And my sales still sucked! In fact, they had gotten worse in Viagra's second year, slipping to 84 percent of quota. Desperate for an answer, I decided that I had been giving away too many samples, thereby decreasing the need for urologists to write prescriptions. If the national average for sexual intercourse in a marriage is six times per month (as we had been told at a meeting once), I reasoned, and there are five 50-milligram tablets in each Viagra sample pack, then I was giving the majority of people a freebie! Thus, the boycott was born.

I stopped giving out Viagra samples altogether. Of course, I needed a story to back it up when questioned by urologists. Shaking my head disgustedly, I'd sigh and simply say, "Production problems in Memphis," as if it were an everyday occurrence with which they were used to dealing. "Somebody miscalculated and we didn't make enough Viagra samples for July. Hopefully, they will get it straightened out by August." Strangely enough, the "problem" was not corrected until nearly the end of September, which just happened to be the last month of our sales year. This did not make many urologists happy. In fact, I got yelled at by a couple of docs. One intuitive guy even called me a liar, saying that I *had to be* holding back.

At six feet tall, I still had to crane my neck to look up and give him my best disbelieving stare. "Now, Doctor, *why* would I do that? What good could possibly come from my making you this angry?"

As he glared down at me, I realized that, of all my urologists I could have pissed off with the boycott stunt, *this* guy was the worst possible; he was rumored to have threatened to "firebomb" the new office a competing group of urologists from another area had planned to build in his town. They ultimately decided not to expand their practice, after all.

Thankfully, Dr. David Banner didn't have an answer for my question as to why I'd want to make him angry, and he let it drop. As it turned out, I didn't get an answer, either. An answer to my prayers, that is.

Aside from aggravating a few urologists, the boycott accomplished nothing. My Viagra sales stayed relatively flat. Which is to say, they stayed relatively shitty, never climbing above 88 percent of quota. This was becoming problematic, because now my career mobility was suffering in addition to my self-esteem.

By the end of 1999, I had managed to climb into the number-eight spot in national Celebrex sales. Combined with my number-seven Trovan position, this made me one of, maybe, three reps ranked in the top ten in two drugs. Obviously, I was going to need a new shelf in my office to hold all the awards headed my way, not to mention I'd have to call the movers because I would certainly be getting promoted out of Farmland, U.S.A.

Mitch returned from the year-beginning manager's meeting in Florida with a promise from the head of Pfizer's training department that I would be considered for one of the upcoming vacancies. "I bumped into him in the men's room," Mitch told me, with a combination of embarrassment and pride. "And when I brought your name up he said, 'Enough about Jamie Reidy, already! If one more person talks to me about him, I'm gonna puke. He's getting an interview.'" I had wanted to be a trainer since Day One of initial training, and now I was actually going to get the chance to make it happen!

Mitch didn't want me just to get a chance, though. He wanted to make it impossible for them not to promote me. "You really need to get your Viagra numbers up, man," he said, having grown oblivious, like all people involved with the little blue pill, to the innumerable double entendres created by the drug. Without my nemesis, I was ranked number one in the district, number one in the western region, and number one in the nation. With Viagra, however, I was third out of five, seventh out of twenty-five region-ally, and in the top quarter nationally. Good, but not great. And you needed great to make it to training.

Always the voice of hope, Mitch told me, "If you can move your Viagra number in the region [twenty-second out of twenty-five] up just three spots, you'll be tops in the district. If you can move up seven, maybe eight places regionally, you'll make VPC [Vice President's Cabinet, the most elite award a rep could earn; I had never had a VPC discussion with a manager prior to that]. Once you've got VPC on your résumé, Jamie, you'll get any promotion you want."

Beside holding my career hopes in the balance, my Viagra sales were also negatively impacting my family life; my father was starting to suspect things were not so *bueno* in Modesto.

My dad loved hearing about my sales experiences. I think they reminded him of himself thirty years ago at IBM. "How's business?" he'd ask cheerfully. What this really meant was, "By how much are you outselling the other guys on your team?" I had always done well with at least one of my drugs, so I tended to focus on the positive rather than share with my father the extent of his eldest child's mediocrity. In other words, I'd lie to him. This tactic worked fine until I got promoted. My moving up the ladder had given him the false sense that I was kicking ass, but two years later that impression was about to change.

My response to his question never changed: "Good. Good," with too much enthusiasm on the first good and the second good thrown in for lack of anything better to say. This meant, "Lousy, but I do not want to admit that to you, Dad." I never quite figured out if he had figured out that I was trying to duck the issue, but at least he never pushed it too far.

From Day One with vitamin V, Dad could not get enough of the stories. A human Rolodex of jokes, he quickly memorized every bit of Viagra humor ever told. He was surely regaling his Wall Street buddies with Jamie's latest real-world installment, boring them to tears with assurances that I was setting the world on fire sales-wise. Then something changed. Anecdotes weren't sufficient anymore, now he wanted stats, too. Sometime in late 1999, he asked about my Viagra sales, specifically. I started to give him the "Good. Good" routine, but he cut me off.

"No, how are your *sales?*"

"Uh, they're okay, Dad, you know, a little flat right now." I thought for sure he'd respond with a "flaccid" quip, and we'd change topics.

"How flat?" he asked, sounding a bit annoyed. There was no escaping him.

"Uh, about as flat as you can get."

"But you're at least making quota, right?" *Once a sales guy, always a sales guy.*

"Uh, no, Dad. I'm not." I decided to come clean. "And, I didn't make quota last year, either." I waited a moment for the deluge of verbal abuse.

"Are you pulling my leg?" I assured him that I was completely serious.

"What's your percent to quota?"

"Eighty-eight percent."

"Ha-ha, ha-ha, ha-ha!" The laugh exploded from deep inside his sizable belly. "This is terrific!" he bellowed. "I can't believe it! Viagra's only the most popular drug *in history* and you can't even make quota?" More laughter, followed by a coughing fit. I thought that was it—that he had spent himself, run out of ammunition.

"Hold on, hold on," he gasped, as if he could see me getting ready to hang up the phone. I held.

"You aren't making quota with Viagra! You just might be the worst salesman in the world!" Hysterical, he had to hang up.

Thanks for the support, Dad. It means the world to me. Keep laughing, too. But I wouldn't go checking the mailbox for those samples anytime soon.

Epilogue

I was driving through the Carolinas in late July 2000 when my cell phone rang.

"How is it?" the caller asked.

I had to shout over the roar of the road—doing eighty with the top down got pretty loud. "How do you think?" He laughed, enviously.

This was the first time Mitch had contacted me since I'd quit Pfizer two months earlier. I'd left amicably, though disappointed.

Boredom and frustration combined to drive me away from my first civilian employer.

As I explained earlier, Pfizer programmed us to deliver the proper message on each and every call. In fact, as one legendary southern California rep said when asked about the secret to his unequaled success, "I say the same thing every time I see a doctor." The questioner probed for clarification, "But what about when—" The twenty-year superstar interrupted and spoke more slowly. "I say the *same* thing *every* time." If forced to follow that mantra, I would have stabbed a Zithromax pen through my eye inside of two days. Even though I never followed the corporate script and more often than not failed to mention my products, I still felt like I was saying the same thing over and over again. The sound of my own voice got old really fast—and this from a guy who *loves* the sound of his own voice. Jobs, like drugs, have side effects, and pharmaceutical sales is no exception. Drug reps universally reported boredom as their primary complaint. Of course, earning $100,000 for working twenty hours a week helped make it more tolerable than, say, stomach cramps.

Unfortunately, nothing could ease the pain of being bored while residing in B.F.E.

As a thirty-year-old bachelor entering my third year of living in a farming community, I was ready for a change of scenery, a promotion to a more populated area. Obviously, the training department in New York was my top choice, but L.A. and San Francisco were also fine with me. Management disagreed—not with the cities, but with the concept. Unfortunately, my poor Viagra sales—I failed to move up from twenty-second in the region—prevented me from having the "breakout year" the higher-ups wanted to see before taking a chance on moving me upward again. They told me to be patient.

Instead, I took the advice of my dot-commer friends and asked for a leave of absence, something they routinely requested and received with ease from their companies.

"Tell them you're burned out and need to take a step back to evaluate things," my wise friend Ranah instructed. "Dude, they've pumped all this money into training you over the years, there's no way they'd let you just walk away." This seemed logical, especially given the fact that Pfizer had recently conducted a retention survey that revealed an alarming attrition rate among salespeople with four to six years of service. My five-year anniversary fell in August, only a few months away. So I put in for a leave of absence. You either work for Pfizer or you don't, I was informed.

By the time Mitch got in touch with me, I had put the top down on my Miata (a knee-jerk purchase made in celebration of northern Indiana's first sunny day of 1997, which came in March; perhaps if I had worked a little harder, I could have afforded a Z-3) and driven from San Francisco to Phoenix to Austin to Little Rock to Nashville to South Bend to New York City to Newark, Delaware, to Ithaca, New York, to Cincinnati to Atlanta to Hilton Head to Jacksonville, Florida, to Greensboro, North Carolina. Not the most direct route, but that was the point. I stayed with friends every night, met babies produced by couples in whose wedding parties I had served, and lowered my handicap by six strokes. Mitch understood my reasons for leaving. I was having a hell of a time when he called.

"Have you heard?" he asked.

"Heard what?"

"You're number one."

I banged the heel of my palm on the steering wheel. All right! Way to go out a winner! "Which drug?"

"No, not with just one drug. With your *territory*. You're number one. Your territory is number one. In the *country*." It took awhile to settle in my brain. "Your Viagra finally came around."

"Are you shitting me?" He was not.

Before quitting, I was ranked in the upper third of the region, and I knew I was "trending well"—my weekly sales numbers kept rising—but I'd had no idea that I would soar to the top.

Pfizer had a two-month lag on its sales numbers, meaning that the sales figures a rep posted in March were really for drugs he had sold in January. I had quit in mid-May; therefore, July's sales numbers were still attributed to me.

I was number one in the country.

"Mitch, I gotta go, man. Thanks for the scoop, but there's somebody I need to call."

He said good-bye, but not before revealing that people in HQ were asking why the number-one rep in the country—the poster child for Pfizer's retention problem—was allowed simply to walk away from the company. Smiling, I pressed speed dial on my cell phone.

"Reidy."

"Hey, Dad! Guess what?"

Epilogue, Continued

WAIT. THAT'S IT? BOOM—YOU JUST QUIT YOUR JOB AND TOOK OFF?

I heard that from a lot of people after my book came out. I did a lousy job of letting my readers inside, allowing them to understand the motivations behind my decisions to that point.

At the start of *Hard Sell*, if I'd simply shared my hopes and dreams and fears, no one would've been surprised by my quitting Pfizer at the end.

But I didn't think anybody would care about the hopes and dreams and fears of some random drug rep who egotistically thought he had a story worth telling. Years later, after reading such moving and impactful books like J. R. Moehringer's *The Tender Bar* and Craig Mullaney's *The Unforgiving Minute*, I know now that readers buy memoirs and, more important, buy *into* memoirs specifically for the author's hopes and dreams and fears.

In that sense, I failed my readers. And myself.

I've always been a storyteller. I remember friends in junior high nudging me to tell the story, even though I hadn't actually been present when it occurred.

I didn't realize I wanted to be a writer until late in my senior year of high school. Mr. Richard Shust was my English teacher, but that doesn't begin to scratch the surface of his impact on thousands of boys he taught in over thirty years at St. Joseph Regional in Montvale, New Jersey.

He assigned us an essay titled "The Object I'll Never Throw Away." I wrote about the catcher's mitt I used to make the single greatest play of my entire life: saving the championship for my sixth-grade Little League team. *No really, you should've seen the catch.* In the essay, I detailed my childhood dream of playing for the

New York Yankees. But, I admitted, "I now realize the only time I'll ever hear my name called over the Yankee Stadium loudspeakers is to inform me that my four-year-old son has been located at the cotton candy stand in Section 12."

Mr. Shust wrote in red pen directly above that line, "Beautiful. *That* is writing!"

You would've thought I'd pulled Excalibur out of the fucking stone. At that very instant, I knew I wanted to be a writer. Mr. Shust didn't just light the fuse to the firecracker of my dream; he built the firecracker, explained to me what it was for, and *then* lit the fuse.

I left his classroom knowing what I wanted to be.

Of course, there's a big difference between having a dream and pursuing one. And it took me a loooooonnnnng time to actually do anything about it.

About a month after I left Pfizer, I got a call from a former colleague named Terry Patzner, a Nebraskan with whom I shared a training class when I got promoted into the Urology Division. Terry left Pfizer shortly after I did and took a job with Eli Lilly's Oncology Division. They were hiring, and he said I'd be a lock.

Work for Lilly? The lying sacks of shit who pushed Prozac for acne? (I made that up. Maybe.) Puh-lease. I'd rather be the head fry guy at Mickey D's. I told Terry as much.

He gushed to me about how different selling chemotherapy drugs was compared to selling Viagra. "We only have to make three calls a day." Instantly, he had my full attention. "The docs don't look at us as shady sales guys, but as *consultants*. Pretty much everything is off label, because who is going to follow the FDA rules when they're trying to save a patient with cancer?" Wow. Consultant? I'd never felt like a physician's peer before. "Best of all?

No samples!" This, I did not understand. "Chemotherapy is *poison*, dude. Reps can't be schlepping that stuff around."

Three calls a day as a consultant with no samples. I sent him my résumé that afternoon.

Two weeks later, I had a series of interviews in Los Angeles. None of the three managers could believe I just up and walked away from Pfizer. I shrugged and smiled, confident in my well-rehearsed answer. "I'm a *specialty* rep. That's what I do. But by the end of my time with Pfizer, I was a specialty rep in name only; we had so many reps calling on urologists that I had nothing unique to offer. I wasn't willing to continue working like that."

The interviewers looked at me like I'd just admitted that my retirement plan hinged on my winning the lottery. I expected that reaction. I leaned back and crossed my hands behind my head.

"Besides, what's keeping me in Modesto? I just turned thirty, and I'm financially set for at least a few months. I don't have a wife or kids . . . when in my life am I going to be able to just drop everything and drive cross country again?"

One of the interviewers was a married father in his midthirties. Another was a single guy in his midthirties who admitted later that he had never driven cross country and, listening to me, realized he might never drive cross country.

I finished up. "So I was having fun visiting friends all over the place when my friend Terry called and told me about this incredible opportunity to be a *specialty rep* again. And here I am."

I got the job. But not the one for which I interviewed, which was known as L.A. West; I mean, how cool does that sound? But my district manager assured me I wanted L.A. Metro. *That* did not sound cool. That sounded dangerous.

And it was. Watts and Compton both fell within the territory. But then he mentioned that L.A. Metro also covers Hawaii. I'd be required to spend one week out of every five or six in the Aloha

State. "You seem like the kind of guy who'd be OK with that." Yes, sir, yes I am. Mahalo.

I moved to Manhattan Beach in October 2000. I will not bore you with details of how great it was to live at the beach. My address read "The Strand," which is the California word for boardwalk. Jackpot.

Work proved less fun. There were considerably fewer jokes in chemotherapy sales than in Viagra sales. But I found oncology infinitely more rewarding than my previous sales role. I sold Gemzar, a drug primarily used for first-line treatment of pancreatic and non–small cell lung cancers, and third- or fourth-line treatment in late-stage breast cancer.

We weren't curing anybody. Instead, Gemzar treatment was intended to extend the patient's life while palliating the symptoms. Victories were achieved when a lifelong smoker lived long enough to see his granddaughter born. I gained an everlasting respect and appreciation for the jobs medical oncologists and their nurses and staff members do every day.

My sales momentum with Pfizer carried over to Eli Lilly. My partner Jennifer and I finished my first year ranked number one in the country. The pharmaceutical future glowed bright on the horizon.

But I wasn't happy.

I'm supposed to be a writer, damn it!

So I started writing. Kinda. I wrote in fits and starts, putting in several long sessions followed by months of inactivity. How I was ever gonna finish the book, I did not know.

I never could have guessed that my writing salvation would be delivered not by an angel from above but by one from Indianapolis: Lilly HQ. Turned out that my trips to Hawaii every five or six weeks didn't just provide me with an enviable job; they gave me twelve hours of uninterrupted writing time. It took several visits for me to realize I was trapped on a plane. No one else determined what I did during those flights. I was the lone person deciding to nap, watch shitty movies . . . or write.

Finally, after years of talking a big game, I started typing.

I completed *Hard Sell* within six months, but I couldn't find a literary agent to show interest in the manuscript. Months went by and the rejection notices piled up. I didn't keep every letter from the start, so I only have twenty-six sitting in my desk as motivation. But there were plenty more.

Then on September 6, 2003, I attended the Notre Dame–Washington State game in South Bend. That date is not etched in my brain because of the Irish's historic comeback from a nineteen-point deficit, or due to the fact that my cousin Mike got me thrown—literally, tossed "like a slab of meat"—out of the Linebacker Lounge, the most famous bar in South Bend. No, that first Saturday in September holds a place of permanent prominence because a friend started me on the path to publishing.

It had been two years since Ed Trifone (he of the dog allergy that I cured with a Zyrtec sample) and I last spoke when I joined him standing at the bar in the Backer. As we caught up on things, he asked about the book. I just shook my head. "Can't get an agent—can't get published. Not looking good."

Ed begged me to give him the manuscript so he could send it to Kathy Andrews, co-owner of Andrews McMeel Publishing in Kansas City. She was on the Notre Dame board of directors, and Ed knew her from his stint in the alumni office. I thanked him for the offer and explained that if everybody who knew somebody at a publisher sent that employee an unsolicited manuscript, then every publisher would require an extra warehouse to store all the pages that would never get read.

But Ed insisted. He wouldn't let it go. Finally, I relented. It was easier to send him the manuscript than it was to discourage him. As expected, he got no response from the publisher.

Two weeks later, Eli Lilly made the same fateful mistake Pfizer had made back in 1998; they promoted me. But this time, I became a field-based sales trainer. The irony was not lost on me: The slacker who once spent three days in London when Pfizer thought he was selling in Fort Wayne, Indiana, was now a shaper of young pharmaceutical minds.

My training territory ran from Los Angeles to Cleveland. Working with two reps per week, I spent nearly as much time in the air as I did on the ground. I flew out at six A.M. on Monday morning and returned late Tuesday night, and then I flew out at six A.M. Thursday morning and returned on Friday evening. This crazy schedule—most field trainers stay out for four days in a row—enabled me to be home on Wednesday nights for my coed flag football league. My mother commented, "No wonder you're single! Who wants to marry someone who sets up his calendar around flag football?"

I loved being a trainer. Best job I ever had. I still miss it.

In January 2004, I got a call from Andrews McMeel. Christine "Chris" Schillig, the editor, told me they wanted to publish my book. My mom called it "another Notre Dame miracle."

I nearly quit my job immediately following the publication offer. Chris begged me not to. "Jamie, rarely do writers make enough money to be full-time authors. Please keep your good-paying day job and wait to see what happens." I love that woman. You see, unless you're Jessica Lynch just back from Iraq, it takes a year to publish a book.

For starters, I had a lot of revising to do. Chris Schillig is one patient woman. Fortunately, Eli Lilly once again helped me out, as my constant flying to sales-training gigs gave me ample time to complete my rewrites in the air.

Working on the book with the publisher made it seem real, but I couldn't forget that I still had a day job. Every time I saw the Indianapolis 317 area code on caller ID, I panicked—I was certain that my secret was about to blow up in my face. My parents begged me to use a pseudonym and remove any identifying specifics (Fresno, etc.) from the text, thus allowing me to continue living my comfortable lifestyle risk-free. But my egomania would never allow that; critically acclaimed or panned, I wanted the world to know Jamie Reidy authored *Hard Sell*. Frighteningly, everyone nearly found out way sooner than I wanted.

In November 2004, I went on a second date with a brunette bombshell named Amanda. She told me she'd read all about me and my book on the Internet. I nearly spit my drink all over her blouse. "H-h-how?!"

She explained that after our first date she went home and Googled me, an action that, at the time, was fairly new. But it convinced her I wasn't a serial killer, so she agreed to go out with me again. At the conclusion of our second date, I raced home and Googled myself. Sure enough, the outside PR firm Andrews McMeel hired to promote the book had posted a "coming soon" page on its Web site. Sweat poured out of every pore in my body. I fired off a panicked e-mail to Chris. Fortunately, the PR firm took down the Web page before anyone at Lilly found it.

Soon after, my close friend and attorney Patrick Sweeney set up a meeting for me at the Gersh Agency, Hollywood's second oldest firm. I met with Steve Kravit and Amy Schiffman, attorney and agent, respectively, to discuss their representing me to sell the movie rights to my book. That seemed highly unlikely to me, but the three of us clicked, and I signed with Gersh.

When the first copy of *Hard Sell* arrived in the mail, I just sat there and stared at the book as I turned it over and over in my hands for ten minutes. I simply couldn't help it. On the phone with my mother, I said, "This must be what newly engaged women feel like."

Andrews McMeel shipped *Hard Sell* to bookstores at the beginning of March 2005. From my friends' reactions, I immediately learned two important rules that every author should know: Anyone you mention in the book will complain about how she was portrayed, and anyone you fail to mention in the book will complain about how he was not portrayed at all.

With the book on shelves, the clock continued to tick down on my Eli Lilly career. I knew I was done. Either the company would pay me a lot of money to go away quietly, or it would fire me—and thus create publicity that would help push book sales. I just didn't know which way Lilly would go.

I told my former sales partner about the publication because I liked him a lot and didn't want him to get blindsided. He chuckled knowingly and said, "Reidy, did you just fuck it up for all of us?"

Amazingly, the company's higher-ups didn't learn about the book until I informed them of its existence in an FYI e-mail on Friday, March 4, 2005. I e-mailed my boss (West Area manager) and his boss (head of the Oncology Division) and cc'ed the Oncology Division's HR person the following message: "Wanted to let you know that I have published a book that will be coming out in the next week or so. *Hard Sell: The Evolution of a Viagra Salesman* chronicles my five years at Pfizer and the craziness of selling Viagra." Completely true, but admittedly not entirely forthcoming.

My boss did not write back.

The HR lady answered, "Wow—congratulations, Jamie! I will have to look for it." My lawyer told me to print that out and keep it someplace safe.

The head of the Oncology Division responded, "I didn't know you were writing a book. I better get a free copy!" Again, my lawyer advised printing the e-mail.

My boss, however, actually went to Amazon.com and did some research. He did not like what he read online. He *really* didn't like what he read when the book arrived at his house. Word quickly spread from there.

A friend of mine who worked inside HQ in Indianapolis told me she had heard that executives at other pharmaceutical companies started phoning their Lilly counterparts, asking why they'd let "that asshole" publish a book. This prompted Lilly officials to start calling downhill asking, "That asshole works for us?" I have no idea whether that story is true, but I like to think it is.

On Monday, March 21, management pulled me out of the field. They flew me to HQ for a meeting to take place on Thursday, March 25.

Across the table from me sat a company attorney, an HR exec, and my boss. They spent the better part of two hours telling me that I was an unemployable scumbag who would never work again. The best thing I could do for everyone involved would be to take their piddling severance offer of four months' salary in exchange for signing a nondisclosure agreement.

I refused. They told me I was crazy, but they didn't know what I knew.

See, Lilly's Scumbag Squad had no idea that the pharmaceutical beat reporters from the *New York Times*, the Associated Press, and CNBC were all waiting to hear from me. A guy I didn't even know, Peter Rost, a former Pfizer VP and whistle-blower, tipped off those media members about my possible firing. The reporters could *not* believe I was ballsy enough—or stupid enough!—to actually publish the book while still employed by the pharmaceutical industry, and they were intrigued by the idea that Lilly would axe me and risk the potential media attention.

All three of these savvy professionals felt sure the company would simply pay me to resign and go away quietly. To paraphrase: "They don't want to give you any more publicity than you'd get normally. And who knows what you can reveal about the way Eli Lilly does business! But call me if they are dumb enough to fire you."

Big-shot friends of mine at huge companies in other industries sought the opinions of their HR executives. *What would we do if we had to deal with a wild-card author like this?* The answers were universal: Pay the asshole to disappear. Now, the amounts each company would be willing to fork over in exchange for an airtight nondisclosure agreement varied from two years' to five years' salary.

But the Scumbag Squad's tactics got to me; I *did* feel like a loser turncoat. So I only asked for one year's salary. The HR woman scoffed, but said she'd get back to me on Monday. When she faxed me Lilly's offer, they hadn't budged—it was still only four months. Patrick Sweeney and several pals who had graduated from law school but don't practice kept pumping me up. "Fuck 'em, Reidy! Don't give in! Make 'em pay through the nose!"

Alone and hung over on a Saturday afternoon . . . the doubts took hold. *Am I a total scumbag? Should I just walk away and not cause Lilly any problems?* Awash in self-loathing, I cracked. I dialed the number on the HR woman's card; I was ready to accept their deal.

I got her work voice mail. Of course she wasn't at the office on a Saturday afternoon. Had she given me her cell number, I would've gotten her on the phone and told her I'd take their deal. Can you hear that gigantic whoooshing sound? That's the "Whew!" I let fly every time I think how close I came to giving in.

On Monday morning, I called my father. He could tell I was nervous about the whole thing and was still wavering. Rich Reidy didn't hesitate. "They're screwing you over. You can always get another job. You're Jamie Reidy!"

The HR woman called at the appointed time. She said the higher-ups had declined my counteroffer. Either I took the $34K, or I left them no choice but to can me. My mouth dried out. Sweat sprang from my forehead. I cleared my throat.

"Then I guess you're firing me."

She didn't say anything for a few seconds. "Jamie, are you sure you want to do this? Everyone will know you got *fired*."

I paced around my room, my head pounding.

"I'm sure." I could almost hear her shrug. And that was it.

I sat down on the floor. I blinked a lot. *WTF? I'm Jamie Reidy. People like me. I don't get fired, I get* hired! I took a few deep breaths.

Then I picked up the phone and called the Associated Press.

On Tuesday, March 29, the AP put a story on the wire with the following headline: LILLY FIRES EX-PFIZER REP OVER BOOK. If I had tried—really put my mind to it—I could not have come up with a better headline. That article appeared in almost every paper in the country. And I appeared live on CNBC's *Power Lunch* that day.

The results were immediate; the book skyrocketed up Amazon's rankings. The peak I saw was #71, but my friend Matt Smith spotted it at #57, which was higher, he pointed out in an e-mail, "than that book about bees that every chick has!" Matt added, "You just became a funnier and more attractive man."

I exited the CNBC studios on a high. My cell phone blew up with congratulatory calls and texts. Several friends inside Lilly HQ called, whispering their messages. All of them basically said the same thing: *Nobody is working! Everybody in this building watched your interview and now keeps talking about it. Everyone wants to know, "How much did this asshole want? Why didn't we just pay him to go away?"* Pfizer issued a one-sentence statement and simply repeated it over and over. "We don't know if this book belongs in the fiction or nonfiction section of the bookstore."

Funny, dismissive, brief. And totally brilliant. When a reporter read that quote to me, I thought, *I'm screwed.*

And then Eli Lilly's spokesman Philip Belt started talking, and he simply wouldn't stop. Belt repeatedly badmouthed me to the press with a personal tone so vitriolic I had to double-check to make sure I hadn't ever dated his wife, sister, or daughter. My mother became upset at the negative light in which Belt portrayed me. That made me angry.

Until a reporter told me, "This guy is making you money!" *Uh, excuse me?* "Pfizer handled this the right way: Issue one comment, let it blow over. This Lilly guy keeps throwing gas on a dying fire. If he'd just shut up, the media wouldn't care anymore. But because he keeps saying things about you, it makes us think there's more to the story."

I appeared four more times on CNBC, once on CNN, and twice more in the *New York Times*. Thank you, Phil Belt!

In June 2005, I spoke with Charles Randolph, a screenwriter (*The Interpreter*) who wanted to adapt *Hard Sell* into a movie. We hit it off, and I liked his ideas, so Charles became "attached" to the project as a writer-producer.

Charles made the rounds of Hollywood pitching his vision for the movie. Megaproducers Scott Stuber (*The Break-Up, Role Models*) and Mary Parent (now the chairperson of MGM) immediately snatched up the rights, changing my life forever.

In mid-2008, the project got a huge boost when A-list director (*About Last Night, Glory, Blood Diamond*) and Oscar-winning producer (*Shakespeare in Love, Traffic*) Ed Zwick came on board to direct. Now all we needed was somebody to play me.

My always-supportive friend Maureen—2009 Cresskill High School teacher of the year—called to mention, "Danny DeVito is available."

In June 2009, I got an e-mail from my sister-in-law Clare. She demanded to know why I hadn't told her that Jake Gyllenhaal had signed on to play "Jamie" in the movie, now titled *Love and Other Drugs*. Clare had heard from a friend who had learned the news from perezhilton.com. It was more than a little embarrassing to explain that while I knew Jake was in negotiations to take the role, none of the producers had let me know the big news. That's me—always in the loop!

My guy friends were much more excited to learn that Anne Hathaway would be playing "my" girlfriend in the movie.

By the way, there is *no* truth to the rumor started by some Notre Dame friends that Jake had to shave his head to play me. I had hair when I was twenty-eight, damn it! FYI: Jake does have dreamy hair.

On Friday, September 17, 2009—aka The Greatest Day of My Life—Ed Zwick yelled "Action!" on the set of *Love and Other Drugs*. This meant two things: (1) my name would be immortalized on screen by an Oscar-nominated actor, and (2) I just cashed the largest check of my life.

The resulting sigh of relief emanating from my parents' home in New York registered on Richter scales in Southern California. My father told me, "I dunno what your mother is gonna do with all this newfound time on her hands, now that she doesn't have to go to Mass every day to pray for this movie to get made!"

In October, the producers flew me to the set in Pittsburgh— thank you, Pieter Jan Brugge!—for what became the best five days of my life. And there wasn't even any drinking involved.

Throughout the week, crewmembers pulled me aside to tell me, "You know that *this* doesn't happen, right?" They'd wave their arms in the direction of Jake dressed as a drug rep, implying, *You know that people don't write nice little books that nobody ever heard of, and then have those books turn into major motion pictures starring one of the acting giants of his generation as you, right?* "You know how lucky you are?"

I did. And I do. Sometimes I still can't believe this is happening to me. It might not even sink in until I'm walking down the red carpet, the flashbulbs reflecting off my bald head blinding all of Jake's fans.

Fox 2000 has scheduled the premiere of *Love and Other Drugs* for November 24, 2010. When a nobody author sells the movie rights to his book, the contract stipulates that he only gets two tickets to the premiere. Like I said earlier, I'm taking my mother. And praying I can schmooze my way into a bunch more tickets for my brother, sister, sister-in-law, girlfriend, lawyers, agent, etc.

Studios are notoriously tight with premiere tickets. This is gonna take some serious selling on my part.

Think I still got it?